The JAPANESE HAIKU

The JAPANESE HAIKU

Its Essential Nature, History,
and Possibilities in English,
with Selected Examples

by

Kenneth Yasuda

CHARLES E. TUTTLE COMPANY
Rutland, Vermont & Tokyo, Japan

Published by the Charles E. Tuttle Company, Inc.
of Rutland, Vermont & Tokyo, Japan
with editorial offices at
Suido 1-chome, 2-6, Bunkyo-ku, Tokyo

© 1957, by Charles E. Tuttle Co., Inc.
All rights reserved by the author

Library of Congress Catalog Card No. 57-8795
International Standard Book No. 0-8048-1096-6

First edition, 1957
First Tut Book edition, 1973
Twelfth printing, 1995

PRINTED IN SINGAPORE

TO
Gedatsukongô

CONTENTS

FOREWORD

IT HAS BEEN SAID that every age produces its Shakespeare. If this be
true, it follows that every age has its own unique poetry—its own peculiar
emotional stance—and, whatever else may be expected of poetry, it is
generally agreed that it should communicate the feelings of its age.
Just how these feelings are to be communicated has been a point of
strong issue between generations. The generation of Pope and Dryden
found Shakespeare to be a barbarian of singular but wasted talent.
Our own generation generally finds the Victorians to be uncongenial
reading. We feel betrayed by the bright optimism and professed realism
of the nineteenth century, and in our resentment often claim its poetry
to be bankrupt. Modern Western poetry clearly records this revolt.
In this milieu, it would seem that the Japanese haiku has its best
opportunity of being understood and appreciated in the West. For modern
poetry and haiku share very basic tenents, as Dr. Yasuda demonstrates
so clearly in the pages that follow. Our generation in the West has
the opportunity, as it has never had before, of reaching a deep and
fundamental understanding with that part of the East which Japan
represents, perhaps not only in poetry, but in the wider realization of
common humanity. The temper of present-day America has much that
can find close kinship with Japanese temperament and culture.

It has been my good fortune to have journeyed to Japan, for periods
of varying length, more than a dozen times since 1927. Each time
I have been impressed increasingly by not only the superb natural
beauty of the country, which is something easily grasped, but also by its
great artistic achievements. The realization has grown that these achieve-

ments are not things of the past, to be seen only in museums and galleries, but form a vital living part of the life of the Japanese people. This art has grown out of that life and continues to be an active part of it.

Each time that I have been a guest in a Japanese home this truth has been further demonstrated. My host shows me some particularly fine painting, recites poetry, or writes in "sumi" a verse for me in incomparable calligraphy that portrays a three-line poems in striking, fluid design. In this and other ways, my host and his family carry me a little way into the living spirit of Japanese art.

This book by Dr. Yasuda, while ostensibly about haiku, in reality penetrates deeply into the totality of this living spirit of Japan. It deals with those aspects which have produced and maintained haiku into the present day. The important key to understanding comes with the realization that in Japanese art one strives always for the absolute. Of the absolute there is no question of degree; it is either attained or lost. Most often, to be sure, it is not attained, but it is the constant striving toward and awareness of that high goal which gives strength and vitality to this living aesthetic spirit which has so impressed me in Japan. It is the failure to understand that which has led some Western critics to claim that *The Book of Tea,* for example, is nothing but exaggerated bombast.

It is this living aesthetic spirit which makes of each trip to Japan a challenging experience. An understanding of this spirit is one of the most valuable contributions that Japan can make to my country. Any book which can give even an inkling of the nature and aliveness of this aesthetic life in Japan performs a most valuable function. Dr. Yasuda has achieved this in his original approach to the problem of haiku.

ROBERT B. HALL

ACKNOWLEDGMENTS

THIS BOOK WAS originally submitted to Tokyo University as a doctoral thesis in 1955 under the title *On the Essential Nature and Poetic Intent of Haiku*. It represents a formal presentation of material—a part of which first appeared in the introduction to my collection of haiku, *A Pepper Pod*—that is the culmination of an interest in haiku dating from many years ago.

I am very deeply indebted to many people for encouraging me to pursue that interest and for their help in clarifying my thinking and poetic practice. Among them are Masao Kume and Kyoshi Takahama in Japan; John Gould Fletcher, Clark Ashton Smith, Babette Deutsch, Mark Van Doren, and George Savage in America. Among Japanese scholars, I should like to acknowledge the great help received from Dr. Yutaka Tatsuno, Dr. Senichi Hisamatsu, and Dr. Isoji Asô, the latter two of whom were kind enough to read the original outline and offer many valuable suggestions; from Dr. Shigeru Nambara, Dr. Shintaro Suzuki, Dr. Naoshiro Tsuji, Dr. Takeshi Saitô and Mr. Kinichi Ishikawa, whose heartening encouragement was so generously given. Thanks are also due to Dr. Robert B. Hall for his kind foreword and thoughtful suggestions, and to Mr. Noboru Takahashi for his help in proofreading and with the many troublesome details connected with the actual publication. Above all I must acknowledge the most fundamental debt of all to the late Archbishop Seiken Okano and Bishop Eizan Kishida.

For permission to quote from the works listed, I wish to make acknowledgment to the following: George Allen and Unwin Limited for

Mysticism and Logic by Bertrand Russell and for *Ariosto, Shakespeare and Corneille* by Benedetto Croce; Brandt and Brandt for "Dirge without Music" from *The Collected Lyrics of Edna St. Vincent Millay,* published by Harper and Brothers; the executors of the James Joyce Estate for *A Portrait of the Artist as a Young Man* by James Joyce, published by Jonathan Cape Limited; Constable and Company Limited for *The Poetical Works of George Meredith;* the John Day Company, Inc., for *The Asian Legacy and American Life,* edited by Arthur E. Christy; Faber and Faber Limited for *The Use of Poetry and the Use of Criticism, Selected Essays,* and *Selected Prose* by T. S. Eliot; Harcourt, Brace and Company for *History of American Poetry* by Horace Gregory and Marya Zaturenska; the Harvard University Press for *Philosophy in a New Key* by Suzanne K. Langer; William Heinemann Limited for *The Essence of Aesthetic* by Benedetto Croce; Henry Holt and Company, Inc., for "The Runaway" from *New Hampshire* by Robert Frost, copyright 1923 by Henry Holt and Company, Inc., and copyright 1951 by Robert Frost, and for "Chicago" from *Chicago Poems* by Carl Sandburg, copyright 1916 by Henry Holt and Company, Inc., and copyright 1944 by Carl Sandburg; Houghton Mifflin Company for "Flame Apples" from *Pictures of the Floating World* by Amy Lowell, and for *Some Imagist Poets,* edited by Amy Lowell; Intercultural Publications, Inc., for "Contemporary Japanese Art," by Chisaburo F. Yamada and James Laughlin, published in *Perspective of Japan,* the January 1955 supplement to *Atlantic Monthly;* Longmans Green and Company Limited for *The Psychologist Looks at Art* by Louis Danz; Macmillan and Company Limited, London, for *Oxford Lectures on Poetry* by A. C. Bradley and for *Aesthetic as a Science of Expression and General Linguistic* by Benedetto Croce; Macmillan Company for *Science and the Modern World* by Alfred North Whitehead; John Murray Limited for *Japanese Literature* by Donald Keene, in their series "The Wisdom of the East"; New Directions for selection "XXI" from *Spring and All—I-XXVIII* by William Carlos Williams, copyright 1948 and 1951 by William Carlos Williams; Open Court Publishing Company for *Substance and Function and Einstein's Theory of Relativity* by Ernst Cassirer; G. P. Putnam's Sons for *Art as Experience* by John Dewey, copyright 1934; Henry Regnery Company for *Achievement in American Poetry 1900–1950* by Louise Bogan; Routledge and Kegan Paul Limited for *Speculations* by T. E. Hulme; Charles Scribner's Sons for *Aesthetic Quality* by Stephen

Pepper and for *Reactionary Essays on Poetry and Ideas* by Allen Tate; The Society of Authors and Dr. John Masefield, O. M., for "Sea Fever"; the Stanford University Press for *Imagism and the Imagists* by Glenn Hughes; the State University of Iowa for *Rhythmic Verse* (Humanistic Study, Vol. 3, No. 2) by J. H. Scott; the University of Hawaii Press for *Essays in East-West Philosophy,* edited by Charles A. Moore; the University of North Carolina Press for *Modern Poetry and the Tradition* by Cleanth Brooks; the University of Oklahoma Press for *The Heel of Elohim: Science and Values in Modern American Poetry* by Hyatt Howe Waggoner, copyright 1950 by the University of Oklahoma Press; Vision Press Limited for *Form in Modern Poetry* by Herbert Read; *Partisan Review* for "William Shakespeare and the Horse with Wings" by George Barker; the *Saturday Review* for "The Proper Pose of Poetry," by Archibald MacLeish; Babette Deutsch for *Poetry in Our Time;* Harold G. Henderson for *The Bamboo Broom;* Ezra Pound for his writings.

Acknowledgments are also due to the following: Shin Asano for *Haiku Zenshi no Kenkyû;* Isoji Asô for *Haishumi no Hattatsu;* Taizô Ebara for *Haikai Seishin no Tankyû* and for *Haikaishi no Kenkyû;* Etsurô Ide for *Meiji Taisho Haikushi;* Chikara Igarashi for *Kokka no Taisei Oyobi Hattatsu;* Masao Kume for *Bikushô Zuihitsu;* Tamio Kuribayashi for *Haiku to Seikatsu;* Nippon Gakujutsu Shinkokai for the *Manyôshû;* Asaji Nose, Kusadao Nakamura, and Isoji Asô for *Renga, Haikai, Haiku, Senryû;* Shinobu Origuchi for *Origuchi Shinobu Zenshû;* Seki Osuga for *Otsuji Hairon-shû;* Masakazu Sasa for *Rengashi Ron;* Kyoshi Takahama for "Haiku no Tsukuri Kata" in *Arusu Fujin Kôsa;* Yûkichi Taketa for *Manyôshû Zenchûshaku;* Yoshio Yamada for *Renga Gaisetsu;* Kenkichi Yamamoto for *Junsui Haiku;* Kiyoshi Yuyama for *Nihon Shiika Inritsu Gaku.*

Special thanks are due to Alfred A. Knopf, Inc., for permission to reprint selections from my book *A Pepper Pod.*

Finally, I should like to thank the publishers of the present book, the Charles E. Tuttle Company, for their part in making this publication possible. In all fairness to them, I should add that, in order to bring the book out as soon as possible, I myself have assumed full responsibility for the editorial style and the proofreading.

Kotaki-en, Tokyo, February 1, 1957

KENNETH YASUDA

INTRODUCTION

MANY QUESTIONS relating to the status of the haiku in English are put to me by interested Japanese each time I come to Japan. On the surface these questions seem simple and insignificant; however, I feel strongly that they represent a basic problem if we consider them in the light of world poetry, especially at present when the East and West have met and the two worlds are more than eager to understand each other. Here are a few representative inquiries:

"Do the English-speaking people understand haiku?"

"Do they write haiku in English?"

"Do the English haiku have any form?"

Such questions represent a problem to be solved not only by the Japanese or by English-speaking poetry lovers alone. For the problem relates to the larger one of mutual understanding among peoples. Considered in this light, these questions on haiku give us a dynamic sense of the impact of the problem of understanding, for they seem to posit some fundamental difference in the understanding of poetry between East and West. There is no such difference fundamentally. The reason for the popularity of haiku in Japan, as a classic as well as a literature of the people, holding their hearts with its irresistible charms and dignity with as much force today as in the past, lies in its nature and in the aesthetic principles that govern it. These same reasons, I feel, are enough to insure the possibilities of haiku in English, as popular with its audience as the Japanese haiku has been in Japan. For it is my contention that the underlying aesthetic principles that govern the arts are the same for any form in Japanese or English.

Along these lines, Donald Keene has pointed out that the words of the dramatist Chikamatsu written about 1720 are curiously echoed by Ford Madox Ford in 1930. Chikamatsu wrote thus of the creation or rendering of emotion: "There are some who, believing that pathos is essential to a puppet play, make frequent use of such expressions as 'it was touching' in their writing, or who when chanting the lines do so in voices thick with tears. This is foreign to my style. I take pathos to be entirely a matter of restraint. . . . When one says of something which is sad that it is sad, one loses the implications, and in the end, even the impression of sadness is slight. It is essential that one not say of a thing that 'it is sad,' but that it be sad of itself."[1] Ford, through his contact not only with the Imagist group but through Joseph Conrad with the nineteenth-century French writers represented by Flaubert and Gautier,[2] voices a similar opinion: "Poetry is a matter of rendering, not comment. You must not say: 'I am so happy'; you must behave as if you were happy."[1] Such instances of similar views shared by both Japanese and Occidental artists and critics are most numerous; many examples will be given in the following pages. They demonstrate the common ground of arts separated by time and great differences in culture. Consequently, I hope that a systematic study on the possibilities of haiku in English may have a significance beyond that which first appears probable.

My purpose, then, is to try to see and explore the possibilities of haiku in English by analyzing its nature and its unifying aesthetic principles so that we can understand it; through such analysis it may be shown that haiku, far from being an esoteric, purely Japanese form, incomprehensible to the West, shares common ground with all art in an important and significant manner. It is also my hope to give one answer to the question that Harold Gould Henderson raises in the following passage: "What the final English haiku-form will be, I do not know. It may be two lines or three or four; it may be rimed or unrimed. But I am sure that whatever it is, it will be a definite form, *for a haiku is a poem and not a dribble of prose*."[3] That definite form, to my mind, can satisfactorily follow the same general pattern in English as in Japanese in regard to the number and length of lines, finding within this framework variations and subtleties as multiple as the poet will need for his vision. Indeed, as will appear from the discussion, I feel that this pattern in English is so fitting a vehicle for the kind of experience that is a haiku that to me at this stage any other vehicle seems completely inadmissible.   Many of the principles of Japanese prosody governing the successful use of this form will be enlightening to the poet in English, as I hope to show in the following pages. He will find that the haiku, like the sonnet in its time, can enjoy great popularity.

Just as the sonnet, when introduced by Sir Philip Sidney into English through his translations, retained its original form, affording such insight to poets that eventually they produced masterpieces in English, so that we know the form as ours, the haiku too can become acclimated, once it is understood. For it is not yet understood, in spite of the fact that the Imagists knew of tanka and haiku as early as 1909 and felt that they were influenced by them, as Glenn Hughes has pointed out: "A poet of [John Gould Fletcher's] wide interests and experimental tendencies could hardly be expected to escape the influence of the Japanese. Ezra Pound felt this influence, and so did Amy Lowell. So have many of their contemporaries and followers. The tiny, clear-cut, suggestive tanka and hokku, the essence of refined imagery and concentration, appeal inevitably to the imagistic poet."[4] Indeed the Imagists created what they thought were haiku somewhat as a finger-exercise for the more strenuous art of other poetic forms.

The English poet Flint recalls the group's efforts: "We proposed at various times to replace [English poetry as it was then being written] by pure *vers libre;* by Japanese *tanka* and *haiku;* we all wrote dozens of the latter as an amusement. . . ."[5] As Horace Gregory and Marya Zaturenska remark, the atmosphere surrounding these earliest meetings of the youthful Imagist group retained the air "of after-midnight conversations held by undergraduates at college. . . . We can then understand how casually a discussion of the Japanese *tanka* and *haikai* took place in a Soho restaurant, and how the young philosopher, T. E. Hulme, as if to prove a point in a discussion which had lasted several hours and was probably forgotten, produced five pieces of unrhymed verse."[6]

It is perhaps in John Gould Fletcher's essay, "The Orient and Contemporary Poetry,"[7] where he discusses his personal remembrance of the earliest years of the Imagist movement, that a full sense of these poets' confused understanding of haiku can be best grasped.* Let me cite one example.[8] In discussing the need for condensation for the sake of

---

* This essay was written by Mr. Fletcher prior to my happy acquaintance with him. He did me the honor of saying after our discussions that certain points in it would have been differently expressed had we met prior to his writing it.

intensity, which was the motive behind the composition of the following "*hokku*-like sentence" of Pound's, Mr. Fletcher declares that it compares favorably with well-known Japanese originals. Ezra Pound's poem reads:

> The apparition of these faces in the crowd;
> Petals on a wet, black bough.

The Japanese poem to which he compares it is the following, in what appears to be Chamberlain's translation:*

> Fallen flower returning to the branch;
> Behold! It is a butterfly.

The comparison between the two poems seems most unfortunate, since the Japanese poem succeeds where Pound's fails, as Fletcher himself points out; Pound's effort is not an unqualified success since "the relation of certain beautiful faces seen in a Paris Metro station to petals on a wet tree branch is not absolutely clear."[9] That is to say, the poem is lacking in unity, in that forceful intensity of poetic vision and insight which alone can weld the objects named into a meaningful whole. In contrast, the relationship between the objects named in the haiku is quite clear.

If Fletcher's thought is carried further, it can be shown that the Imagists, with their concern for "what could be pictorially and vividly stated,"[10] had forgotten that the naming of objects alone does not constitute an image. As Cleanth Brooks has remarked, this tendency arose as part of the general revulsion of the twentieth century against Victorian poetry: "It revealed itself in a tendency to rest in the mere objective description of things (the kind of poetry which John Crowe Ransom has defined as physical poetry, a poetry of things without ideas.)"[11]

Bashô himself, one of the greatest haiku poets, seems to warn against the practice, noting that it can degenerate into mere copying: "The masters of the past took such care in composing [haiku on natural scenes] that they created only two or three in their lifetime. For beginners, copying a scene is easy, they warn us."[12] As the Japanese haiku poets have tried to remember, the totality of the poem is the image, within which there may be one or more objects. The interest of the Imagists

---

* Except for inconsequential differences in elision and punctuation, the two versions are the same. For Chamberlain's version, see his *Japanese Poetry* (London: John Murray, 1910), p. 212.

in Japanese poetic forms was only one phase in their restless experimenting arising from their dissatisfaction with Victorian poetry, and in their somewhat nebulous search for poetic values they understood only the most obvious characteristics of haiku. Consequently, interest in haiku, leavening though it was for a time, faded away.

Pound thought better than he practiced in this particular instance, for his Metro poem was supposedly a pure example of what he meant by Vorticism: "The image is not an idea. It is a radiant node or cluster; it is what I can, and must perforce call a vortex; from which and through which and into which ideas are constantly rushing. It is as true for the painting and the sculpture as it is for poetry."[13] This definition of Vorticism, as fragmentary as it is, seems a suggestive description of what I have called a haiku moment: that moment of absolute intensity when the poet's grasp of his intuition is complete, so that the image lives its own life. Such an image is the kind of poetry the West yet seems timidly to accept as valid, for reasons which critics have only recently come to understand. It is a poetry without ideas, though there may be ideas in it, as Isoji Asô, the noted haiku scholar, puts it: "What governs such an art [as that of haiku] is not a concept or logic, feeling or rationalism. . . . Even if we find an idea in it, that idea is something diffused throughout the entirety of the art product, like the air."[14]

A successful haiku renders then a speaking, vibrant image. It is another purpose of this book to show what haiku in English can be and that the haiku form in English will prove to be one of the means of writing poems that "should be equal to," and "should not mean but be," as Archibald MacLeish has said in his "Ars Poetica."[15] The examples given then are offered, not as translations, but as haiku in English, although whenever translating, I have attempted to be as faithful as possible to the original.*

The examples given are for the great part my own work—translations and some originals—mostly from my collection of haiku entitled *A Pepper Pod*,[16] since I was unable to find among other translators a consistent use of what I believe is the norm for the English haiku form.

---

* In this regard, it is interesting to note what Chamberlain said of his own earlier translations: "The writer's taste has changed. He has gone over to the camp of the literalists and cares for no versions whether of prose or of poetry, unless they be scrupulously exact." (*Op. cit.*, p. vii.)

Acknowledgment is made where the work of other translators has been used.

As for the book's organization, after some considerations of a basic aesthetic attitude and its application to haiku, I proceed to a discussion of certain aspects of English prosody applicable to the English haiku. Since my purpose is to present only the possibilities of the haiku in English and not a thoroughgoing philosophical dissertation on aesthetics, where the subject demands discussion of aesthetics, I speak only as a poet and not as a professional philosopher. What I was able to grasp from those philosophers so heavily quoted in the following pages seemed to parallel my own experiences both as reader and as writer so closely that I felt encouraged to include a discussion of those aesthetic concepts which seem to me to illuminate the nature of haiku. The observations of Japanese thinkers and poets on haiku have been utilized where they seemed pertinent to the discussion of the haiku in English, both to clarify and to reinforce it. They will also, I hope, serve to indicate the scope, depth, and clarity of Japanese critical thinking, which is not generally known in the West or available in translation. Unless otherwise acknowledged the translations of such Japanese material have been done by me.

In Chapter V I have included a history of the development of haiku. Such history is not directly pertinent to a discussion of the English haiku, but since the form in English will approximate that of the Japanese, I felt that some knowledge of its development and background in the East would round out an understanding of it. How the haiku evolved historically will become evident from the historical summary, but why it developed as it did and other related questions which have remained controversial in Japanese haiku theory will, I hope, find one answer here. Nor is it surprising that the discussion of the English version should be pertinent to the Japanese form, considering the basic aesthetic principles which I assume are universal to all poetry. Since I am dealing primarily with the English form, the historical material has been placed after the main body of discussion, although otherwise it would perhaps be more conveniently included as introductory material.

Finally, through this study I hope to reaffirm Henderson's judgment on the universality of the haiku: "The haiku form is peculiarly Japanese, but I believe most strongly that it has characteristics which transcend the barriers of language and nationality, and which fit it for a special place among the forms of Occidental poetry."[17]

The JAPANESE HAIKU

CHAPTER ONE

AN APPROACH TO HAIKU

A DEFINITION OF the term haiku which will cover not only its formal
characteristics but will also embody something of its breathing beauty
and its allusive life is a difficulty which probably faces the definers of
any art form. An additional hurdle in the case of haiku is the tendency
of critics in the past to dismiss it as inconsequential for a variety of
reasons which seem to have no relationship to its function and no appreciation of its accomplishments. We are not, however, so rich in
beauty or tranquillity or joy to be able to discard any creation so directly
concerned with these qualities as is the haiku, concerning which Bashô
noted: "From ancient times, those with a feeling for refinement...find
joy in knowing the truth and insight of things."[1] For as the haiku is a
major poetic form in Japan, I feel that it can become so in other
countries, given some understanding of its nature and its aesthetics and
its sort of power, a power which is similar in some respects to that of
painting. I shall begin then by comparing haiku to painting.

Each time I look at an old painting on rich silk by a Chinese master
of the T'ang Dynasty—especially one of the monochromes in Chinese
ink, *mo,* by such a painter as Wang Wei or some later master of the
Sung period—I am left speechless, my breath taken away in admiration.
The effect of the picture, in black and white and with subtle grada-
tions from white to black, is one of mysticism and extreme delicacy.
Unlike an oil painting, this fills the space without filling it; as a sampan

rises out of a silver mist on the Yangtse River, the faint outlines of distant mountains appear far beyond, and a pagoda's darker lines float between and above the misty veil over the rich valley.

A picture, whether the scene described above or a portrait painting, is easy to appreciate; even the inexperienced in matters of art can enjoy it just by looking at it. This is called intuition. Intuition is immediate, as the perception of color is immediate. In its essence it is non-judgmental, amoral, non-verbal, and uncritical, although after the intuiting moment the spectator may be filled with scorn or praise, and so on. Thus I hold with Croce, Dewey, and other thinkers on aesthetic matters that any work of art can be enjoyed through this act of immediate perception without conscious effort or reasoning.

The same holds true of poetry and, to a degree undreamt of in the West, of haiku in particular. Perhaps the inability of Western readers and critics to grasp the nature of haiku lies here. They are not yet accustomed, in spite of the efforts of the Imagists and their heirs, to a poetry that as Ford Maddox Ford said arouses "emotions solely by rendering concrete objects, sounds and aspects."[2] Perhaps as a vestige of the Victorianism they decry, an explicit interpretation is somehow felt as a necessity, not only by the reader but even by the poet. A far more complex reason, and one which serious Western critics have lately exposed as fallacious, probably lies in the attempts of poetry to justify its sort of intuitive material against the empirical successes of scientific thought; the age, unable to understand or to accept the values of poetry, assigns to it didactic, humanitarian, or propagandistic functions, a phase through which a certain Japanese group also passed.[3] As Allen Tate has said, "we are justifying poetry by 'proving' that it is something else, just as, I believe, we have justified religion with the discovery that it is science."[4]

Is there almost a fear that the concrete experience, the intuition, is somehow "not enough" in the following comments of Cleanth Brooks on the general structure of Robert Penn Warren's poems, which he finds on the whole admirable?

> There is a rich and detailed examination of the particular experience with the conclusion, which may be drawn from the experience, coming as a quietly ironical statement or as modest and guarded understatement. It is as though the poet felt that only the minimum of commentary was allowable if he was not to do violence to the integrity of the experience.[5]

It would perhaps be a sly question to ask how much commentary is so minimum as not to "do violence to the integrity of the experience." And it is interesting to note that in discussing Yeats' poem "Blood and the Moon," Brooks finds that its value resides in part in the poet's refusal "to define the moralization except in terms of the specific symbols."[6]

The question as to whether "minimum commentary" is a valid part of the long poem or of certain types of subject matter is one which I do not feel is within the scope of this book. If this appears to be an ambiguous area in certain types of Western poetry, the attitude of the haiku poet is sharply defined. There can be no commentary, no conclusion; the concrete, sensuous material to be intuited must stand alone. While the latter concept is by no means strange to Western poetic thought, it may be that the clear-cut position of the haiku form may serve a useful purpose within the large body of Western poetry. Where Brooks has said that some poems demand a revision of our ideas of poetry, perhaps haiku can force a clarification of them.*

Even that most persistent of imagistic poets, William Carlos Williams, would not escape censure from Japanese critics, even though he has maintained that "all art is necessarily objective. It doesn't declaim or explain; it presents."[7] Yet the function of the explicit, prose statement in the first line of the following, beautiful poem seems primarily explanatory:[8]

> so much depends
> upon
>
> a red wheel
> barrow
>
> glazed with rain
> water
>
> beside the white
> chickens

Let us compare this with the following poem by Bashô, remembering that enjoyment that comes from a haiku comes intuitively and immediately, rather than through logical reasoning:

> On a withered bough
> A crow alone is perching;

---

* "From time to time poets appear, who if they are accepted at all, demand a radical revision of the existing conception of poetry." *(Modern Poetry and the Tradition,* p. vii.)

Autumn evening now.

How clear it is that a great deal depends upon the crow, perching upon the withered bough; yet Bashô, complying with the exacting standards of haiku poetry, conveys its importance only through the concrete objects. Perhaps this is part of what he meant when he said: "The haiku that reveals seventy to eighty percent of its subject is good. Those that reveal fifty to sixty percent we never tire of."[9]

We feel instinctively that the air is clear in Bashô's haiku; the sky hangs gently above the horizon like a cobalt mirror. There, against a tranquil background of the autumn blue turning almost into deep black-purple, we can see the tall tree standing, distinct and still, above the gathering gloom of the autumn twilight, and a black crow perching alone on one of the withered branches. A loneliness is there, and a mystic power which holds us close with an acute feeling akin to melancholy sadness, tinged with acceptance. The three objects mentioned—the withered bough, a crow, autumn evening—have the same feeling and we are moved by and impressed with this common emotion existing among those three; and only through them can we feel that emotion, that sense of the essence of this autumn evening, through our intuition.

Here we want no adjective to blur our impression; the picture speaks for itself. We seek no metaphor or simile to make the picture clear, but simply let the objects do their part. If the picture is so beautiful that he who looks must admire, how superfluous and intrusive would it sound if the author were to exclaim, "Oh, how beautiful it is" and the like. If sad, we do not want him to tell us so, but we demand that he make it sad; then our understanding will supply the necessary adjectives. One advantage of this method, as Hughes has remarked, is that " there is a kind of force gained from the expression of this emotion once and once only through an appropriate image."[10] Indeed, the simple treatment of this kind, whether of a picture or of a haiku, is always the most difficult. It demands the true, mature artist, like the master Bashô.

Here is another example:

> Underneath the eaves
> A blooming large hydrangea
> Overbrims its leaves.

Here we see the hydrangea growing with its large disks of clustered flowers by the house. "Overbrims its leaves," the poet puts it, to say aesthetically how the flowers bloom among and above the deep-green enamelled leaves. The poem has a bright light; it gives the impression of a rich oil painting drawn with the dynamic strokes of a masterful hand.

Another equally colorful picture is this haiku:

> Scattered the peony!
> One beside another pile,
> Petals two or three.

The beauty of the splendid peony expresses itself. The richness of the flower has a magic touch to keep our attention; yet here, viewing its large petals piled one upon another rather than lying one above the other, we can feel their movement, a sense of weight exquisite enough to give the living texture of the petals, further vivified with a definite number of the petals—"two or three"—to give a concrete impression. Contrasted with the softness and barely perceptible weight, how appropriate is the dynamic cadence, "Scattered. . . . !"

Color can be as important to haiku as to painting:

> In the twilight gloom
> Of the redwood and the pine
> Some wisterias bloom.

There is a twilight touch to this scene. The lovely wisterias hang their clusters against the background of the semi-darkness of the redwood and the pine, whereby the sweet purple of the flower gains in softness and visual contrast. It reminds us of the rich coloring of some exotic painting, especially of the southern school of Wang Wei in the Sung period.

Thus haiku has something in common with painting, in the representation of the object alone, without comment, never presented to be other than what it is, but not represented completely as it is. For if the haiku poet moves us by presenting rather than describing objects, he does so by presenting the particulars in which the emotional powers of the things or scenes reside. And from these particulars comes the significance and the importance of his particular haiku. He renders in a few epithets what he experiences, so that imagination will fill those spaces with all the details in which the experiential value of the images reside. He does not give us meaning; he gives us the concrete objects which have meaning, because he has so experienced them. When we read such a poem, how true it is that the "meanest flower can give thoughts That do oft lie too deep for tears."

CHAPTER TWO

BASIC PRINCIPLES

IN THE FOREGOING chapter we have seen what haiku is like when compared with painting. For the more than five hundred years that Japanese poets have been composing haiku, they have found it a fit instrument for giving utterance to their experiences; it is the most compact, evocative verse-form crystallized by Japanese talents. Santei, the haiku poet with whom I lived for almost two years, has well expressed the supreme position that the form has for the Japanese literary artist; even though he attained great success as a novelist under his actual name, Masao Kume, he felt that the haiku was the greatest and most enduring flower of Japanese art:

> For me haiku was truly the gate which opened my literary career and even now I think of and yearn for the joy of appreciating and creating haiku as a haiku poet. Often I wonder why I did not spend my whole life as an artist as a pure haiku poet. . . . In regard to a unity in life, art, and mental attitude, there is no other artist for whom it is so harmonized as for the haiku poet. . . . Though Bashô and Issa are matters of the past, even now there are haiku poets like them. So the feeling that in a country like Japan haiku will always be the first and last art form is deeply held.[1]

Its long history, in itself, shows that it is able to satisfy certain poetic needs. Its ability to do so is, I feel, because its underlying aesthetic principles are the same as those for any art form in the East or West.

A haiku can be a thing of joy to any reader for the same reasons that a sonnet can be, although the techniques may seem so different that even as acute a reader as John Gould Fletcher, the noted Imagist poet, could occasionally be led astray in his judgment of it.* I hope therefore in the following pages to discuss the aesthetic nature of haiku, following generally the theories of Benedetto Croce, John Dewey, and others, many of whose basic positions seem to me shared by those Japanese haiku poets whose random observations have been preserved and by Japanese critics. Such a discussion will have two purposes: first, to organize and unify basic aesthetic theory in regard to haiku; and second, to demonstrate that haiku, far from being an esoteric, purely Japanese form, incomprehensible to the West, shares common ground with all art in an important and significant manner.

1. AESTHETIC ATTITUDE

Let us suppose that a poet is looking at a rye field one sunny afternoon with two friends, one a farmer who owns the field and the other an entomologist. The farmer is explaining how lovely and rich his field is and how many bushels of rye it produces every year. While they are thus talking, a red dragonfly passes before them, and immediately the entomologist notices it. Perhaps he classifies it as an idle mental exercise, and may even remark on its beauty aloud to his friends. The poet, standing beside them, also sees the dragonfly and notices it light on a blade of rye, as do the other two. He is immediately interested in the dragonfly—in its color, form, and quality.

This is a happening shared by the three men. The farmer, in seeing the dragonfly, may have agreed with his friend the entomologist about its beauty, but it does not affect him. He is probably thinking of something else; perhaps he feels very proud of the rich rye field he owns. The value he places on his field is directly referable to the price the grain will bring him in the market place. His attitude might be called commercial.

The entomologist's attitude is scientific. As soon as he sees the red

* "The relationship of the Chinese classical poets to the Japanese *tanka* and *hokku* poets is, psychologically speaking, like the relation of full-grown and mature human figures to a group of rather small and temporarily attractive children. The *tanka* or the *hokku* poem is nothing more than a sketch. . . ." ("The Orient and Contemporary Poetry" in *The Asian Legacy and American Life,* p. 159.)

dragonfly, he ceases seeing it directly and sees it only as a part of his system of categories. If he had not recognized it, he would most likely have observed its characteristics by counting the number of its wings, legs, and so on, in reference to his entomological knowledge, and tried to arrive at some sort of conclusion. As Allen Tate has concisely put it, the scientific statement is "about a thing, a person, an experience, which relates it to something else, not for the purpose of giving us intensive knowledge of the thing, person, or experience, in itself and as a whole; but simply to give us, in varying degrees depending upon the exactness of the science under which it is viewed, the half-knowledge that limits us to the control of its extensive relations."[2]

In contrast to these two attitudes, the poet's is neither commercial nor scientific. His attention is directed not to his knowledge about the dragonfly, nor to the value of the rye field. He is interested in the object for its own sake. Furthermore, he is not aware even of how beautiful the object is or of how he is affected by it. An attitude such as this is aesthetic. I shall call it a haiku attitude.

This haiku attitude is a readiness for an experience for its own sake. The value of the experience does not lie outside the object as the value of the rye field lies outside of the object for the farmer; for the scientist, the value of the dragonfly lies in the object, but only as that object can be classified, generalized about, and related. Nor does the aesthetic value lie in the observer's emotion about the object or in the emotion aroused in him by the object, as when the scientist casually remarked on its beauty. A poet, when he is being a poet, cannot make such a statement. That is to say, he cannot interject anything of his personal or egoistic needs between himself and the experience; and it is interesting to note that Japanese critics and poets are most insistent upon the importance of this point.

As Otsuji,* a noted poet and one of the greatest haiku theorists, puts it: "[We can enter the world of creation] when we are completely sincere and humble before nature, yet free and fearless; when we are never separated from nature; when we do not introduce idle fancy or fall into cogitation."[3] One aspect of the sincerity and humility he calls for is the poet's willingness to surrender cherished intellectual concepts before the reality of his experience: "It is unnecessary to believe in some ideo-

---

* Seki Osuga is referred to throughout by his pen name of Otsuji.

logy or personal philosophy in order to compose haiku, because, since they contain ideas, there is a danger that the poet will compose haiku through logic where pure feeling should be the motive."[4] This understanding is of course shared by Western critics such as Allen Tate, who points out that while there are poets who understand "the poetic use of their ideas," still a "conscious cultivation of ideas in poetry is always dangerous."[5]

Bashô notes that the poet must also surrender personal vanities and attitudes: "The verse of some poets tries to speak with charm but, on the contrary, is completely without it; the quality of charm is not to speak of charm. ... Again the verse of some is over-ambitious and loses its sincerity."[6]

As for the poet's emotions, Otsuji remarks, as have many Western thinkers,* that far from aiding him toward clarity of vision, they will actually hinder him when they are of a certain sort: "When one is overwhelmed by sorrow, that sorrow cannot produce a haiku. When one is joyful and immersed in happiness, that feeling cannot produce a haiku."[7] Asô calls such emotions crude and hints at the reason why they have no place in aesthetic experience; they do not arise from the experience: "[In the aesthetic attitude] what we call feeling is not human feelings like joy, sadness, anger, etc. In Bashô's art of *haikai* these fresh, crude feelings are rather avoided. Such feelings as joy, anger, sadness or delight are subjective and are merely another form of subjectivism."[8] For, as Rainer Maria Rilke has said, "Verses are not, as people imagine, simply feelings; they are experiences."[9] The whole question of the role of emotion in experience is dealt with more fully in the succeeding pages.[10] I wish here only to point out that it can serve to separate the poet from experience.

When a person is interested and involved in the object for its own sake, then, a haiku attitude is formed. It is therefore said that a haiku attitude is a state of readiness for an experience which can be aesthetic. Without such an attitude it is impossible to have an aesthetic experience. However, the relationship between the attitude and the experience is not causative; when a person with a haiku attitude looks at an object, he does not necessarily have an aesthetic experience. Therefore I call

---

* E.g., John Dewey: "Portrayal of intoxication is a common device of the comic stage. But a man actually drunken would have to use art to conceal his condition if he is not to disgust his audience...." (*Art as Experience*, p. 80.)

it a state of readiness, of receptivity. As Otsuji has remarked, "the writer faces these conditions [which produce a haiku attitude] and his sympathetic activity is very strong; this alone cannot produce haiku."[11]

This readiness, moreover, must be for a disinterested form of single-minded activity. If it is not disinterested, it will be commercial, the farmer's attitude, or scientific, like his friend's. If it is not single-minded —i.e., for the sake of the experience alone—there will be only a relationship, not an experience. To clarify this point, let us remember that both the farmer and the entomologist related to the dragonfly; the act was casual, fleeting, and did not involve them in any serious manner. What is meant here by single-mindedness will be explored in the following section.

2. AESTHETIC EXPERIENCE

I have stated that a haiku attitude and an aesthetic experience are inseparable and co-exist, but that a haiku attitude does not necessarily cause an experience to be aesthetic. Here the question arises as to the nature of the aesthetic experience which has been characterized above as being among other things, single-minded. By this is meant that during such an experience the observer has no awareness of himself as separate from what he sees or hears, from what he is experiencing. As he contemplates and experiences, becomes submerged in the object, there comes in Coleridge's phrase "a coalescence of subject and object" into one. As Otsuji has said, then "consciousness is completely unified"[12] and "the poet's nature and environment are one."[13]

John Dewey has called this state the "common pattern of experience": "The outline of the common pattern [of experience] is set by the fact that every experience is the result of interaction between a live creature and some aspect of the world in which he lives."[14] The condition exists until we reflect upon it. As Ernst Cassirer has put it, "If we consult immediate experience unmixed with reflection, the opposition of subject and object is shown to be wholly foreign to it . . . . What is grasped by consciousness here and now 'is' and is precisely in the form offered by direct experience."[15] Otsuji has expressed almost the identical thought, indicating that the immediate experience is the aesthetic experience: "**At** the instant when our mental activity almost merges into an unconscious state—i.e., the relationship between the subject and object is forgotten—we can experience the most aesthetic moment. This is what is implied when it is said that one goes into the heart of created things and becomes one with nature."[16]

The "form of direct experience" is the realization of what the object is, in its unity and oneness, in and for itself. It is an experiencing of what, in being itself, the object is, so that it becomes unique. It is, as Croce has maintained, an experiencing of the quality of the object.[17] The form of the color red is red—as we see it. The form of the crow, as Bashô saw it, is the crow. Experience then is always the interaction of a man and his environment.

What then are the uses of such words as *subject* and *object*—a dualism that has long plagued Western philosophy*—in dealing with aesthetic experience? They are convenient tools to distinguish aspects of a whole, to deal with its parts, and to analyze it. They are useful terms, as long as it is remembered that, in the aesthetic experience, the subject cannot exist without the object, nor the object without the subject, since they are one. Only as they are one, in a concrete and living unity, is there an aesthetic experience.† Otsuji, too, remarks on how inappropriate these dualistic terms are as applied to haiku arising out of a true aesthetic moment: "When one reaches the state where he is unattached and sings naturally, he can produce true haiku. The haiku composed under this condition transcend what we call the subjective or objective attitude."[18]

So far I have dealt with the role of the object in the aesthetic experience. To consider the role of the subject, let us begin with the question as to a particular artist's choice of a particular object out of the limitless objects available. That is to say, not all objects speak to an artist, inviting contemplation and absorption into an experience. Which one

---

* Alfred North Whitehead, in his enormously influential book, has suggestively described the situation: "The enormous success of the scientific abstractions, yielding on the one hand *matter* with its *simple location* in space and time, on the other hand, *mind*, perceiving, suffering, and reasoning, but not interfering, has foisted onto Philosophy the task of accepting them as the most concrete rendering of fact." (*Science and the Modern World*, p. 81.)

† These particular terms have never become as rigidly dualistic in Japan as in Occidental thinking and their oneness in experience is generally understood and accepted. Due to the historical associations around words such as *subject* and *object*, or *form* and *content*, the English words themselves seem immediately to suggest separate entities rather than distinguishable aspects of a whole. Wherever these terms occur hereafter, they are to be understood as defined in the text.

will become a part of a realization is dependent upon what Dewey has called "funded experience."

Let us take a musician, a painter, and a poet who are looking at a scene in which all three find a mountain, a brook murmuring through a flowering dale, and birds singing. As Dewey has observed, they cannot face this scene with no interests and attitudes, with no meanings and values drawn from their prior experience; he goes on to say: "Before an artist can develop his reconstruction of the scene before him...he observes the scene with meanings and values brought to his perception by prior experiences.... They cannot vanish and yet the artist continue to see an object."[19] Waggoner maintains the same position, emphasizing the reciprocity between object and subject:

> The poet today then...must constantly concern himself with the immediately presented data of experience.... But concrete experience has meaning,— indeed, it has form, has existence—only in terms of values.... Even on the rudimentary level this is so: the phenomenon of attention, without which experience could not be said to exist because it would be, if anything, an indescribable blur, means exclusion as much as it means concentration. We contribute a part of the meaning. We interpret even as we see, not simply after we have seen. Awareness is a dynamic and purposeful activity....[20]

So categorical is the role of the observer's funded experience in his experience of the environment that Cassirer points out that "thus no content of experience can ever appear as something absolutely strange."[21]

The way, then, that each of our three artists synthesizes his experience is different not only because of their respective fields of art, but in Dewey's words because of "those memories, not necessarily conscious, but retentions that have been organically incorporated in the very structure of the self."[22] Otsuji, in referring to "our real life" in the following passage, seems to mean what Dewey calls the "very structure of the self": "The spirit of composing haiku must be a searching which is both passive and active, to feel the dignity of unadorned nature in such a way as to reflect our real life, in all its diversities."[23] Croce, in dealing with the same concept, reveals the flexibility of the artist's funded experience and its capabilities for growth and change:

> The research of which we speak does not concern the superficial but the profound character of the man; it is not concerned with the congealed and solidified stratum [e.g., any political beliefs, any openly professed religion] but with the tide that flows beneath it.... Presuppositions are the philoso-phemes that everyone carries with him, gathering them from the times and

from tradition, or forming them anew by means of his observations and rapid reflections. In poetical works, they form the condition remote from the psychological attitude, which generates poetical visions.[24]

In expanding what Croce above calls the poet's presuppositions gathered from the times, Waggoner concurs in the following manner: "All poetry exhibits to a greater or less degree—greatest of all in didactic poetry... and least in pure lyrics...—the patterns of assumption, attitude, and idea of the age and of the poet."[25]

Consequently, even were our three artists poets, they would not experience the common scene except differently, for in virtue of their different funded experiences, any aspect of the scene is potentially significant. As Bashô has said, "There is no subject whatever that is not fit for hokku."[26] What each selects out of the scene is what meaning he finds as the quality of the experience he realizes.

Why the artist contemplates this aspect of his environment rather than that is not his concern. Indeed, he is not completely free in the choice. He is solely interested in experiencing the object that does present itself, in and for itself. When he contemplates a scene, in virtue of his funded experience, any object that has meaning resonatory enough to respond to and answer the impulsion generated in him becomes his subject. He becomes so aware of it that his self is that awareness; he does not reflect on it. He is like a tuning fork placed before a vibrating one of the same frequency. When he contemplates the impassionate, living object he immediately realizes its quality just as the sound from the tuning forks will become audible. He is in a state of aesthetic resonation, a harmonized whole of all the meaningful experiences he has had, brought to bear upon the moment of aesthetic contemplation.

Every man, poet or not, as Dewey remarks, possesses a funded experience through which his insights are indeed his own: "I have tried to show...that the aesthetic is no intruder in experience from without, whether by way of idle luxury or transcendent reality, but that it is the clarified and intensified development of traits that belong to every normally complete experience."[27] But often we see only superficially, through the eyes of convention, prejudice, or tradition; as I have said, we can relate casually to objects instead of experiencing them. This is fatal for the poet, as poet. His perceptions can become sharp only as his funded experience becomes easily available to him, as he strives to be sincere, to be devoted single-mindedly to the realization that is his.

Only by doing so can he achieve an aesthetic experience or, as Otsuji calls it, a unity in life, arising from the poet's very being: "Before a poet can compose haiku, he must find a unity within his life which must come from the effort to discover his true self."[28]

It is in this area that questions of what sincerity, morality and truth in art are can be most satisfactorily resolved, without reference to standards that lie beyond the concern of art. Bradley has shown the comic implications of evaluating art by direct reference to other values:

> If we [determine the intrinsic value of poetry by direct reference to other human values] we shall find ourselves maintaining what we did not expect. If poetic value lies in the stimulation of religious feelings, *Lead Kindly Light* is no better a poem than many a tasteless version of a Psalm; if in the excitement of patriotism, why is *Scots, wha hae* superior to *We don't want to fight?* if in the mitigation of the passions, the Odes of Sappho will win but little praise; if in instruction, *Armstrong's Art of Preserving Health* should win much.[29]

Mistaken notions as to what constitutes poetic sincerity are many: an attempt to espouse good "humanitarian" principles, to re-affirm without qualification the values of religion, or a given moral or political position, or to deal with "beautiful" subject matter rather than what a reader finds gross or crude. As both perceptive Japanese and Western critics have maintained, such concepts of artistic sincerity are irrelevant. They can result in sheer sentimentality, as Cleanth Brooks declares:

> [An older view] expresses itself as a vigilance which keeps out of the poem all those extraneous and distracting elements which might seem to contradict what the poet wishes to communicate to his audience. It is the sincerity of the conscientious expositor who makes his point, even at the price of suppressions and exclusions. Poetry which embodies such a conception of sincerity, when it is unsuccessful, has as its characteristic vice, sentimentality. For sentimentality nearly always involves an over-simplification of the experience in question.[30]

Rather, as he goes on to say, a more tenable position will deal with art in its own terms; sincerity lies in a single-minded devotion to the totality of the realization:

> The second conception of sincerity...reveals itself as an unwillingness to ignore the complexity of experience. The poet attempts to fuse the conflicting elements in a harmonious whole.[30]

In dealing with the experience, Asô has pointed out that Onitsura, one of the outstanding haiku poets of the seventeenth century, had pertinent observations to make to poets. For aside from the necessity of rejecting the claims coming from without the area of art, the poet must also be sincere in his own artistic practice:

> At the center of Onitsura's haiku theory is his statement about truth. Everywhere in his writing he uses the word *makoto*. This term is used in various ways and its meaning is not fixed. However, he uses this term in the sense of *sincerity*. In his writing entitled *Soliloquy,* he said, "When one composes a verse and exerts his attention only to rhetoric or phraseology, the sincerity is diminished."
>
> .   .   .
>
> The fact that no artistic effort in the form or no decorative expression in the content [should be present] is Onitsura's ideal, which is the way to sincerity.[31]

And as has been previously pointed out[32] the poet can become single-mindedly devoted to his experience only as he abandons the needs of the self and submits humbly to his vision.

Here also lies the crux of the question of morality in art, which is synonymous with the poet's sincerity of devotion to his realization, not with his treatment of morally enlightening subject matter or with pious conclusions appended to his works. This is not to maintain that a valid work of art cannot have morally sound effects or should not treat of moral subject matter; but morality *per se* is not the artist's concern. Rather it is the experience, which is unique if it is truly his and which it is his function to grasp. Such an experience may be profoundly moral and religious, as indeed the Zen quality is in many of Bashô's haiku; but it was not his concern to make his poems so. His concern was to grasp the intuition. As Croce has maintained, "if art be beyond morality, the artist is neither this side of it nor that, but under its empire, in so far as he is a man who cannot withdraw himself from the duties of man, and must look upon art itself—art which is not and never will be moral—as a mission to be exercised as a priestly office."[33]

The importance of the artist's attitude toward his art is a commonly recognized concept by Japanese thinkers, who maintain further that his "life, art, and mental attitude"[34] must be unified and harmonized, so great must be his devotion to his "priestly office." Asô's comments on Bashô may be taken as representative:

> In the life of a haiku poet, his attitudes from day to day were very important.

The haiku he composed each day was his "death verse"* for that day, according to Bashô.... [Consequently] the art of haiku should be the outbursting of attitudes he holds every day.... The attitude of the haiku poet is to find the way of art in the common modes of living.

• • •

One of the outstanding characteristics of Bashô is that life and art are in perfect harmony.... In his work, art is the expression of the whole man, and in it, the whole man was able to emerge in the art.[35]

Otsuji expressed the same idea: "Therefore as regards the attitude necessary for composing haiku, it requires endless effort to find a unity in life and to make life an art."[36]

Unlike the Japanese, Western critics have for the most part tended to avoid such phrases as to make "one's life an art," not insisting upon the relationship between an artist's mode of life or sense of artistic morality and his works. The hesitancy is due undoubtedly to a wish to escape any identification with the school that cultivates a so-called aesthetic life, which usually degenerates into an esthete, pseudo-Bohemian display in which the arty rather than art became the standard; or with the school that adversely criticizes the art product because of the unconventionality or irregularities of the artist's life—a remnant of the Victorian attitude. Students of art have also tended to feel that the matter lay outside of their area, which is perhaps another instance of the fragmentation of learning in the West. As Allen Tate makes clear, however, there is an awareness of a connection between literary practice and the problems of morality: "I assume that a poet is a man eager to come under the bondage of limitations if he can find them. As I understand John Peale Bishop's poetry, he is that eager man. It is a moral problem, but that phase I cannot touch here."[37]

Morality lies then in the artist's sincerity as he searches for artistic truth. When Onitsura states that without truth there is no haiku, he is not referring to actual truth, but rather to what something, actual or not, is. The true in the sense of the actual is not what the artist presents. In the case of one of Bashô's poems, this point is well illuminated. He wrote the following haiku on the seashore of Kuwana:

> Fallen snows are light,
> And the lancelets appear
> No more than an inch white.[38]

---

* Following Japanese tradition, each poet was supposed to compose one final poem shortly before his death, which was then his "death verse."

The poem represents what Bashô saw on a beach where the snow had fallen lightly. This is factual, not the poetic truth that Bashô was seeking. For in composing the poem, he was too much bound by factual truth and failed to grasp a deep insight of what it was that he saw, actual or not. Of course I do not mean by this that the factual is not important, but rather that, through factual truth, the poet can realize poetic truth. Bashô, apparently feeling some dissatisfaction with the above version, perhaps along some such line of reasoning as that presented, later changed the poem to read:

> In the dawn twilight
> There the lancelets appear
> No more than an inch white.[39]

He made the following remark about his revision, which is recorded in the Sanzôshi: "This verse was first composed beginning with the five syllables, 'Fallen snows are light.' It is a matter of great regret to me."[40] It may be said that, from the factual point of view, the revised version is false, since the happening did not occur in this way. However, it is poetic truth, of the sort that not only Japanese but Western poets try to realize. As Eliot has remarked of philosophical theories when they have entered the realm of art, the first kind of truth then becomes irrelevant: "A philosophical theory which has entered into poetry is established, for its truth or falsity in one sense ceases to matter, and its truth in another sense is proved."[41]

Suzanne Langer points out, too, that factual truth is not artistic truth, for this arises from the total poem: " 'Artistic truth' does *not* belong to statements in the poem or their obvious figurative meanings, but to its figures and meanings *as they are used,* its statements *as they are made* . . . in short, to the poem as 'significant form.' "[42] What she means by significant form may be illustrated in the way Bashô realized his insight based on the actual happening. When we compare the two poems above, this point becomes clear.

In the first version we find a small, actual world, flattened by the seashore on which the light snows are white; the whiteness of the snow and that of the lancelet destroy each other's life and nothing remains significant. There is only the actual scene, which is no more than a mere fragment of the poet's intuition. But in the revised verse the seashore becomes a part of the great universe aesthetically wrapped in the twilight of dawn. And the lancelet, no more than an inch white, breathes in significant form, its transparent beauty alive against the atmosphere at early dawn.

Otsuji has pointed out why it is essential for the poet constantly to apply effort and discipline in the realization of his intuition: "A sense of immediacy does not come alive for a poet with any deep significance without such past effort."[43] That is, with such effort, every experience can become excitingly and meaningfully his own, not arrived at second-hand. Only thus, too, can his critical judgment be sharpened and enable him to recognize falseness in his work. Kyorai, a disciple of Bashô's, reports that Kyoroku, another follower, put it thus: " 'I am tired of my self of yesterday.' What a good saying this is. The deceased master [Bashô] often spoke thus...."[44] What Kyoroku meant, one supposes, is that he is wearied of the self who yesterday created a haiku that today he finds false.

The aim of aesthetic contemplation, then, is intuitive insight into the nature of experience, "the total revelation" in Allen Tate's words.[45] That the revelation is knowledge is somewhat defensively maintained by Western critics. For example, Stephen Pepper: "[Aesthetic experience] is the most illuminating of activities. It gives us direct insight into the nature of the world. It shows us what is real there, it realizes events. ... Art is thus as fully as cognitive, fully as knowing as science, so that the contextualists are fond of calling intuition of quality a realization."[46] One of the uses of that knowledge, as Croce points out, is to provide the insights which may lead to concepts or generalizations:

> If we have shown that the aesthetic form is altogether independent of the intellectual and suffices to itself without external support, we have not said that the intellectual can stand without the aesthetic. This *reciprocity* would not be true.... Concepts are not possible without intuitions.... Intuitions are: this river, this lake, this brook, this rain, this glass of water; the concept is: water, not this or that appearance and particular example of water, but water in general....[47]

Another use which both Whitehead and Dewey point out is that the artist's direct intuitions are correctives against the fallacy of "misplaced concreteness," the name Whitehead has given to the error of mistaking abstract logical constructions for the concrete fact: "Wordsworth, Shelley are representative of the intuitive refusal seriously to accept the abstract materialism of science."[48] As Dewey puts it: "The conception that objects have fixed and unalterable values is precisely the prejudice from which art emancipates us."[49]

Yet what that knowledge is that art yields through insight is still a difficult question. For example, although Waggoner states that "poetry deals with, includes, is in some sense knowledge," still he is forced to admit that what the knowledge is has not yet been "adequately defined or agreed upon."[50] The background of this question as Western critics deal with it is of course the low esteem to which all disciplines based on an intuitive approach, not publicly demonstrable— e.g., art, religion, philosophy—fell, during the nineteenth century particularly, because of the stunning successes of science and of the scientific method. Reality, as painted by science for its own needs, has been mistaken for ultimate reality, which, being based on a positivistic, mechanistic naturalism, wrought havoc with traditional religious, philosophic, and aesthetic assumptions. As has been suggested,[51] recent thinkers have demonstrated that a "denial of a large part of man's experience because a smaller part seemed to demand it"[52] is unnecessary. It is, in fact, impossible. As Cleanth Brooks has put it: "The refusal to accept the scientific account in matters where the scientific method is valid and relevant is unrealistic, but there is nothing 'escapist' about a hostility to science which orders science off the premises as a trespasser when science has taken up a position where it has no business to be."[53]

Although I do not feel that it is within the scope of this book to explore this question fully, it may be interesting and perhaps enlightening to see how similar are the pronouncements of Japanese haiku scholars to those of Western critics in this area. The similarity seems to me to demonstrate that, no matter how vague or unprecise the language used, as compared to scientific language, to describe the nature of the knowledge yielded by art, there is a common core to their discussions. Moreover, the Japanese as yet unburdened by invidious comparisons between science and art, are not so defensive as the Western thinkers and speak more freely.

A common point of departure seems to lie in Waggoner's following statement: "The poet working as poet includes more of total meaning than the scientist or the practical man does, and works more intimately with the concrete wholes that make up the material of total meaning

than the philosopher does. . . . [Therefore] poetry conveys more humanly
relevant, which is to say more meaningful, more philosophical knowledge
about life and man than science does."⁵⁴ When the haiku poet or critic
speaks of the "knowledge about life and man" that haiku conveys, he
almost invariably does so in terms of man's knowledge of nature, and in
terms of his insights into it, leading eventually to a realization of his
relationship to nature. Representative statements along this line follow.
Let us first take Otsuji: "What is expressed in a haiku is a very small
aspect of phenomena; yet what the poet experiences is the reality hidden
behind what he expresses, which may be said to be a universal feeling
arising from the union of the poet with nature."⁵⁵ Asô's description
of the thinking of both Onitsura and Bashô is revealing:

> Once an abbot asked Onitsura what the essence of haiku art was, and he
> replied: "In front of a garden, a camellia tree blooms with white flowers."
> Since the truth of the universe lies even in a single flower, insight into the
> universe and into God can be grasped by understanding this truth. . . .
> Onitsura thinks that the true way of haiku art is to discover poetic refine-
> ment in the truth of natural phenomena, whether in the snow, the moon,
> or flowers, with a selfless attitude.

                    •   •   •

> [Bashô] tried his utmost to master the hidden aspects of nature and to reveal
> its secrets. What he tried to find was not the outward appearance of nature,
> but to touch its very heart.⁵⁶

The master Bashô himself said: "In the sound of the frog leaping from
the bank overgrown with wild grass, a haikai is heard. There is the
seen; there is the heard. Where there is hokku as the poet has felt it,
there is poetic truth."⁵⁷

For the Japanese haiku poet, insights into nature are most usually
expressed through the important element called by them the seasonal
theme—a concept explored in later sections of this book. Briefly described,
it refers to the inclusion in a haiku of the sense of the season of the
year with which the haiku deals. Otsuji, in one of his characteristically
penetrating insights, declared that once the concept was accepted as
absolutely essential to haiku, a most important consequence followed:

> Viewed against the popular idea that the seasonal theme is a man-made
> concept, the contention that it is unnecessary to haiku has some justification;
> however, if one comes to my idea that the seasonal theme is the natural object
> itself in all its naturalness—that its function is to symbolize nature—then for
> the first time will he come face to face with the problem of the relationship

between nature and himself. Here the poet should think deeply of the problem of the self.[58]

One supposes that W. M. Urban had the same thought in mind when he said that the language of poetry, among its other concerns, always says one thing, "namely, that human life and man are unique, free, and self-determining parts of nature."[59] Although the Japanese might not agree with the characterization of man's relationship to nature as given by Urban in his three adjectives, he would unequivocally agree that haiku dealt with it, and deals with it because, as Asô says, insight into it will reveal the "truth of the universe"[60] or what Waggoner calls "the supreme or unifying value."[61]

To summarize, aesthetic contemplation is, then, a disinterested awareness of an object. The scientist also shares this awareness, but he, in scientific contemplation, has no other end than scientific knowledge of it. The artist, on the other hand, is not occupied, as is the scientist, in drawing conclusions from the object observed. Nor is he interested in making any judgments about it. He is interested in the object only for its own sake. Aesthetic contemplation is also characterized by single-mindedness, for in the state of aesthetic contemplation the subject and object are one. Only as the poet remains completely devoted to the totality of experience in contemplation does the concept of artistic sincerity have meaning. Morality for the artist also lies in his sincerity as he searches for poetic truth; the concept applies to the art work only in reference to the sincerity of the poetic intent and not to values outside the area of art. Poetic truth also arises from aesthetic sincerity, for it is a function of a realized insight, and is not to be determined only by reference to fact or actuality. During the state of realization the quality of the object is grasped. The anecdote is told of Seihô, the famous Japanese painter, that in looking at a picture of a chicken drawn by a student he clucked several times. Here awareness of the object was his whole being and he became that chicken. But had he exclaimed on the beauty of the painting, he would have been separated from the object he was observing; he would have been passing judgment upon it and would no longer have been one with it; and the experience would no longer have been aesthetic. The content of aesthetic experience is judged to be a kind of knowledge, different from the scientific, offering intuitive insight into the deepest levels of meaning.

3. HAIKU MOMENT

Aesthetic contemplation is contemplation of an object and the object's quality which the artist, in virtue of his funded experience, can experience. When an aesthetic contemplation is completed and the quality of the object is fully realized, the artist having felt the perception as a totality, this I call an aesthetic moment. At this moment, and indeed just prior to it as we sense that it is about to come into being, "one's feeling already has reached an enlightened, Nirvana-like harmony,"[62] timeless since "the poet's nature and environment are unified," as Otsuji has said.[63] This moment is common to all art. It is characteristic of it that the completion of the reading of, let us say, a full-length novel or of the hearing of a long symphony does not end its effects. These persist, as many can testify, as did Gustave Flaubert when he said that he loved best those works which made him "dream all day long";[64] as did John Gould Fletcher, who remarked of certain poems that they had the "extraordinary power to set up echoes in the reader's mind";[65] or as did Bashô, who said that experiencing was a "going back."[66]

What these remarks seem to refer to is what might be called the power of "resonation" of the aesthetic moment, which arises of course from the words of the work. However, the relationship between the words and the resonation is that while a temporal element is inherent in the reading of the words, the insight into what is expressed through them, as they attain their full meaning simultaneously, is immediate. In this simultaneity and immediacy, obviously impossible with a novel, a sonnet, or even a quatrain, the words, although of course they give rise to these effects, do not function directly. It is physically impossible for them to do so, where possibly a hundred thousand or so words, as in a novel, are concerned. It is, as I stated, even impossible in a sonnet or a quatrain. Yet there is a literary form in which the words themselves can occur as a simultaneous happening. When this kind of aesthetic moment does take place, I call it a *haiku moment*.

A haiku moment is a kind of aesthetic moment—a moment in which the words which created the experience and the experience itself can become one.[67] The nature of a haiku moment is anti-temporal and its quality is eternal, for in this state man and his environment are one unified whole, in which there is no sense of time. The total implication of the words in the realization of experience creates that sense of immediacy which Ezra Pound declared was essential for art: "[The image is] that which presents an intellectual and emotional complex in an instant of time. . . . It is the presentation of such a 'complex' instantaneously which gives that sense of sudden liberation; that sense of freedom from time limits and space limits; that sense of sudden growth, which we experience in the presence of the greatest works of art."[68]

The truly realized haiku moment is the goal toward which every haiku poet strives. It is as difficult to create a haiku arising from it as to create a tanka or a sonnet. But if a poet overcomes its difficulties, we are charmed by its perfections. It is this that "moves Heaven and Earth—strikes devils and deities with pity—softens man and woman."[69] The haiku challenges the great poets, taxing their power and revealing vividly their individuality and differences in temperament. Rare indeed is the well-realized haiku, as Bashô repeated to his disciples in many ways:

> He who creates three to five haiku poems during a lifetime is a haiku poet. He who attains to ten is a master.
>
> •   •   •
>
> [A disciple said]: "Does even a master sometime nod?" The answer was: "In every poem."[70]

This seemingly quixotically high standard was shared by Ezra Pound: "It is better to present one Image in a lifetime than to produce voluminous work."[71] The haiku moment results, then, in a new insight or vision which the haiku poet must render as an organic whole. It is aesthetic truth, wherein beauty lies and sincerity, when the poet is devoted to realizing it alone. It is all that a poet can accept.

Nor are such moments and experiences confined to artists alone. For when the ordinary man confronts a work of art, or indeed experiences aesthetically any object, his process of realization is identical to that of the artist. Insofar as he experiences it, he realizes its quality, what kind of thing it is. As Croce has said, there is no difference between the artist and his audience in the kind of experience each has: "Great artists are said to reveal us to ourselves. But how could this be possible unless there be identity of nature between their imagination and ours and unless the difference be one only of quantity? It were well to change *poeta nascitur* into *homo nascitur poeta;* some men are born great poets, some small."[72] The artist, then, when he is successful, communicates an experience valuable to the spectator for the new insight afforded him. The artist, however, must be able, as the layman need not, to embody and objectify his realization in terms of his particular discipline and of his individual insight. This leads to a consideration of various aspects of form and technique.

I wish to limit this area to haiku and to show how the preceding general remarks on aesthetic experience are illustrated in this form which is the gem of Japanese poetry.

CHAPTER THREE

HAIKU NATURE

1. FORM AND CONTENT

WE MAY TAKE IT that an artist's chief concern is to form, to create, to set before himself his insight so that he may know what it is. To return to the poet in the rye field, we might assume that he saw a red dragonfly, but what he saw of it we do not know, for there is no poetry yet. Is it enough to say he saw the dragonfly in order for us to know what he saw? Hardly. That sentence gives no experience, no sense of the insect's nature. It is a paraphrase, perhaps, but it gives no experience. Poets being what they are, he, if he were told he had seen a red dragonfly in just those words, would probably not agree at all.

At this particular stage of the aesthetic process, he himself would not be able to say what he saw. He is perhaps aware only of what Bradley has called "a vague imaginative mass": "Pure poetry is not the decoration of a preconceived and clearly defined matter; it springs from the creative impulse of a vague imaginative mass pressing for development and definition."[1] The poet must yet strive to discover for himself what he did see, to formulate it, to create a form which will be his insight. Unless he does so, he may know he had an experience, but he will not know what it was. It will remain vague, nebulous, teasing, and perhaps irritating to him for life, for actuality. Otsuji is quite explicit on this point: "The suffering that accompanies the creation of expression is the suffering to grasp the world of real insight, and between these two activities there must be no space."[2] All else prior to form is potential. Once it is realized, by that very fact alone, it is formed; as Cassirer has said: "What is grasped by consciousness here and now 'is' and is precisely in the form offered by direct experience."[3]

Therefore, as Croce and Bradley, among others, have so magnificently propounded, there can be no separation of form and content. For it is only in their identity, as Croce points out, that art is possible: "Content and form must be clearly distinguished in art, but must not be separately qualified as artistic, because their relation only is artistic—that is, their unity, understood not as an abstract dead unity, but as concrete and living...."[4] Western aesthetics, as the following passage from Bradley suggests, had previously considered them as separate entities:

> [The poem] is a unity in which you can no more separate a substance and a form than you can separate living blood and the life in the blood. This unity...has various "aspects" or "sides";... if you try to examine one, you also find it is the other. Call them substance and form, if you please, but these are not reciprocally exclusive.... They are one thing from different points of view, and in that sense identical.[5]

Demands for a special kind of content—ideological, moral, doctrinaire, modern, etc.—are generally based on the assumption that content is separable from form, and that indeed art itself is only a prettifying of some practical point of view to make it acceptable to the masses or to explain some aspect of the world of confusion in which we are said to live. Along with such demands attempts are generally made to destroy traditional forms and charges of dilettantism or sheer virtuosity are leveled at poets who continue to remain interested in their poetic function.* For, as Tate maintains, it is not the function of poetry to "explain our experience":

> If we begin by thinking that it ought to "explain" the human predicament, we shall quickly see that it does not, and we shall end up thinking that therefore it has no meaning at all.... But poetry is at once more modest and, in the great poets, more profound. It is the art of apprehending and concentrating our experience in the mysterious limitations of form.[6]

---

* Interestingly enough, such demands were made in almost identical terms in France during the nineteenth century and in Japan during the late Meiji period. See Albert Cassagne, La théorie de l'Art pour l'Art en France (Paris: Hachette, 1906). Also see pages 36–39 following.

Recently, however, so well has the position been maintained, the assumption of the identity of form and content is commonplace, as is apparent from the very wording of Waggoner's following statement: "One of the most valuable of the many contributions of the new criticism has been its insistence that form and substance are, or ought to be, one. I take it that this idea is as permanently true as any that we are apt to arrive at."[7] For what is formed has content. Without its being formed, there is nothing. The "content" of what our poet saw may be paraphrased by saying that he saw a dragonfly in a rye field. But this is not "what" he saw; this is not his experience. "What" he saw will be his poem and can be expressed and experienced only in his poem. As Brooks has put it, "the total poem is...the communication and indistinguishable from it."[8]

Let us deal briefly with the question of what constitutes failures in form—briefly, since the topic has already been touched on here and there in the foregoing pages. The primary reason for a failure in form is succinctly stated by Otsuji:

> If one does not grasp something—something which does not merely touch us through our senses but contacts the life within and has the dynamic form of nature—no matter how cunningly we form our words, they will give only a hollow sound. Those who compose haiku without grasping anything are merely exercising their ingenuity. The ingenious become only selectors of words and cannot create new experiences from themselves.[9]

The failure to have experienced genuinely can manifest itself in many ways, as has been suggested in the foregoing pages: the intrusion of the poet's own emotion rather than an emotion arising from the experience; his desire to ride his pet intellectual hobbyhorse; an all too human vanity in wishing to be thought charming or profound; following a suffering to grasp the world of real insight, and between these two fashionable convention until it has become a cliché, a danger against which Kyorai says Bashô warned his disciples: "When one composes ordinary verse, there are certain fashionable types. These types change as is natural. [Bashô], recognizing this very well, said that we should not continue long in a single fashion."[10] Failures in form, then are always failures in content, for there has been no genuine coalescence of subject and object, leading to a true insight.

If, as has been maintained, there can be no separation of form from content, another question arises as to the meaning of words that name forms, such as sonnet or tanka or haiku. The answer lies in the fact that a distinction between the two elements can be made, for the sake of convenience, so long as it is clearly understood that neither could exist without the other. Another question, far more difficult to explore, concerns the relationship between the insight and one of the traditional forms above named. To return to our rye-field poet as he struggles to form his perception and to realize it, following only the necessity of realizing it and knowing what it is, how is he so fortunately able to form at the same time a sonnet or a haiku? For assuredly aesthetic experiences do not come in ready-made packages to be labelled haiku or tanka. As Otsuji has ironically remarked, "When we try to express our emotion directly, we cannot know beforehand how many syllables will be needed."[11] Rather, as the coalescence of subject and object takes place, the form of the experience is in the quality of it: the red of the dragonfly, the green of the rye field, the shapes, the light, what it engages of the poet's funded experience. Every experience, in becoming actual, creates its own form. No form can be pre-determined for it.

If we examine individual, successful haiku, we will see, indeed, that no two are alike. Variations in rhythm, in pauses, tonal quality, rhyme, and so on are marked throughout; later pages will deal with these areas as they render an experience most concretely. But the more important point to be noted in answer to the question raised lies in the general type of experience which haiku renders.

2. HAIKU EXPERIENCE AND LENGTH

I know that when one happens to see a beautiful sunset or lovely flowers, for instance, he is often so delighted that he merely stands still. This state of mind might be called "ah-ness" for the beholder can only give one breath-long exclamation of delight: "Ah!" The object has seized him and he is aware only of the shapes, the colors, the shadows, the blendings. In a brief moment he sees a pattern, a significance he had not seen before in, let us say, a rye field and a crimson dragonfly.

> A crimson dragonfly,
> As it lights, sways together
> With a leaf of rye.

There is here no time or place explicitly for reflection, for judgments, or for the observer's feelings. There is only the speaking, impassioned object, with its "extraordinary powers to set up echoes in the reader's mind."[12] For Otsuji this is the most aesthetic moment, a true haiku moment:

> At the instant when our mental activity almost merges into an unconscious state—i.e., when the relationship between the subject and object is forgotten—we can experience the most asthetic moment. This is what is implied when it is said that one goes into the heart of created things and becomes one with nature.[13]

To render such a moment is the intent of all haiku, and the discipline of the form. It is dramatic, for is not the soul of drama presentation rather than discussion? The image must be full, packed with meaning, and made all significant, as the experience is in aesthetic contemplation. This, then, is the kind of experience that occurs frequently and that the poet wishes to render, in all its immediacy.

Haiku then is a vehicle for rendering a clearly realized image just as the image appears at the moment of aesthetic realization, with its insight and meaning, with its power to seize and obliterate our consciousness of ourselves. Or rather, when a poet wishes to render such an experience, the haiku form seems supremely fitted for it, not because he writes or wishes to write a haiku, but because of the nature of the experience.

When such an experience does occur, the duration of the state of "ah-ness" is, by physical necessity, a breath's length. What I call "ah-ness" Herbert Read has called an "act of intuition or vision," going on to describe its physical effects thus: "All art originates in an act of intuition, or vision.... This act of vision or intuition is, physically, a state of concentration or tension in the mind.... [The words which express this vision] are arranged or composed in a sequence or rhythm which is sustained until the mental state of tension in the poet is exhausted or released by this objective equivalence."[14] The "mental state of tension in the poet" during the kind of experience I am discussing durates one breath-length, for as the poet exhales, that in itself draws the haiku moment to its close, and his vision is completed. Consequently, to form the experience, the length of the line for a haiku thought must have the same length as the duration of the single event of "ah-ness," which is a breath's length, even as Igarashi has pointed out.[15] Consequently, the length of a verse is made up of those words which we can utter during one breath. The length, that is, is necessitated by haiku nature and by the physical impossibility of pronouncing an unlimited number of syllables in a given breath.

As I have stated before, what is uniquely characteristic of this moment in regard to the form in which it is conveyed, is the identity between it and the words which realize it. One aspect of the haiku form which contributes to this identity is the length of seventeen syllables, which, as will be discussed later, is the average number of syllables that can be uttered in one breath. Kenkichi Yamamoto has acutely described the situation:

> As long as a haiku is made up of the interlocking of words to a total length of seventeen syllables in its structure, it is inevitable that it be subject to the laws of time progression; however, I think the fact that it is a characteristic of haiku to echo back as a totality when one reaches its end—i.e., to echo back from the end to its beginning—seems to show that in its inner nature a haiku tends to deny in itself the temporal element inherent in its poetic form. That is to say, on one hand the words are arranged by the poet within the seventeen syllables in a temporal order; on the other hand, through the grasping insight of the reader, they must attain meaning simultaneously.[16]

Every word, then, in a haiku, rather than *contributing* to the meaning, as words do in a novel or sonnet, *is* an experience. It must have been some such thought as this that Bashô had in mind when he told his disciple Kyorai: "In Bonchô, a verse has only seventeen syllables. Not a single word should be carelessly used."[17]

To test the idea further, let us imagine trying to convey to someone the experience of reading a novel. We will talk *about* the plot, the characters, the ideas, the fine effects, and so on. But we can hardly give the words in which the experience was conveyed. The same holds true even of shorter forms such as the sonnet or quatrain, as has been maintained; for with most readers, no matter how meaningful the experience of them has been, a certain conscious effort at memorization is necessary to remember their exact words. This is not true of the haiku. If we consult our experience with them, I think it will be agreed that memorable haiku can be remembered after the first reading. Nor is this due to their brevity alone, as will be clear if we recall how easily forgotten are telephone numbers, short messages, or pithy epigrams based on intellection rather than aesthetic realization.

This is why I question Mr. Yamamoto's statement that there is a friction between the temporal element inherent in the succession of seventeen syllables one after another and the simultaneity of the experience. For he goes on to say: "The nature of haiku seems to arise from the endless friction and battle between those two characteristics—the temporal element in the poetic form and the anti-temporal element of its inner nature. Haiku is the poetic form based on a contradiction."[18] Rather, as I have tried to show, haiku is the poetic form based on the identity between these two elements, toward which its very length of seventeen syllables strives, matching as it does the length of the experience of "ah-ness."

What Yamamoto has to say in the way of analyzing the relationship between form ("seventeen syllables in a temporal order") and content (what he calls "meaning" or the "anti-temporal element of its inner nature") is to my mind most keen. But when he suggests that there is a contradiction between these two aspects of the *total* haiku experience, he seems to separate what can only exist as one. Even in those literary forms other than haiku where, as I have suggested, the words used *contribute* to the total experience, they cannot be separated from it, for the experience can arise only from the words. I am maintaining that there is a difference between a contribution and a contradiction. If my definition of a haiku moment as one arising from a form in which the words and the experience *are* one is granted, it will follow that a contradiction between them is impossible.

It is from such an identity that there arises the freshness of experience which Bashô delighted in:

> In the *Sanzôshi* it is stated: Freshness is the flower of haiku art. What is old, without flower, seems like the air in an aged grove of trees. What the deceased master [Bashô] wished for sincerely is this sense of freshness. He took delight in whoever could even begin to see this freshness.... We are always looking for freshness which springs from the very ground with each step we take forward into nature....[19]

Such freshness arises from an immediacy of feeling, as Otsuji points out: "When we are dealing with nature, the more immediate the feeling, the greater the degree to which haiku can keep an eternal freshness and give to the reader and the poet a true and everlasting delight."[20] Such successful haiku can be read again and again without growing stale, for as Otsuji puts it, there is no space between the expression and the insight.[21]

To a reader that moment of inspiration or state of "ah-ness" comes from reading the haiku, as each word in it is experienced. During a

breath's length he reads, tensions are harmoniously maintained in rhythmic continuity to elevate his soul, and as he pauses at the end of the
verse, a sense of beautiful completion arises, giving a feeling of perfect
finality no less exquisite than the state of "ah-ness" that the poet first
conceived. In this way, a haiku re-creates the true image of beauty in
the mind of the reader, as it was experienced by the poet. Thus the
length of a line may be expressed by the number of syllables that can
be uttered in a breath during the state of "ah-ness."

Now let us read in one breath lines from famous poets:

> Under yonder beech-tree single on the greensward,
> Couched with her arms behind her golden hair...[22]

> Come and show me another city with lifted head singing
> So proud to be alive and coarse and strong and cunning.[23]

> Once when the snow of the year was beginning to fall,
> We stopped by a mountain pasture to say, "Whose colt?"[24]

These lines are a little long to be read at a breath. Let us next try
the following:

> More precious was the light in your eyes than the roses
> in the world.[25]

> It was many and many a year ago
> In a kingdom of the sea.[26]

> I must down to the seas again, to the lonely sea and the
> sky.[27]

These can easily be read in the span of one breath. Thus we find that
the longest lines in English to be read at one breath contain between
sixteen and eighteen syllables. This is true, not only in English, but also
in the other languages. For instance, the songs written in the antique
tongue employed by Homer in the *Iliad* and *Odyssey* and by Virgil
in the *Aeneid* are in dactylic hexameter. And in *Evangeline,* where the
classic meter is imitated by Longfellow, the meter consists of five dactyls
and a final trochee, varying the number of syllables from sixteen to
eighteen. Therefore we can say that the number of syllables that can
be uttered in a breath makes the natural length of haiku. This is why
it is written in seventeen syllables, matching the length of the experience.

Historically, the development of haiku can be traced from *renga* to *haikai* to *hokku* to haiku.* The haiku period dates roughly from 1650 to the present, and ever since its beginning, when the seventeen-syllable pattern was recognized as a separate entity, there have been attempts to modify the form. For example, during Sôin's day, although there was no conscious, organized attempt to establish another length, casual experimentation by the addition of syllables was carried on. However, the norm continued to be seventeen syllables. In contrast, during the 1900's there was a deliberate attempt to substitute a longer length and a different line pattern, e.g., three lines of eight syllables each, and the like.

The problem has greatly occupied the attention of Japanese poets and critics, and Shiki, the able critic and poet who revived the vitality of haiku during the latter part of the nineteenth century, gave a wise and tolerant answer:

> If the question is raised as to what haiku is, the answer is that it is a kind of literature; in addition, the unique characteristic which sets it off from other forms lies in the rhythm of 5–7–5. [That is, three divisions, consisting of five, seven, and five syllables respectively.] The rhythm of 5–7–5 is surely one of the greatest elements in haiku. However, even though 5–7–5 is its most common rhythm, haiku are not necessarily limited to this rhythm. For example, if we look into the older haiku, we will find examples of sixteen, eighteen, and up to twenty-five syllables; even in a haiku of seventeen syllables, there can be other rhythms beside 5–7–5.... We want to give the name of haiku to all kinds of rhythm. Moreover, verses widening the scope from fourteen to fifteen to even thirty syllables, may be called haiku. To differentiate these from haiku of the 5–7–5 rhythm, we may call them haiku of fifteen or twenty or twenty-five syllables or the like.[28]

Shiki held these views until he sensed that the new freedom he endorsed was going too far, just as Pound felt that Amy Lowell had carried the free-verse movement in the West to such ridiculous flexibility that poetic form had ceased to exist. The reasoning advanced by the new haiku school, differing from that upon which Amy Lowell based her experiments, is an interesting repetition in some respects of the arguments that flourished in France during the latter nineteenth century and in America during the 1930's to justify so-called new approaches to literature. For example, Hekigodo intimates that changed social conditions make innovations in poetry imperative:

* For a detailed account of the historical development of haiku, see Chapter V. Definition of the above terms will also be given there.

The periods of Genroku [1668–1703] and Tenmei [1781–88] were built upon despotism, in which politics, economics, manners, customs, and education were based upon a class system. Haiku was born and perfected during this time. The present Meiji period [1868–1911] has developed from a liberal ideal, in which politics, economics, manners, customs, and education are based upon a system of equality. Haiku that are related to the age will not end as imitations of those of the Genroku and Tenmei periods. Genroku and Tenmei were impressed almost equally by the restrictions arising from despotism and the class system. However, even the Tenmei period exhibited the characteristics of its time differently from the Genroku period. Today, when the class system has been abolished and despotism has been replaced by the liberal ideal, it is unnatural for haiku to retain yet its old form. Here the new direction for haiku is born. For this reason, it is called the greatest change—a revolution—since the beginning of haiku history.[29]*

That there is a relationship between a definable period and its art— that is to say, its art forms—is unquestionable. But it seems most questionable whether that relationship is based *primarily* upon those characteristics of any period named by Hekigodo—the class system or the system of equality and the liberal ideal—and whether it is as mechanical as he implies. Even greater doubt arises when it is remembered that the establishment of the "system of equality" and the "liberal ideal" in Japan arose, not as a long, developing evolution in society, but rather as a sudden and dramatic change; that it was in a sense an external change that may in time deeply and fundamentally change the Japanese *Weltanschauung* but has not yet done so seems demonstrable through the many references that Japanese scholars themselves make to the remaining remnants of "feudalism" in the Japanese consciousness.

What Hekigodo seems to be urging in his new program is that the poet *should* feel the necessity for change; but the poet, no matter how worthy the cause Hekigodo pleads, can deal poetically only with what he does feel and experience. In his call for some sort of modernity, Hekigodo has fallen into the same position as that of Maxime DuCamp, one of the most naive of the proponents of utilitarian art in France during the nineteenth century, who maintained that literature should "explain" science: "One must belong to one's age, no matter what."[30]

---

* Cf. Gustave Planche, one of the more conservative of the advocates of *l'art utile:* "The ideal novel will be able to vivify the highest questions of social reform. Without becoming dogmatic, or exchanging imagination for instruction, it will be able to trouble the blameworthy, and revive the quivering courage of the humiliated." (*Nouveaux Portraits Litteraires,* Paris: D'Amyot, 1854, II, p. 421.)

The superficial sense in which he feels that one can be of one's age is revealed in the following, representative statement: "The steam-engine has been discovered, but still we sing of Venus. . . . This is absurd!"[31]

Because Hekigodo pleads for change in the name of political progress based on an admirable humanitarianism, and DuCamp does so for the obviously more easily rejectable notion of material progress, it may be difficult to see that both men are putting the cart before the horse. As Hulme put it: "It is no use having a theory that motorcars [or superior political systems] are beautiful, and backing up this theory by working up an emotion not really felt. The object must cause the emotion before the poem can be written."[32] What I am maintaining is that art grows out of its society as an expression of the deepest qualities and motives in it, and that the structuring of that growth is a complex process that has yet to be clarified.

In yet another passage Hekigodo, urging that the influx of Western ideas into Japan will inevitably change "the interests of haiku," seems to draw a sharp line between the "old thought" and the new "scientific way":

> Although it does not need comment especially now, the current of world thought after the great [Russo-Japanese] war of 1904–05 has brought confusion especially to our world of ideas. Even those who confined their interests to haiku only have not escaped this influence. Touched by the new influence, we can laugh at the ignorance which wishes to maintain its own position. We will not push back the current of thought by closing the gates of the castle of haiku. Even though we wanted to push it back, our power could not do so. To tell the truth, those minds which were cultivated in the old thought have felt a shock. Moreover, those who have been educated in the scientific way and are interested in haiku naturally cannot help but be moved. With the situation as it is, is it not wrong of those who think that they do not yet see a change in the interests of haiku? For the development of the interests of haiku, have not the circumstances around us progressed favorably in every respect?[33]

That part of Hekigodo's attack which was aimed at a blind conservatism which conspired to close "the gates of the castle of haiku" seems vindicated in some areas. Most critics today, for example, would readily agree that successful haiku can be written on modern themes. But when he chose to name the scientific attitude or education as a representative aspect of the new ideas that will change haiku—specifically, destroy the length of seventeen syllables—one feels that in his enthusiasm he had lost sight of the difference between the nature of science and poetry, which has been explored in previous pages.[34] As Tate succinctly puts it, "The aim of science is to produce a mechanical whole for the service of the practical will. Our *experience* of a machine—even if our world were mechanical—is very different from our capacity to run it."[35]

A third approach to the justification of breaking down the norm of seventeen syllables is the argument that a "feudalistic form" such as haiku is too small to serve as a propaganda weapon for political ideologies:

> The unique characteristic of haiku lies in its feudalistic form—that is, the fixed form of 5–7–5—and in the seasonal theme. Such a feudalistic form breaks down as the development of society takes place, and soon it dissolves into general poetry. Free haiku is merely its transitional form. This fact means that such a small form cannot fully express a content which is proletarian and revolutionary. If we adhere strongly to a form like this, it can only show a twisted content and a twisted ideology. To establish a short form within the realm of poetry means to surrender it to bourgeois haiku. Therefore the proletarian haiku should dissolve into poetry.[36]

The assumption on which such statements are made is that poetry is an instrument to be used for the furthering of a political dogma*—a familiar dictate of communist thinking. As is evident, my contention is that such is not its function; rather, as Tate has said, it "is the art of apprehending and concentrating our experience in the mysterious limitations of form,"[37] so that we can know what the *meaning* of that dogma is. Tate continues: "It is in this sense that poetry is most profoundly the criticism of life. . . . Let the [social] plans be well-wrought indeed, but let the arts teach us—if we demand a moral—that the plans are not and can never be absolutes. Poetry perhaps more than any other art tests with experience the illusions that our human predicament tempts us in our weakness to believe."[38] As was previously pointed out also, such demands for a special content—in this case, proletarian and revolutionary—are based to my mind on a mistaken concept of the relationship

---

* Cf. P. J. Proudhon *(Oeuvres Complètes.* Paris: Librairie Internationale, 1867–70, XVII, p. 41). He berates writers for not having been active in the Revolution of 1848. "Did literature prepare the way for it? When has Victor Hugo ever defended the rights of workers?"

between form and content in art.[39] Moreover, I note in passing that Bashô did not consider the haiku form too "small" to express his realizations of not-so-simple an attitude as that of Zen. Therefore, it would seem that the problem of this particular proletarian and revolutionary group is not that the form is too "small" but that the group itself has yet to produce its poets who can create great haiku out of complex political material.

As has been stated, Shiki retreated from his original stand, in face of what he felt was the destruction of the poetic form:

> [In their new rhythm] there is no fixed rhythm and it becomes close to prose rhythm. It is already prosaic, yet is still bound by twenty-three to twenty-four syllables and cannot free itself entirely from verse. It is neither of prose nor verse—and does it create anything? Judging this kind of writing, so far as I can tell, what is called the new rhythm is merely a temporary phenomenon, which cannot flourish for any length of time. It merely exists as an anomalous form of haiku. . . . Whether this is an advance, a retrogression, or a destruction, at any rate at present it cannot last permanently.[40]

He felt that complexity was possible within haiku: "No matter how complicated we try to make our verses, or how clearly we try to make an impression through them, we can at the end reach perfection easily within a limited number of syllables—only seventeen or eighteen."[41]

Kiyoshi Yuyama has advanced the interesting suggestion that possibly one reason why there has been such a concerted attempt to lengthen the haiku beyond its usual limits of seventeen syllables lies in the fact that, generally speaking, modern man has lost his ear for sounds in poetry and consequently tends to read for meaning alone, which is a much quicker process than reading for the full content of a verse arising from rhythm, sounds, etc. He can thus take in longer lines, since he absorbs only one aspect of them. The obverse of the lengthened haiku, as Yuyama points out, is the very primitive, short verse, which also fails to exploit all the resources of communication, once again because the modern has lost his ability to enjoy poetry fully.[42]

Eventually all attempts to destroy the traditional haiku length of seventeen syllables have suffered the fate of fringe movements, and the central impulse of haiku as a seventeen-syllable poem is no longer seriously challenged. Perhaps Kyoshi Takahama, the greatest living haiku poet today, has touched in an unassuming statement on the central reason for its persistence:

I recognize that to express a thought in a certain fixed form is a technique, and the technique itself does its most effective work when it transfers the thought to another.... People generally accept haiku as a poetic form of seventeen syllables arranged in three lines of five, seven, and five syllables each. They express their thoughts and feelings as freely as they can in this form and appreciate it with each other. That, I believe, is one of the great reasons why haiku exist in the world of poetry.[43]

That is to say, since poetic communication can take place only as it is formed, and since, as I have attempted to show, one aspect of the haiku form—i.e., its length of seventeen syllables—has its *raison d'être* in the experience to be communicated, the return to that form is not surprising.

Most Japanese students of haiku, in considering the matter of its length, have seemed to substitute a historical account of its development for an examination of the values in its structure, thereby committing what Waggoner has called the "genetic or analytical fallacy," in which "complex values are explained away by reference to their parts, their mechanisms, their origin."[44] Yet even in Bashô's day, when the term haiku had not yet received its modern, clear-cut definition, the pattern of the form had nevertheless been defined, as Otsuji points out: "What has been called the 5-7-5 pattern is merely a historical step, showing how it branched out from *waka,* and even in the period of Bashô, the haiku had already developed a pattern of *niku isshô* (i.e., two parts make one whole). [For] the intervals between the three lines 5-7-5 do not occur with the same time stress or length."[45] Shin Asano, reaching even farther back into the history of Japanese verse, has remarked that in the Japanese language the poetic groupings of seventeen syllables existed long before it was identified as haiku, with all its later refinements, suggesting thereby that the number of syllables is not only a historical accident: "[Haiku] did not come from chained verse nor from *haikai* verse. It originated from the main stream of basic poetic elements in our language (mainly word groups, centering around seventeen or eighteen syllables). In short, these poetic elements which appear in the lyrics of ancient times surge forth on the tide of the flourishing period of *haikai.*"[46] What I am maintaining is that the length of the haiku has in itself a *raison d'être,* quite aside from its historical development; otherwise, as I have tried to show in the foregoing discussion, it could never have so successfully resisted for three hundred years all efforts to change it.

3. THREE ELEMENTS

As has been maintained, in haiku the poet usually attempts to present a speaking object, around which and in which he has had an experience; and this in a breath-length's space. There are certain basic attributes of an object which serve to identify it and locate it amid the constant barrage of impressions which impinge on consciousness. Objects, that is to say, are located in time and space.* Let us take an actual experience had by a poet. Bashô, let us say, was passing through a field one autumn evening and a crow on a branch caught his attention. Similar scenes had doubtlessly been seen by many people before him, but he is the one who made it a memorable event by forming his experience of it in the following haiku:

> On a withered bough
> A crow alone is perching;
> Autumn evening now.

For him, a bough, a crow, and the evening are essential elements, without which the aesthetic experience cannot be formed. This is not to maintain that haiku can be broken into three disparate sections, for, as Otsuji warns us, "in discussing the method of expression, those who consider it by dividing the haiku into many parts are wrong."[47] For it is the relationship between these three elements which together are the experience, and which appear one in each of the three lines of the haiku, that is basic to the haiku experience. They are:

WHERE	*On* the withered bough
WHAT	*A crow* alone is perching;
WHEN	*Autumn evening* now.

The "where, what, and when" then are the properties which constitute that experience, the necessities to make that experience meaningful and alive. Without them the experience cannot be fully realized, nor can a haiku moment be created completely.

Let us then consider these three elements more fully.

* Lest I shock the purist, I should hasten to add that I am far from maintaining that these are the only attributes which are valid in identifying objects or in dealing with experience.

WHEN

As has been often remarked, many a successful haiku, if not all, has in it a sense of a vivid yet subtly elusive air, filling every corner of the haiku, imponderable, yet making its presence felt. This is a live atmosphere that comes from a sense of the season with which the haiku deals, adding clarity and fullness to the other elements in the haiku, as well as bringing to bear upon the haiku moment the many riches already belonging to it as a part of our funded experience.

Such a seasonal feeling arises from either the theme of the poem or from the inclusion in it of a so-called seasonal word. For example, in the following poem by Ryôta *haze* is the word which informs us that the season is spring:

> From the long hallways
> Voices of the people rise
> In the morning haze.

Here is beautifully suggested the liquid light of a very early spring morning, with a tender haze from which rise the voices of unseen people. (Note how accurate the seasonal touch is, which demands the word *haze* and not *mist,* which is colder, wetter, and thicker in feeling. Mist is actually used as an autumn theme.) The clear new air which only spring can create rises into the spaciousness of the long hallways from every word in this haiku. When a seasonal word is thus fully realized, it is an aesthetic symbol of the sense of seasons, arising from the oneness of man and nature, and its function is to symbolize this union.

The necessity of having a seasonal symbol in a haiku has been a matter of some dispute as is evidenced for example in the following statement by Ippekirô:

> There are those who say my verses are haiku. There are those who say they are not haiku. As for myself, what they are called does not matter.... My feeling is that my verse differs in its point of view from what have been called haiku up to now. First, I am indifferent to an interest in the seasonal theme, which is one of the important elements in haiku. It is not a matter of concern to me whether there is a seasonal word or not. I believe I have freed myself completely from the captivity of the seasonal theme.... I do not write verse with the intention of putting seasonal words in them, or of leaving them out. I write freely as my thought arises.[48]

His position can be understood when it is realized that in the past, poets, sometimes incapable of grasping the symbolic significance of a seasonal word or theme, blindly contended that the inclusion of them in a haiku was enough. Asano observes that there was little realization around the concept: "In Sôkan's day the degree to which the connotative meaning of the so-called seasonal words was recognized was slight. The word which pointed out the season in which the poet composed the haiku was enough, and although seasonal words were used, we can assume that the content of such words was not fully realized."[49]

This was due to the fact that the seasonal feeling as one aspect of experience was not fully realized and was treated only conventionally. Indeed, so conventionalized and artificial had the seasonal words become that *saijiki,* or collections of seasonal themes which were usually used in haiku, were compiled, classifying them as belonging to certain, predetermined seasons. For example, cherry blossoms denoted spring; dragonflies, summer, etc. Such words were then called seasonal words. Poets forgot that such terms were only arbitrary, and that the concept could be given life only as the word was realized, as Otsuji states: "Terms such as seasonal word or seasonal theme were named arbitrarily. Since the seasonal theme refers to natural objects as they are, it is not a man-made concept, but exists. Seasonal themes have been classified according to the four seasons for the sake of convenience in editing anthologies of haiku, but aside from that, they have no meaning."[50] When he says further that a "sense of season cannot be formed without haiku," he again emphasizes that it is a *part* of the haiku experience, not a requirement forced upon the material of the verse: "Those who consider a sense of season as a feeling arising from the seasonal theme apart from haiku undoubtedly think of the sense of season as a conceptual symbol. In actuality, a sense of season cannot be formed without haiku, and for us who consider that it arises from the total poetic effect of the haiku itself, it is a symbol of feeling."[51] What Otsuji says of the seasonal theme is indicative of the oneness and unity of a haiku experience of nature. From such an experience arises a realization of quality, *which is the seasonal theme:* "It is immaterial whether the peony is classified as a spring or summer theme. The peony has its own quality and characteristics; that quality or characteristic is the seasonal theme."[52] This statement seems to me to be the essential key to an understanding of what the seasonal concept means. The things of nature are born and fade away in the rhythm of the seasons. Realization of their quality must take into account the season of which they are inseparably a part.

Obviously, without a seasonal theme—i.e., without a realized quality —the state of oneness is not achieved. The objective correlative is not adequate to convey the experience; and its omission shows that the poet did not become one with nature. Haiku written from such a basis run the danger of being *about* an experience, rather than *becoming* an experience. Otsuji, in recognizing this pitfall, suggests what the function of the seasonal theme is in haiku and what its meaning is:

> A haiku in which each concept is lined up in a row sometimes becomes merely an accumulation of concepts and, losing realistic poetic feeling, becomes dull. This is a shortcoming inevitable to haiku which are composed by an analytical mind. Something which is more than capable of meeting this danger is the seasonal theme. Since the seasonal theme is a feeling that arises in seeing disinterestedly and praising the dignity of unadorned nature, the interest in haiku poetry lies here where everything is harmonized and unified with this feeling. Therefore, the development of interest in haiku can be said, in short, to be the development of the seasonal theme in haiku poetry. The interest in the seasonal theme, in other words, is an enlightened, Nirvana-like feeling. The atmosphere in which a haiku is written will be born from this interest in the seasonal theme. Therefore, to write haiku without it is either an unsuccessful attempt at copying amusingly without any real poetic impulse or results in a kind of unpoetic epigram whose main objective is witty irony. For this reason the seasonal theme is one of the elements which cannot be omitted from the haiku form.[53]

The reason why the Japanese poet stresses the seasonal theme, then, as Otsuji does, arises from a recognition of man as a part of nature, of man's inescapable involvement in nature—an awareness suppressed by Western urban life—and this recognition is given actuality through the seasonal theme. Thus, even human affairs, when treated of in haiku, are not purely human affairs, as Otsuji observes:

> When even a part of human affairs is considered as a phenomenon of nature, there is a grand philosophical outlook, as if we had touched the very pulse of the universe. Herein we find the life of haiku. . . . Human affairs as they appear in haiku are not presented as merely human affairs alone. Both human affairs and natural objects are inseparably woven into a haiku. Both the appreciation and the creation of haiku should be based on such a concept.[54]

A haiku can thus open up greater understanding of what a man is, of what his relationship to the world is. In it, that relationship is changed from a concept to an experience—as it must be in order for it to have the alive meaning that art can give it. Since, to experience in art, an objective correlative* is needed, the seasonal theme is one way to actualize experience, to achieve a genuine objective correlative. For the Japanese poet this achievement is impossible without a sense of nature, for man is a part of it and only from his relationship with it can the basic meaning of man's self become apparent. It is against such a background of thinking that Otsuji makes the following key observation, which though previously quoted will be given again because of its importance:

> Viewed against the popular idea that the seasonal theme is a man-made concept, the contention that it is unnecessary to haiku has some justification; however, if one comes to my idea that *the seasonal theme is the natural object itself* in all its naturalness—its function is to symbolize nature—then for the first time will he come face to face with the problem of the relationship between nature and himself. Here the poet should think deeply of the problem of the self.[55]

When a poet confronts the problem of the self through the relationship between himself and the nature of which he is a part, he will understand what Hulme meant by the classical in verse: "What I mean by classical in verse, then, is this. That even in the most imaginative flights there is always a holding back, a reservation. The classical poet never forgets this finiteness, this limit of man. He remembers always that he is mixed up with earth. He may jump, but he always returns back; he never flies away into the circumambient gas."[56] Thus a sensitive Western soul recognizes the fact that, in the most basic sense, we cannot find a deep meaning of life without exploring our relationship to nature. Indeed, as has been previously pointed out, the influential writer W. M. Urban indicates that poetry may deal with many subjects, but always deals with one: the contention that "human life and man are unique, free, and self-determining parts of nature."[57] Thus the importance of the seasonal theme for the haiku poet can be realized. It is not without meaning for us, therefore, to find such statements as the following one by Otsuji: "The area of haiku is limited by the fact that it is always accompanied by a sense of season."[58]

---

* I feel that some aspects of T. S. Eliot's concept of the "objective correlative" (his phrase) are too much a product of a conscious method; his use of nature symbols such as gulls, hyacinths, etc., seems overly conscious and thin.

Let us see how the seasonal theme actually functions within a haiku, using Bashô's crow poem for the purpose:

> On a withered bough
> A crow alone is perching;
> Autumn evening now.

Here the season is autumn and the time is evening. The air of this haiku is greatly dependent on the seasonal element. Were it to be changed, let us say, to a summer evening, the whole effect would be lost, for the seasonal air is as important to a haiku as light is to an impressionistic painting. From the very alone-ness and darkness of the crow, from the very bareness of the bough arises the autumn, becoming an actuality in the haiku and creating the air of the haiku with which a poet fills the space. The felt-object, being thus steeped in and blended with it, becomes superlatively significant. That the autumn arises from that same dignity of unadorned nature which Otsuji named[59] as one of the sources of the seasonal feeling, is quite clear in the simple, tranquil naming of the bough and the crow and the evening. Here too is the enlightened, Nirvana-like feeling Otsuji called for in the complete identity of the poet with the scene he has intuited. One sign of how successful the realization has been is the rising up of the sense of autumn from the whole haiku, unifying and filling the haiku world.

In Bashô's haiku, the naming of autumn is an abstraction, since the word is not the name of a concrete object. But the abstraction becomes concrete because of the absolute totality and reality of the intuition which is the haiku. In the following poem the season is only implied or suggested:

> The nightingales sing
> In the echo of the bell
> Tolled at evening.

The seasonal aspect is suggested by the element of "what"—nightingales, whose song is most closely associated with spring. The very use of the words *imply, suggest,* and *associate* raises an interesting question, which can illuminate the difference between the Japanese grasp of the seasonal sense and a Western one. For the Japanese the sense of season is so implicated in natural objects that the nightingales themselves *are* spring. They do not merely suggest or imply spring. They contain it; they incorporate it. It is in this sense that *imply, suggest,* and *associate* are to be taken, not as indicating something separate from the nightingales, as a first reading might lead one to believe. So in such haiku as the foregoing, the object and the time often coincide. Here, by implication, the evening is a spring evening. And from our own associations, which are a part of our funded experience, there rises up the delicate sweetness of such a balmy evening, filling the haiku, caressing and becoming one with the sounds in it.

Let us take another example:

> A crimson dragonfly,
> As it lights, sways together
> With a leaf of rye.

Here the significant element of "when" is that single moment as the dragonfly lights and sways. This moment is by implication in autumn,* since the dragonfly suggests the autumn in which it lives; again the seasonal feeling is incorporated in the object. It cannot be explicity separated from other elements, as it could in the first example; yet this haiku is strong in its "early autumn air," flooded with crisp, clear sunlight.

In the three haiku quoted above, it will be noted that while the season is indicated in each one, the time element is not necessarily confined to it alone. From the season, the time element can be narrowed down to the day or night, and even more narrowly to a particular moment during the day or night. This difference in the degree of specificity arises from the quality of the aesthetic experience realized by each poet and is a part of the organic unity which is the inner necessity through which the complete realization of that haiku moment becomes real and significant.

WHERE

In the three haiku used as examples in the foregoing section, the place of the objects is clearly identifiable in a "place" line: "On a withered bough"..."In the echo of the bell"..."With a leaf of rye." In each case the name of the place, as can be seen, adds to the quality of the haiku and is in harmony with it, as well as with the seasonal element.

---

* A red dragonfly is an autumn theme; when unqualified, the dragonfly is a summer motif.

The three elements, it is clear, must reinforce each other and become one unity if we are to avoid a mere enumeration. As Otsuji has said, "a haiku in which each concept is lined up in a row sometimes becomes merely an accumulation of concepts and loses realistic poetic feeling, and becomes dull."[60]

Of the three elements, however, the designation of the place seems most dispensable. Consider the following poems:

> "Summer thinness, dear,"
> I replied to him, and then
> Could not check a tear.

> Warm the weather grows
> Gradually as one plum flower
> After another blows.

> Here at parting now,
> Let me speak by breaking
> A lilac from the bough.

In none of these poems is the place specifically designated, although we are easily led to visualize the scene. In the first, although the physical place is absent, what may perhaps be called the psychic location—that is, a scene between lovers—is so clear that the omission is not felt. In the second, again the place, while omitted, is easily supplied by the reader: a garden perhaps or a grove of trees by a roadside. In the third, the lilacs themselves provide their own place.

The reason why the indication of the place may be omitted seems to lie in the reader's ability to supply it, as it is suggested in the object, and also in the relative stability of place as compared to time. The plum tree in a garden will always be in a garden, but its appearance will change radically during the various seasons of the year, or the various times of the day. However, in the majority of haiku the place is usually named, lending concreteness to the image. At times, of course, depending on the poet's vision, the place is the all-important element in the haiku, while the object and the time may be only attributes of it. For example:

> Some one from below
> Is looking at the whirling
> Of the cherry snow.

WHAT

The common pattern of experience, as noted before, is always an inter-action between a live creature and some aspect of his environment, as Dewey puts it.[61] I have said that what the haiku poet feels as characteristics of his environment necessary to his kind of experience includes time and place; this may be peculiar to haiku and perhaps is not felt with the same urgency by poets working in the sonnet or lyric form. But what is common to all poets is the object, in the largest sense, in his environment, which can become significant. Without a significant object there can be no aesthetic experience; without it, a haiku becomes, in Yamamoto's words, "a mere proverb": "A haiku comes into being through inspiration arising from a special object meaningful to the poet. If such a special object...is lost from view, the haiku becomes akin to a mere proverb."[62]

An experience becomes significant when it is placed in an object that is, in T. S. Eliot's phrase, "an objective correlative" to the emotion of the experience, that is, when the emotion truly rises from the experience, and therefore the presented object can arouse a sense of significance complete and relevant to itself. As Otsuji has said, the feeling is objectified: "The joy of a haiku lies precisely in the point that the writer's feeling has been objectified and not that a condensed picture of nature has been shown."[63] The object becomes truly a felt-object, rather than one around which the poet's feelings flow, more or less haphazardly adhering to it. Asô has put it clearly: grasping an insight into an object is accompanied by the feeling arising from it.

[It is said in the *Sanzôshi*]: "If the haiku does not arise naturally from the object, the object and its observer become two, and the observer cannot realize the feeling of the object, since his self intervenes." When one writes about the appearance of nature, what the poet must do is to grasp a basic insight into the object. Otherwise a separation arises between the poet and the object. This is what Bashô meant by saying, "Learn of the pine from a pine; learn of the bamboo from a bamboo." The way is not to divorce oneself from the pine and to see it with his own feeling, but to divorce the self and to enter the pine with a selfless interest. Then a real insight into the pine arises. Thus will it become a pine into which the human heart has entered. . . . It will become sentient, instead of remaining a natural object, viewed through the five senses objectively. And furthermore contemplating the human feeling infused into the object, the poet expresses it through the illumination of his insight, and when that feeling finds its expression, it becomes the art of haiku.[64]

The question may arise as to how, if "human feeling [is to be] infused into the object," the poet is to avoid the sentimentalism of seeing his world only in terms of his own emotions. The key to the difference between the object viewed sentimentally and the valid objective cor-relative is the word "subjectivism" in Otsuji's following statement: "If we think, with shallow subjectivism, that every natural object possesses life, this is a ridiculous misunderstanding."[65] For, as Asô has pointed out above, "the way is not to divorce oneself from the pine and to see it with his own feeling, but to divorce the self and to enter the pine with a selfless interest."

Emotion, then, is the unifying, creative force in experience. As Croce has said: "What gives coherence and unity to the intuition is feeling; the intuition is really such because it represents a feeling and can only appear from and upon that."[66] The feeling, however, is not the poet's solely, but rather feeling as it arises from the fusion of subject and object in experience. Emotion, then, is a quality of experience, as Dewey has said: "In fact, emotions are qualities, when they are significant, of a complex experience that moves and changes."[67] And since all emotion, he continues, unless pathological, moves toward or arises in objects, every aesthetic experience centers in the object: "An emotion is *to* or *from* or *about* something objective, whether in fact or idea."[68]

As for the presentation of the felt-object in haiku—that is, the crow, the nightingales' song, and the dragonfly in those quoted above—it seems to me highly significant that the naming of it is always direct. Haiku eschews metaphor, simile, or personification. Nothing is like something else in most well-realized haiku. As Bashô has said: "Learn of the pine from a pine."[69] Learn, that is, what a pine tree is, not what it is like—one supposes this is what Bashô meant. This avoidance of metaphor or simile arises, I feel, from the poet's need to render directly and concretely the vision he has had, and only that vision. Almost he seems to aim at the paring down of his medium to the absolute minimum, so that the least words stand between the reader and the experience! The result can be what Babette Deutsch has called a "naked poem" as she noted in speaking of the art of William Carlos Williams: "Not merely rhyme and metre but sometimes metaphor itself became an imperial interference between him and the sun."[70] Metaphor is always an interference for the haiku poet. His aim is to render the object so that it appears in its own unique self, without reference to something other than itself,—which is where vision ends and intellection begins—and so that it can never be mistaken for any other object than itself.

There is also another value to be found in poems of this "naked" sort, which is based on the haiku poet's concept of vision and form, or rather, perhaps, of the formed-vision he is dealing with. This it is which is the motive for his poetry. Not poetic embellishments, not as Herbert Read puts it, paraphrasing Goethe, "the profoundness of single thoughts, not the richness of imagery, not the abundance of illustration," but "that power of execution which creates, forms, and constitutes"[71] is the essence of haiku, as it is of all art. It seems to me that in the absolutely direct statement of haiku we get a rewarding example of this insight being consistently incorporated in poetic practice. By foreswearing all the devices to make his poem attractive or pleasing, the haiku poet lays all the emphasis upon "that power of execution" which is a test of his poetic powers as well as of his poetic vision. What else can hold together in transcendent meaning Bashô's naked statement about a crow?

> On a withered bough
> A crow alone is perching;
> Autumn evening now.

It is in poetry of this sort that we can find the ultimate examples of the self-sufficiency of a work of art, which, once formed, exists independently of its creator, the circumstances under which it was written, or any historical event or allusions. Asô has noted: "It is said that a haiku poet composes a haiku and then sets it aside. . . . The haiku poet will never leave any attachment between himself and the haiku he composes."[72] For if the poem depends for its completion on something outside itself, it ceases to be an intuition, a realization which is entire and accomplished. Such extraneous information, valuable for other than aesthetic reasons to, for example, the literary historian, must not be essential for the experiencing of the poem. If our insight into it must depend on some event in the poet's life—the death of someone close to him, let us say—and we cannot grasp it without that knowledge, I would say that the poem was to that extent a failure. For it has failed to communicate on the deepest level, toward which all art strives— the largest denominator of experience.

Moreover, to have to interrupt the aesthetic experience to receive an "explanation" which is not an intrinsic part of it shatters the unity essential to it. The single-mindedness of the reader is distracted, and to that extent the experience is not aesthetic for him. James Joyce has amusingly described the relationship between the author and the living, self-sufficient being of his creation:

> The dramatic form is reached when the vitality which has flowed and eddied around each person fills every person with such vital force that he or she assumes a proper and intangible aesthetic life. The personality of the artist ...finally refines itself out of existence, impersonalizes itself, so to speak.... The mystery of aesthetic, like that of material creation, is accomplished. The artist, like the God of creation, remains within or behind or beyond or above his handiwork, invisible, refined out of existence, indifferent, paring his fingernails.[73]

Here the emphasis is entirely upon the realized, speaking object.

Of course, the poet does not strive to give a "carbon copy" of the object or, as the school of realism used naively to believe, to present it as it is. Such a procedure can lead only to triviality or to a miscellaneous collection of odds and ends, as Yamamoto points out:

> The true intention of Shiki was to appreciate and respect the objective world. Yet, even as great as he was, his appreciation was transferred to real facts [i.e., actuality]. For this reason, many of the haiku he wrote were trivial.... In the last analysis a haiku is a complete world. If a fragment of a fact which is experienced casually is only transferred to words, that fragment remains only a fragment.... By this alone it cannot give the work a sense of completeness.[74]

As I have defined the process of aesthetic contemplation, the artist cannot present an object "as it is," for such a statement is meaningless. He can only present his realization of the object, as that realization and experience have grown from the interaction of the object and himself, his funded experience. The deeper he has seen, the more profoundly his experience has been a vital growth between the object and himself, the more sharply realized his insight will be. The importance of the intensity and necessity of the growth lies in the ultimate value of all art, i.e., in the tendency toward the universal. For as John Dewey has said, "there is no limit to the capacity of immediate sensuous experience to absorb into itself meanings and values."[75] Universality is a property of art by which it can refer to great areas of human experience and meaning, so that in the greatest of art, the intensely realized particular object can "set up echoes in our mind," as Fletcher has said. Ultimately, this is the "knowledge" that art can convey, "the more humanly relevant...the more meaningful, more philosophical knowledge about life and man" of which Waggoner speaks.[76] It is the "reality hidden behind what [the poet] expresses, which may be said to be a universal feeling arising from the union of the poet with nature," as Otsuji has said.[76]

Let us analyze a bit the already-quoted haiku:

> The nightingales sing
> In the echo of the bell
> Tolled at evening.

This is a haiku of the ear, full only of sounds. I do not feel that it is necessary for me to see either the birds or the temple bell, but when in the trailing voice of the bell, the nightingales' melody rises and the two become one as I hear them in the spring dusk, I sink into reverie, led perhaps to appreciate the dignity and grandeur of the bell's voice as it contrasts with the birds'. Both speak somehow of beauty. The bell, of the beauty man has made to worship his God; the birds, of the beauty God has made for his own joyous reasons. How good it is that the two should be one in this moment! How this speaks, touching the deeper springs of being in a man effortlessly. I am held. Just as with the booming temple bell, the echoing experience spreads farther and farther out, from this single haiku.

This surely is the highest value of all art, and what ultimately each artist strives to communicate, to form. Yet he can communicate most intensely in this area only through the speaking object, or as Dewey says, through the "immediate sensuous experience." Contrast the haiku above with the prose analysis. The haiku *is* the experience; the analysis *about* the experience. And the haiku is the experience because the poet has rendered the objects as he experienced them. This I believe is the reason for the insistence upon the directness of rendering the object in haiku. As stated before, haiku tradition rules that the use of metaphor, simile, or personification impedes this aim.

Again for the sake of directness, relatively few adjectives and adverbs are used in haiku. Indeed, as Kyoshi Takahama has pointed out,[77] there are a number of Japanese haiku without a single verb, adjective, or adverb. Truly, haiku could be called the poetry of the noun, which George Barker has said is the simple fact about it, after all the complexities have been explored: "Poetry is calling things names. I learned that from William Shakespeare."[78] This point was also recognized by Ezra Pound, one of whose "chief aversions" was a "superfluity of adjectives."[79]

4. RELATIONSHIP OF THE THREE ELEMENTS

Although the three elements of object, time, and place are necessary for haiku, it is the relationship among them in a unified whole that is a haiku. A poet must see how the three elements exist, in one, as parts of a whole, without which they do not become an experience but only remain in a relationship to each other. They are in the latter case simply placed side by side or "gathered together." As Bashô says: "Haiku should not be composed, as you do by gathering together two or three things. Would that we could have a haiku like a sheet of hammered gold!"[80] If we examine well-realized haiku, we will see that the three elements are so unified that they are immovable and that no substitute is possible. There is an air of inevitability about them, what Otsuji calls a "Nirvana-like sense," which can arise out of the connections they create within themselves: "A Nirvana-like sense will be expressed by the organization of and placement in order of appropriate objects, in such a way as to create the same sense of harmony as when, at a glance, we experience them intuitively."[81]

A poet, then, tries to form and create the kind of relationship that truly exists within the elements, which is indeed an organic force that holds them together in a harmonious whole. This organic force, arising within and among the elements, determines the rhythm and flow which he feels, dispassionately, and tries to realize by word-rhythm and flow. Out of this effort, a verse comes in its original meaning of the term *versum,* a turning. For a poet tries to create a haiku moment with words in temporal order. Those words will group themselves according to the rhythm and flow of the organic force which holds the three haiku elements in a whole. Much as music proceeds in phrases, the haiku proceeds in lines, by turning.

The construction of these lines cannot be arbitrarily imposed by the poet; he cannot determine that he will end a line here and turn into the next line there. Rather, the aesthetic realization itself, forming itself in groups of words, pausing, going on, will determine the place for a turning, out of its own being and through the inner necessity of expressing itself. I do not mean to suggest here that the realization is some sort of magical power and regulator. For course, while it has life, it does so because the poet experienced it. It is the poet's own realization of the object that will control the forming of the lines and determine the points of termination and beginning, which is the flow. In Bashô's crow haiku, the turning occurs where the rhythmic flow within each element is formed; one line deals completely with one element. Let us name this type a "one-for-one" haiku. It is perhaps the simplest type of turning within a haiku and emphasizes the calm tranquility that is its tone. The impossibility of turning otherwise than Bashô does can be tested by actually terminating the flow of the rhythm differently. For example:

> On a withered bough, a crow alone
> Is perching;
> Autumn evening now.

The effect of the second line is to place too great an emphasis on what the crow is doing, whereas it is the stillness of the crow that is harmonious with the mood of the poem, not its activity.

Let us take another example, to show how turning is determined by the inner necessity of material quite different from Bashô's:

> Brushing the leaves, fell
> A white camellia blossom
> Into the dark well.

In this haiku, one might ask why the turning takes place at the word "fell," rather than at the word "leaves." Should it be written as follows?

> Brushing the leaves,
> Fell a white camellia blossom
> Into the dark well.

The poet, it might be argued, preferred the first version in order to obtain the traditional five syllables for the first line of the haiku, as well as to have a rhyme with the third line. However, a moment's consideration will show that the "turning" should occur as in the first version, not for the mechanical reasons suggested above, but rather for those arising from the material itself. This may be sought in the inner nature of the rhythmic flow within the element of "when," which consists of the moment suggested in "brushing" and "fell." The time element is the motif and heart of this experience. At first reading, the rhythm of the line seems very abrupt and harsh to the listening ear, as the two accented words come at the end of the line, but this apparent discord is appropriate to the action so characteristic of the camellia—the surprising abruptness with which it falls. If we place the word "fell" at the beginning of the second line, this characteristic action, the soul of the haiku, cannot be fully created, and the essence of turning so vital to poetry loses its significance.

Let us try another version:

> Brushing the leaves
> A white camellia blossom fell
> Into the dark well.

Aside from the lack of an element of surprise, I feel this version is quite flaccid and soft. Further, the two action words which support and complement each other—"brushing" and "fell"—are here weakened by their separation. For *the leaves were brushed as* the flower fell; the two actions were simultaneous, but the version above does not suggest this. Again, it is this moment of the simultaneous action that is the heart of this haiku and that makes this falling camellia unique.

Here is a fourth possibility:

> Brushing the leaves
> A white camellia blossom
> Fell into the dark well.

The tone here in the last line, with its doggerel-like rhyme that seems to emphasize the "fell" action, again separated from its vivifying complement, makes the poem prosaic. There is nothing to distinguish this flower's falling in particular from all the other blossoms which fall. The significant moment has not been captured.

Let us take another one-for-one haiku to see how turning takes place in regard to the elements of the object and the place. The normal order of the haiku is as follows:

> The nightingales sing
> In the echo of the bell
> Tolled at evening.

Suppose we change the position of "sing" and place it at the beginning of the second line:

> The nightingales
> Sing in the echo of the bell
> Tolled at evening.

Here the sense of "The nightingales sing" does not come off vividly, for "sing" gets undue emphasis in this position, both as idea and in its verb aspect. For in reality, as was maintained previously,[82] this is a haiku of sound; it is not the *action* of singing that is wanted here, but rather the sound. That is to say, the verb "sing" has the force of a noun and might almost be said to be the object of the haiku, with the word "nightingales" serving as a modifier. In the second version, we cannot help but feel that something is being hampered and notice a flaw in the harmony, for the symphonic beauty of subtle delicacy is lost, the elusive quality of a superb symphony in nature as experienced by the poet. Likewise, the rhythm will be marred if "tolled" is placed at the end of the second line:

> The nightingales sing
> In the echo of the bell, tolled
> At evening.

It seems apparent that "tolled" belongs as a part of the rhythmic unity of the time element, through which the sounds are harmonized as true to the experience.

So far I have used examples of turning all in the one-for-one pattern— that is to say, with the turning and the end of the rhythmic flow in each element coinciding. This does not necessarily occur in every haiku. Turning takes place where it should by its own necessity due to the nature of the experience, which the poet tries to realize sincerely. The following is an example:

> Warm the weather grows
> Gradually as one plum flower
> After another blows.

In this haiku one might ask why the adverb "gradually" is placed at the beginning of the second line when logically it modifies the verb "grows" and might well be placed with it. However, if we do so, the sense of "how gradually the plum flowers blow" is lost. The heart of this haiku lies in the *matching* of the gradually warming weather and the gradually blowing plum flowers. This is the insight grasped by the poet, which he expresses in the turning and endues with significant life.

It is also noted that turning takes place at the word "flower" and the rest is expressed in the third line, placing emphasis on how gradually the blossoms blow, one after another from the branches of the plum tree here and there. Note the effect if turning takes place as follows:

> Warm the weather grows gradually
> As one plum flower after another blows.

I feel that the haiku has gone flat, losing its elusive quality. The delicate, matching effect has not been captured, nor has the insight been formed.

Turning, as I have tried to define the term, differs from a thought-pause, since it is a sense-pause, dictated by aesthetic perception and by the poet's attempt to realize his insight as he feels it as a totality. A pause in the thought, as far as it can be distinguished in a poem, arises as Otsuji says from the attempt to objectify it aesthetically: "Though our thought exists as one unity, by developing individual ideas included in it, we can achieve objectification of it aesthetically, just as a single firecracker, shooting upward, scatters and creates many jewels. . . . . Pauses are used to show clearly the points of distinction between the general ideas in the arrangement."[83] *Versum* and the thought-pause can, of course, coincide, as is obvious from a consideration of Bashô's crow haiku, where a *versum* and the thought-pause occur together at the end of the second line; Otsuji remarks that the thought-pause is usually indicative of an ellipsis in the haiku and goes on to describe its placement:

> From the point of view of content, there is one strong pause within a single haiku, which arises from an ellipsis. This strong pause, which occurs at the end of a line, has the effect of tightening the rhythm of the whole haiku. That is to say, the pattern is generally as follows, showing the two parts making up one whole: 5–pause–7–5; 5–7–pause–5. . . . Comparing the pauses of old and modern haiku, we find that the latter tend to have a pause in the middle of the haiku after the eighth or ninth syllable, instead of after the fifth or twelfth syllable.[84]

An example of the modern placement of the thought-pause is illustrated in the plum-blossom haiku, analyzed in the preceding pages, where the thought-pause occurs after the ninth syllable and does not correspond with either of the two *versum* points within the poem. Otsuji goes on to say that while the latter placement of the thought-pause has not become dominant even in modern haiku, it arises from the more finely differentiated rhythm arising from syllables which the moderns have cultivated—an area which is dealt with more fully in later sections of this book.[85]

It should also be briefly pointed out here that the modern placement of the thought-pause as related to syllabic rhythm is also in some cases connected with a basic difference in the kind of experience that is dealt with. The so-called "New Trend School" of haiku of which Hekigodo was the leader, evolved a concept of the rectangular form of a haiku, which followed the pattern of 5-5-3-5 syllabic groupings. The thought-pause then tended to occur as follows: 5-5-pause-3-5. As Etsurô Ide points out, of all the experimental forms that occupied the school's attention only this one lent itself to a pleasing syllabic rhythm:

> During this period [circa 1910] the demand for a change in the haiku form was very strong. Many new forms were experimented with. In order to have complexity of concept, they all became rectangular. The rectangular form is a form which could be easily settled upon, as far as syllabic rhythm is concerned.... Among the rectangular forms, 5–5–3–5 is the best from the point of view of odd-numbered syllabic rhythm.... 5–5–5–3 is not as good as 5–5–3–5.[86]

As for the thinking behind this type of haiku, it will be dealt with in the following section.

To return to Otsuji's observation that the thought-pause usually marks an ellipsis within the haiku, it is of course both a grammatical ellipsis and a poetic one. The grammatical ellipsis is plain between the second and third lines of Bashô's crow haiku, where the missing words might well be either "in" or "it is."

> On a withered bough
> A crow alone is perching
> [In the] autumn evening now.

> On a withered bough
> A crow alone is perching;
> [It is an] autumn evening now.

The omission of such words, which add nothing to the meaning of the verse and make it rather prosaic and heavy, needs no justification. As for the second function of the ellipsis, it is my feeling that from it comes much of the suggestive power of the haiku. Out of the pause rises a whole aura of things left unsaid that fills out the verse, just as an artist in *sumi* painting fills the space of his silk without filling it. I have spoken of the universality which is an attribute of art. Perhaps it would not be too fanciful to say that from the thought-pause which is also an ellipsis comes part of that reference to greater areas of experience and understanding than are literally named in a poem. It is some such richly experiential function that a thought-pause serves in a haiku, rather than being only a simple pause in thought such as is found in prose.

In English the thought-pause can be distinguished only through reading experientially for the pause it marks. In Japanese, however, it can be clearly marked by the so-called "cutting words" or *kire-ji*, for which there is usually no English equivalent. Around their use some discussion and controversy arose, since the usage tended to become inflexibly formalized, with some maintaining that verses without a *kire-ji* were doubtfully classed as haiku. However, such meaningless formalism was blocked and, as in English, "verses without a *kire-ji* but with a well-defined thought-pause based on the meaning were considered hokku," in Otsuji's words.[87] It should also be noted in passing that Japanese poets recognized that the ellipsis or thought-pause could also coincide with the end of the haiku, although this type of placement is rare.

I have hoped by this discussion to illustrate what I mean by inner necessity, especially as it relates to the division into three lines within one breath-length; it is a fidelity to the exact nature of the experience, or rather, an exactness of experience, arising from the single unique entity that experience fully realized is.

5. FIVE-SEVEN-FIVE

In the haiku quoted already, it is noted that the turning occurs where it should by its own necessity, often coinciding with the completion of the rhythmic flow within each element. In other haiku, there is often an over-lapping, so that one element often occupies one line and continues into the second, as in the plum-blossom haiku. In both types, the turning usually happens at the fifth and twelfth syllable.[88] This does not mean that turning must take place in a 5-7-5 pattern in every haiku. Yet when it does so take place, because the material itself dictates the necessity for it, the resulting poem has a quality of balance and symmetry, of a well unified whole. It seems that there is in the 5-7-5 pattern itself a sense of harmony and balance, due to the kind of relationship that exists in length alone among the three lines. To take the first line of five syllables and the second line of seven syllables, it can be seen that one half of the first part goes into the second part approximately three times. This proportion of two to three is almost like the proportion of the golden section, which represents in art the desire for aesthetic balance. Lightner Witner, among many others, has described it thus:

> It seems to be true that the development of taste leads to a preference of proportion to symmetry.... But the cause of this is not the demand for an equality of ratios, but a demand merely for greater variety. Symmetrical figures are divided into parts monotonously alike; proportional figures have their parts unlike. The amount of unlikeness or variety that is pleasing will depend upon the general character of the object, and upon the individual's grade of intelligence and aesthetic taste. The ratio of "proportion" is not fixed as is that of symmetry. It is only as a very rough approximation that the ratio of 3:5 can be said to represent the most pleasing mean between a too great inequality or variety and a too great equality or sameness.[89]

The harmonious effect of such a proportion seems eminently suited to the kind of experience that is dealt with in haiku, while the concluding line of five syllables, balancing as it does with the first line, adds symmetry.

Let us consider the effect of an arrangement of 5-5-7 or of 7-5-5 syllables, both of which patterns still adhere to the length of seventeen syllables as found in most haiku. While it is true that the ideal proportion of two to three is preserved, the sense of balance between the two five-syllable lines is lost by their juxtaposition. Rather, either of the two patterns seems to suggest a stanza form in a poem of several stanzas, and not the closed, self-sufficient pattern of contrast and identity that is in the 5-7-5 order.

What kind of experience is in haiku, then, which seems to correspond to the formal, balanced pattern of 5-7-5? I feel that above all a haiku experience, as is any genuine experience, is an organization in perception; in itself, experience or insight brings, in Coleridge's classic phrase, order out of chaos. Western art often deals with the process of bringing order out of chaos, presenting entanglements and conflicts, and showing how they are resolved. As Brooks has put it, "[The modern period views] the poet, the imaginative man, [as having] his particular value in his superior power to reconcile the irrelevant or apparently warring elements of experience."[90] But in a haiku moment of one breath-length, there is only the resolution. Whatever conflict or disharmony there is has preceded the haiku moment, in which the nature of things is grasped in clear intuition. The world, in the haiku moment, stands revealed for what it is. We are filled with "ah-ness," with a sense that, indeed, this is the way it truly is, with the perfection of finality. For the art of haiku, as Asô has said, "is that of beauty arising from harmony."[91] It is not "the art of passion; it is an art that attempts to grasp the intimations of things or the atmosphere arising from the tension of emotion rather than the emotion itself. Consequently it is the art of synthesis rather than of analysis, of intimation, rather than realism."[92] Indeed, Otsuji advises that the haiku poet would do well to abandon the haiku if he wishes to deal with materials which are better dealt with in other forms: "A part of the field which haiku covered in the past should be surrendered as prose develops. At the same time there is no obstacle that we can find to a haiku poet's becoming a novelist or a dramatist. According to the objectives, form should be selected."[93]

The insight into felt objects at the haiku moment can be grasped only through a unified, well-ordered whole corresponding with the insight. For this reason, a formalistic structure, of which balance, harmony, and symmetry are qualities, seems best suited for realizing a haiku moment. As was demonstrated, the 5-7-5 pattern is such a formalistic structure. It is an instance when the insight and the pattern create each other, for, as Allen Tate has noted, "it is probable that there is an intimate relation between a generally accepted 'picture of the world' and the general acceptance of a metrical system and its differentiations into patterns."[94] It seems to me that haiku, both in its length of seventeen syllables and their division into three parts of five, seven, and five syllables, tends to substantiate Tate's conjecture. Ideally, the formalized structure is congruent with the inner turnings of the material itself, as was shown in the analysis of turning given above.

In considering haiku which do not follow the usual pattern, there are perhaps four reasons for the deviation. The first may be that the poet's perception in itself is not clear or fully realized. Perhaps he has not succeeded in isolating the most significant place or time for his object, the one which will set it off in its only possible setting. Perhaps he has not succeeded in realizing the crucial organic force which holds his perception in one totality. Any personal emotion—the desire to be thought witty or sensitive, for example—will stand between a poet and his insight.

Secondly, the poet may not be a master of his medium; he may have no feeling for the precise word, no ear for sounds, no sense of rhythm.

The third and most valid reason may be that the poet rightly refuses to force his perception into a pattern that is not its form. His insight may be clear and profound, and demand another pattern. There is room for giving play to the poet's individual vision, Otsuji says: "When we try to express our emotion directly, we cannot know beforehand how many syllables will be needed. Moreover, each poet has his own way of expression, characteristic of himself, and how he divides the lines should be left up to him."[95] Yet he is still under the necessity of producing an effect of balance and symmetry which is in his realization. If he is a master of his medium, and to be a poet, he must be, he can usually do so in English by the use of unaccented syllables, liquid sounds, and polysyllabic words. As Bashô points out, the desired effect is not dependent on the number of syllables alone: "Please examine verse with three, four, five, or even seven extra syllables to see whether it sounds well or not. Also examine verse with only one extra syllable, which can disrupt the rhythm."[96] If the longer line deals with a lighter object or a lighter color as compared to the shorter lines dealing with heavy, massive objects and intense or dark colors, balance can be maintained. Various other methods will be discussed in the following chapter dealing with the art of haiku.

A fourth and most interesting reason arises from the intent of the poet, as that was illustrated by the New Trend School headed by Hekigodo. They felt that the experience they wished to deal with differed from the kind found in haiku formed on the 5-7-5 pattern, and characterized it in various ways. Seisensui declared that a haiku must express "a dynamic rhythm of impressions": "The significant fact is that the old form was broken [i.e., the 5-7-5 pattern]. In a haiku which must express a dynamic rhythm of impressions, there should be no form based on syllabic numbers."[97] Ide points out that the new poets wished to deal with "complexity of concept,"[98] expressive of the "new sensitivity" and enabling the poet "to fulfill the self."[99] Kuribayashi points out that by dispensing with a formalized interest in the seasonal theme, a newer sense of atmosphere and mood could be attained: "In a rectangular form [the seasonal theme] is not necessary. So we can be freed of such a formalized interest in the seasonal theme and can depict atmosphere and mood freely."[100] Hekigodo, as I have shown, felt that changed social conditions and new intellectual attitudes introduced from the West called *ipso facto* for a new haiku, naming specifically the liberal ideal in society and the new scientific attitude.[101]

Their point of view that the older classic form of 5-7-5 was triangular in concept, while their new form was rectangular is described by Kuribayashi:

> If we consider tne old 5–7–5 form as a three-sided form (i.e., triangular), the form of the New Trend School can be considered as made up of two triangles (i.e., a rectangle); if we consider the triangular form as having one center, the rectangular one will have two centers. Thus it can depict atmosphere and mood. Since a triangular form is arranged with a seasonal theme as its center, it tends to fall into a formalized interest in the seasonal theme. However, in a rectangular form, that is not necessary. So we can be freed of such a formalized interest in the seasonal theme and can depict atmosphere and mood freely.[102]

The two centers of interest in the rectangular form were generally expressed in a 5-5-3-5 pattern of syllables, with a thought-pause occurring between the two points of interest.[103] Kuribayashi goes on to compare a haiku by Shiki in the older form with one by Hekigodo in the newer. Translations adhering to the syllabic patterns of both follow:

> Toward those short trees,
> We saw a hawk descending
> On a day in spring.
> —*Shiki*

> The day we saw the hawk
> On a churchyard tree,
> A kite too
> Was in the far sky.
> —*Hekigodo*

Kuribayashi's paraphrase of Seisensui's comments on the two poems follows:

> Comparing these two poems, in the first the interest lies in the harmony among the three individual ideas—i.e., the tree, the hawk, and the spring day (in short, in the formalized interest in the spring day). However, in the second, the lines—"The day we saw the hawk / On a churchyard tree"— are considered the front scene; and the next two lines—"A kite too / Was in the far sky"—is the back scene. Through the placement of two centers of interest, one in the closer and one in the farther scene, the poem expresses atmosphere. So it does not consist of a formalized interest in the kite as a seasonal theme.[104]

When the newer poets rejected the injection of the seasonal theme in haiku as a worn-out convention, they were only agreeing with the old, classical masters, as has been shown.[105] But having rejected the seasonal theme *in toto* and thereby one of the great unifying elements of haiku,[106] the new poets were free to "fulfill the self" through the subjective element inherent in the grounds for relating the two centers of interest. For if we examine Hekigodo's representative verse given above, it seems to depend for its interest on the relationship—and these can be in the nature of conflicts, contrasts, complementation, and so on—between the two points of interest. Without an objective criterion for the relationship, then, in the hands of lesser poets, the relationship between the two elements became unclear and prohibitively private, with results similar to Pound's Metro poem, where the unrelatedness is a disintegrating force and the experience is not unified:

> The apparition of these faces in the crowd;
> Petals on a wet, black bough.

As previously pointed out,[107] John Gould Fletcher's comment on Pound's poem seizes on the essential point of weakness in this poetic method: "The relation of certain beautiful faces seen in a Paris Metro station to petals on a wet tree branch is not absolutely clear." Extreme examples of subjectivity and privacy of meaning incommunicable to another are strikingly similar in the writings of both the Imagists and the New Trend School (as well as in the Free Haiku School which followed). Let us compare one of Amy Lowell's short pieces with one of Seisensui's. The American poem reads:

> Little hot apples of fire
> Burst out of the flaming stem
> Of my heart.[108]

Seisensui's, in which I have retained his pattern of syllable groupings, is just as bizarre:

> A ginko tree of my own
> As well as my breast
> Budded forth
> With young little leaves.[109]

What Otsuji has to say of verbal playfulness without content in his comments on the Japanese poem seems equally applicable to Western poems of this type, though one suspects that Amy Lowell's verse arose more from an ingenuous lack of discrimination and from a striving for effect rather than from a deeper and perhaps more evil triviality: "An expression like 'My breast/Budded forth/With young little leaves' is a product of a trivial life of words without any content. How can a work be aesthetic when one's life is already only a playful game? Here the state of boredom and wearisomeness has reached its extreme."[110]

That another of the objectives of this school—namely, complexity— is attainable through an emphasis on relationships seems clear. It is of course not arguable that a kind of complexity is not a desirable element of verse, but when it arises not from fully realized particulars, but from an intellectual and conceptual process, I feel it has no place in poetry, which must above all render experience. If we consider the following verse, it seems clear, I feel, that neither of the two objects mentioned has been realized or has become an adequate objective correlative of some felt insight of the poet:

> My house where my mother is ill
> Lies before my sight,
> And the dragonflies
> From the fields.[111]

The dragonflies here do not lead a life of their own, but depend rather on the relationship to the house; consequently, the poem depends upon a conceptual, rational idea rather than upon a felt insight. Another example of a "dead" listing of a word follows:

> Fluttering its wings,
> A small sparrow
> Has come to perch upon a branch.
> Morning.[112]

Otsuji has unerringly picked out the "dead" word: "This word *morning* does not have enough content to balance with the lines that precede; it does not balance their importance."[113] That is to say, the quality of the morning has not been realized so that it is felt. This becomes very clear if we remember how alive and meaningful the autumn evening is in Bashô's crow haiku.

> On a withered bough
> A crow alone is perching;
> Autumn evening now.

The strictures I have made on some aspects of the objectives of the newer school of haiku poets are not related directly to the syllabic pattern employed—the norm of which seems to me close enough to the 5-7-5 pattern, with a thought-pause in the second syllabic grouping, to assume the balanced characteristics of the older form as previously described—but rather to the concept of haiku with two centers of interest, both apparently equally operative in one poem. That this is possible in what Vivante, an Italian aesthetician, calls "constructive thought" but is not the *modus operandi* of poetic vision seems particularly well brought out in his following observation:

> In the poetic period not only the attribute, but every word, every moment of thought, gathers up, renews the whole. The subject is recalled in its concept in every word of the proposition, that is, it progressively takes fresh value, fills up of itself and governs every new moment. Thus reality at every point is drawn up from the unknown. The new expressive moment in its particular significance forms itself in the meaning of the whole, which in the new moment is not inferred but renewed: and myriads of *nexus*—resemblances, accords, unities, *ex principio*—form themselves. On the other hand, constructive thought loses the *nexus* or necessities of principle proper to thought in its integral originality: if we except the *nexus* belonging to formal logic, to a conception schematically material and spatial—a position of mere existences and of spatial and quantitative relations and ideal abstract identities. In other words, in constructive thought *nexus of inherence* are comparatively prevalent, in poetic thought *nexus of essence*.[114]

It would seem to me as I have said both as regards the length and syllabic groupings of haiku that it emphasizes a unity in perception, arising out of immediate sensuous perception, in which all things are one in, as Vivante has said, a *nexus* of essence. It is only when we step down or away from the experience that it can break up into parts, whose relationship interests us. Perhaps this relationship can become a legitimate concern of other forms of poetry, but not, I feel, of haiku, which is not to say that complexity and relationships of another kind, the basis of which has been described, are not dealt with in successful haiku.

It should be noted that Hekigodo's New Trend School led to the development of the Free Haiku School, headed by Seisensui, who was more extreme than Hekigodo in demanding freedom of and from form. His position is made clear in the following statement.

The fact that during the period of the new trend, the 5–7–5 form was broken and the rectangular form of 5–5–3–5 was created has no meaning in this new form. The significant fact is that the old form was broken. In a haiku, which must express a dynamic rhythm of impressions, there should be no form based on syllabic numbers. This is very important. Therefore the later period of the new-trend movement, when haiku settled down in a kind of fixed form, seems after all not consistently logical.[115]

In the demands for freedom from form, this group forgot that art exists and is communicable only through form. What they wished would have resulted in the destruction of poetry itself, and as a result, their influence has become negligible. At present, the classic school based on the 5-7-5 pattern, headed by Kyoshi, the great living disciple of Shiki, who revived the haiku during the latter 1800's, is the dominant one.

Asô has perhaps given the definitive answer of the classicist to Seisen-sui's position; form, far from being restricting, can be a liberating force:

Simply to be contented with achieving a certain form has no value. However, the effort to maintain that form must be the expression of a humble sincerity, intent upon defending that art form. It is no less than the artist's effort to master his art, by negating the self, not by flaunting his ego or his personal eccentricities. When such an attitude of self-refinement is present, the form for that man is not a mere dead thing. He will realize a wonderful state of inspiration as the result of self-discipline. To experience such a state is to arouse in the poet a realization of the strength of the poetic faith in him, which will undoubtedly issue forth as a great talent.[116]

CHAPTER FOUR

CRYSTALLIZATION

IN THE PRECEDING PAGES, mention has been made of the organic force which arises in experience and unifies it. It is the feeling that belongs to a consummated experience.[1] In and around the words through which the haiku poet attempts to form the world of his aesthetic experience, must flow the feeling of the experience. It alone will control the selection of words, their order, sound, rhythm, and cadence. When all these elements within a group of words are bound in and with the emotion, the resulting haiku is a crystallization. Much as crystals are held together by the inner force of their pattern, so a crystallized haiku is held together by the organic, emotional force of the experience. In this chapter I shall discuss these word elements, beginning with some consideration of words as they relate to each other in groups.

1. HAIKU ART

The two functions of words—namely, denotation and connotation—I shall call their static aspect or sign function and their dynamic aspect or organic-force function. As words function dynamically, in poetry, they cease as in prose to *stand for* objects and concepts; rather, as the force of crystallization binds them together, the words themselves can *become* the things they stand for. Herbert Read has put the matter succinctly: "Words are generally (that is to say, in prose) the *analysis* of a mental state. But in the process of poetic composition words rise into the conscious mind as isolated objective 'things' with a definite equivalence in the poet's state of mental intensity."[2] To illustrate, let us consider that groups of words can vary from meaningless juxtapositions, to arrangements that deal only with their static aspects, to organizations which exploit to the full their dynamic, connotative properties. Any of these three groupings can be put in a 5-7-5 shape as the following will show:

> JUXTAPOSITION: Precious more the was
> In the light eyes your all than
> In roses the world.

Each word here is static. It stands alone and independent. Since the group retains only its sign function or what may be called its noun meaning, and since none of its parts relate to each other, the group has no force as a whole. Let us relate these words to each other:

> ARRANGEMENT: More precious was the
> Light in your eyes than the
> Roses in the world.[3]

Meaning now arises from relating the denotative function of the words to each other. The group of words is shaped like a haiku, contains the three haiku elements of object, time, and place, and is sixteen syllables long, close enough to the ideal haiku length. But it obviously is not a haiku. Far from affording a vivid insight into a lover's feeling, it is banal in the extreme. Although it has a haiku shape, it is not a haiku form, for there is no felt, organic force that holds it together. As Otsuji says, the words give only "a hollow sound":

> If one does not grasp something—something which does not merely touch us through our senses but contacts the life within and has the dynamic form of nature—no matter how cunningly we form our words, they will give only a hollow sound. Those who compose haiku without grasping anything are merely exercising their ingenuity. The ingenious become only selectors of words and cannot create new experiences from themselves.[4]

In the present context it can be said that the connotative, dynamic element of the words has not been exploited. To illustrate this, let us take the word *roses* used in the third line. Its use here does not bring out the meaning of the rose, nor does it give a sense of season or render that fine feeling of a spring atmosphere* although the word *roses* itself has the intrinsic quality and meaning of such a feeling. Here I shall use the following verse to make this point clearer:

ORGANIZATION :   Here at parting now,
Let me speak by breaking
A lilac from the bough.

In this poem, *lilac* is a word appropriately chosen to show the season, and even more, the moment of speaking, when it is broken from the bough. We see how this word, being an adequate objective correlative for the heartfelt feeling expressed in the verse, acts as a dramatic symbol with its delicate purple of clustered flowers, and the spring in which it blooms, of the sentiment in the poem. The person who speaks here is, perhaps, a beautiful girl addressing her young lover.

Observe how solidly imbedded in the haiku is the word *lilac*, because the connotations have been brought into play. Observe how easily some other object can be substituted for roses (e.g., rubies, laughter, sunshine, etc.) in the preceding one, which I call an arrangement because the words are static, like so many wooden counters. Organization, however, is that kind of grouping by which the function of a word changes from static to dynamic. In such a grouping is force, which cannot be arranged, but only organized. Only when words can be organized will a crystallized haiku result.

Both Brooks and Otsuji are agreed that a poet's use of words, as they arise from insight and are held by the emotional force of the experience, can give originality to his expression. As Brooks says, this is what is meant by poets' "building a more precise sort of language": "Keats... like all other poets, is really building a more precise sort of language than the dictionaries contain, by playing off the connotations and denotations of words against each other so as to make a total statement of a great deal more accuracy than is ordinarily attained."[5] As previously stated, Otsuji castigates those who compose haiku without having grasped something which "contacts the life within." They are only "selectors of words and cannot create new experiences from themselves."[6]

As for diction, it is interesting to note that both Bashô and the

---

* Note that although we customarily say "summer rose," we do not feel it necessary to say "spring rose."

Imagists are insistent on the use of common language,* as contrasted to the pretentiously poetic phrase, and are agreed as to the poet's role in using them. Bashô says: "In the poetry of haikai ordinary words are used,"[7] and adds that the value of poetry is "to correct ordinary words."[8] The first statement in the famous Imagist credo found in their 1915 anthology declared: "To use the language of common speech, but to employ always the *exact* word, not the merely decorative word."[9] For as Hulme, who according to Hughes, "reasonably may be called the 'father of imagism,' " declared: "Plain speech is essentially inaccurate. It is only by metaphors...that it can be made precise."[10] That is to say, using the words of ordinary language, the poet attains precision— as Bashô says, he corrects ordinary words—only as the words *are* the experience. The ultimate extent to which the words can become the experience, organized by the poetic force that belongs to a realized perception, has been vividly described by Eliot, so that truly, as Paul Valéry said, the poet is consecrated to building "a language within a language."[11] It seems to me that the following is one of the most successfully suggestive descriptions Eliot has written of part of the poetic process:

> [The poet possesses] the feeling for syllable and rhythm, penetrating far below the conscious levels of thought and feeling, invigorating every word; sinking to the most primitive and forgotten, returning to the origin and bringing something back, seeking the beginning and the end. It works through meanings, certainly, or not without meanings in the ordinary sense, and fuses the old and obliterated and trite, the current and the new and surprising, the most ancient and the most civilized mentality.[12]

When every word in the poem has rooted itself so pervasively beyond consciousness, beyond history, beyond artifice, we get, it seems to me, verse like Bashô's crow haiku:

---

* Eliot seems to suggest that a return to the "common language" is a return to a basic function of poetry—communication between persons. "So while poetry attempts to convey something beyond what can be conveyed in prose rhythms, it remains all the same, one person talking to another.... The immediacy of poetry to conversation is not a matter on which we can lay down exact laws. Every revolution in poetry is apt to be, and sometimes to announce itself as, a return to common speech." ("The Music of Poetry," *Selected Prose,* ed. by John Hayward. Harmondsworth, Middlesex: Penguin Books, 1953, p. 58.) Kyoshi Takahama, the greatest contemporary haiku poet, has a similar observation on the basic function of haiku: "[People] express their thoughts and feelings as freely as they can in this form and appreciate it with one another. That I believe is one of the great reasons that haiku exists in the world of poetry." *Cf.* p. 40.

> On a withered bough
> A crow alone is perching;
> Autumn evening now.

Or the following:

> In the twilight gloom
> Of the redwood and the pine
> Some wisterias bloom.

Here the tranquillity, far from being passive, is an active force. The two haiku are held in a pulsing stillness, achieving the ideal state of a poem which Yeats described as being "as cold/And passionate as the dawn."[13]

The process of crystallization not only creates an organization among words, but its function also lies in selecting objects of a size and color that will embody forth the intuition. Even on such seemingly small details does form depend, for as Louis Danz has said, "Form is that kind of organization to which nothing can be added and from which nothing can be taken."[14] And I would add: in which no substitutions can be made. As Bashô said, "Hokku without an air of inevitability are not true hokku."[15] For example, let us consider the following change in the crow haiku:

> On a withered bough
> A *crane* alone is perching;
> Autumn evening now.

How noticeable is the changed effect, the loss of the gem-like. The aesthetic value of a crane in and for itself is no less than that of a crow; as Otsuji remarked: "I do not recognize the contention that natural objects are either superior or inferior to each other."[16] But the aesthetic significance of that value and meaning cannot be fully translated and brought out on a withered bough in an autumn evening, for the elements do not harmonize with each other in a single mood. For example, the intense whiteness of the crane in this subdued haiku of blacks and grays and fading light receives emphasis, but the reason for such emphasis in terms of the total perception is not clear. The proportion between the size of the crane and its bough is such that the object seems too large for its stand. On the other hand, substitution of "sparrow" for "crow" immediately shows how too small an object is undesirable also.

The same may be said of the other elements, as can be seen in the following:

> On a *willow* bough
> A crow alone is perching;
> *Summer* evening now.

It is needless to say that there is no color and mood harmony in this changed version, created with the green of the willow, the blackness of the crow, and the shape and voluptuousness of the summer evening and its light. Certainly a completely different haiku compared to the original, nevertheless it does not create its own mood for the objects do not adhere to each other with that absolute oneness of the original. What Bashô experienced was the quality of mystic profound alone-ness and the mood that comes with it. He created color and mood harmony without describing what that was; and he did it by presenting the particulars in which the experiential value of that quality resides.

The following haiku shows how all important a single color can become:

> Piercing crimson red
> Is the autumn setting sun
> On the cockscomb head.

There is here a violent yet restrained air, filled with the fiery red of the setting sun forming on the stately cockscomb. Bathed in the flood of light, the cockscomb gains in the fierce touch of flaming beauty a visual richness just as the poet experienced it.

Color and mood harmony in both the above haiku is formed through either subtle combination and harmony of color or through insistence on a single one. However, contrast in color, emotion, and tone can produce its unique haiku mood also as the following will illustrate:

> Cast by morning light,
> The stamen's shadow is black
> On the calla white.

The mood created is one of serenity, edged with a sharp, poignant air. This is a harmony realized by contrasting colors in the word image.

A third area to be considered in thinking about words in groups is their order within the group. A poet creates a crystallized haiku through that kind of organization in which a definite order is found, just as that order exists in the realized aesthetic experience. Analysis of a few poems will show one aspect of that order, as it can be found in certain types of haiku. Let us begin with the following:

> White swans, one or two,
> Drew near, pushing the water
> For the food I threw.

Suppose a painter sees the scene of the above poem. He might draw one or two swans facing the food, and a few curved lines in front of the birds denoting the waves or ripples in such a way as to give the impression of the swans approaching. Painting thus enables us to visualize the moment of action or movement by presenting a certain form and appropriate positions for the object in space; on the other hand, haiku can give that spatial form by stating the movement of the object with such a phrase as "pushing the water." Consequently, it may be said that painting is spatial and haiku temporal. That is the fundamental difference between them as far as their mode of expression is concerned; yet, analyzing haiku further, one soon discovers that the methods used for the realization of space, direction, dimension, atmosphere, and perspective in scene or landscape can give it almost the same freedom as painting in these areas in certain cases. Within the limited scope of seventeen syllables, some haiku can become three dimensional.

As a quick resumé, I may suggest that the verb gives us the elements of perspective; words such as *far* and *near* suggest distance; *right, left, beginning, middle, end,* etc., denote the direction and position of the object. Just as the artist can project a three-dimensional world though he works with silk or paper, so can the haiku poet. The last-quoted haiku is an illustration. There the poet placed the swans at the far end as the painter would draw them; the ripples are expressed figuratively by the phrase "pushing the water," and the position of the birds is indicated by the verb *drew* and the adverb *near*. This is further pointed out, and the relations are made clear and distinct, by placing the food in the third line as it would be in a painting.

Let us suppose Hokusai, the famous painter, were to draw a picture of Buson's poem:

> In the rains of spring
> An umbrella and raincoat
> Pass by, conversing.

Perhaps with a few subtle strokes he would draw a simple picture in which we could see the two persons, one with an umbrella and the other with a raincoat, and also a few dozen lines slanting down from above, indicating the rain. In the painting, the rain of course would be above the umbrella and raincoat; the position of these objects to each other would be kept, for otherwise perspective might be lost. This is also true in the haiku; they are kept in their usual position to each other. Let us read it again. We see the rain above the umbrella and raincoat!

Thus the word order in certain haiku can have the same importance as composition and design in painting. For although haiku is a scene reduced to a two-dimensional world in word-print on paper, as soon as the time element is introduced by the movement of our eyes along the lines and the time we require to read the words, a haiku world can become a three-dimensional world. As we read every object reduced to print begins to rise, and we see clearly the trees in their own position and heights. The mountains, the lakes, and all that may be found in the haiku world take their respective places in natural order. Thus objects in haiku can become alive before the reader.

Accordingly, when word order (i.e., the placement of objects) in a haiku proceeds with some awareness of the spatial relationship dominant, it can perhaps be roughly classified as vertical, horizontal, or a combination of the two. The haiku by Buson cited above is vertical in feeling while the swan poem is horizontal. Another example of the second class may be given here:

> On the bench I wait
> For the second gust to come
> Through the garden gate.

We see the bench at one end and the gate at the other. Between, there is nothing but the cool summer gust passing freely at evening.

The next haiku presents an interesting aspect:

> In moonlight, half-hid
> By the silhouettes of leaves
> Twits the katydid.

This poem at first seems vertical, since we might see the moon above everything else; but the moon is not at its zenith because then it is impossible to have vivid silhouettes. Therefore we must consider that the moon, in this case, is at the far end. This haiku world might then seem horizontal. The position of the moon, in this seemingly horizontal scene, indicates the time distinctly: it is the rising moon. However, it can be assumed that the moon's position is high enough to give the clearest aspect of the haiku world. Consequently this poem is in the third group, a combination of the horizontal and the vertical.

Observing the perspective in this poem, we notice that the poet puts the leaves as close to the insect as possible, indicating that some of them are in front of and some behind the katydid. This is further indicated by the word *half-hid,* and also the plural *silhouettes.* Suppose we change the natural order of the things, i.e., the word order, in the following manner:

> From the leaves, half-hid
> In the moon-cast silhouettes
> Twits the katydid.

Then we have (1) leaves, (2) silhouettes—moon, and (3) katydid in this jumbled order, which detracts from the immediacy of the verse. When we add the third dimension to this picture by reading the poem, visualization is difficult, through the words as they occur. Only as we "think" the picture through, can we grasp the spatial relationships, by which act, of course, we remove ourselves from the object and destroy the coalescence with it which is aesthetic.

The spatial relationships in the camellia haiku might appear at first glance confusing, but analysis will show how intimately involved they are with the poet's realization.

> Brushing the leaves, fell
> A white camellia blossom
> Into the dark well.

Let us imagine a frame around this picture. From the upper edge, where the dark-green leaves are quivering, the eye travels to the succulent perfection of the blossom falling into the dark well. Note that the poet does not wish to tell us, in complete chronological order, that the flower dropped, then brushed the leaves and fell into the well. Otherwise the haiku would read:

> The white camellia blossom
> Brushes the leaves and falls
> Into the dark well.

The original haiku does not describe the entire history of the falling flower, for this one has already dropped from its branch and is *already falling* as it enters the haiku moment. The poet has selected only what he felt as the significant portion of that history, and the spatial relationships are accordingly projected in the poem. Consequently, the leaves are placed above the camellia.

Structuring a haiku in regard to spatial relationships much as a painter composes his picture is only one of the ways in which a poet achieves immediacy. As previously stated, not every haiku is written in this technique, since the governing principle is not realistic spatial relationships, but rather the forming of the realization. The following poem by Bashô seems to be an example, since the placement of the objects is inverted if compared to that in a painting:

> Wild the rolling sea!
> Over which to Sado Isle
> Lies the Galaxy.

If, in a schematic sense, the first line is thought of as the top of the painting, the inversion is clear. However, one supposes that Bashô's experience began and proceeded in the order given, and the haiku was formed by it. In spite of the similarities between haiku and painting, since they are different art forms, the limitations imposed on a painter are not the same for a haiku poet.

Therefore, even if a haiku is formed to mirror the natural order in a scene or an event, such order may be inimical to the crystallization of the experience, since other factors equally important must be considered. For example, as I have tried to show in the discussion of how verse "turns"[17] the order of placement of objects in a poem (i.e., word order) is determined by the rhythmic flow of the organic force which holds them together. Only as the poet is true to his experience will he remain unconfused and his creation be aesthetic. In this connection, let us consider the following line from George Meredith, where the placement of the single word *gathering* affects the significance of the live image. The original version reads: "We saw the swallows gathering in the sky." If, however, we change the word order slightly to read "We saw the gathering swallows in the sky," then we notice immediately that the swallows' action becomes dead and the whole line loses vividness. Thus organization gives significance to poetry by changing the relationship among the words into a definite, immovable order to create a form from a shape. On the other hand, arrangements deal with words only mechanically, giving us sign posts through experience, but not the experience itself.

2. HAIKU RHYTHM

Beyond cherry brumes,
Is the bell at Asakusa
Or Ueno that booms?

In reading this famous haiku by Bashô, one cannot but feel the vibrating
rhythm, rising from the aesthetic emotion. It is rhythm, not meter, of
one kind with the mood and meaning of the experience. Here *cherry
brumes* holds all the charms and rich, echoing overtones of the temple
bell. In listening to the inspiring gong, Bashô wonders where the bell
is being tolled, and looks toward Asakusa and then Ueno in marvel
before the soft-pink mist of the blooming cherries. This aesthetic feeling
seems to be the basic rhythm of the haiku, expressed organically in the
sonorous echoes of the temple bell, tolled at evening, rising in a perfect
circle, fringed with cherry mist and expanding in the air to the listening
ear.

Here rhythm is manifested first as aesthetic feeling.* It is no less
than the pulsation of experience which vibrates in our awareness,
coming through a medium, when it is crystallized, just as that pulsation
the poet feels dispassionately demands expression in words. For "rhythm
creates itself and should not be pre-arranged," as Otsuji puts it.[18]
Therefore, whenever the poet wishes to compose a poem, he tries to
crystallize the rhythm of experience as true and subtle as the original
feeling. Only in this sense can the rhythm be "an integral part of the
communication;" in Brooks' words, "the rhythm of a poem is one of
the conditioning factors modifying the tone, supplying emphasis, cor-
roborating and underlying the play of the thought."[19] Here the words
—the English words, since we are dealing with the possibilities of haiku
in English—required for the expression are the means in which lie all
the poetic possibilities as well as the limitations. Consequently, every
poet, especially every haiku poet, must face them and handle them
skillfully to make his art unique and comprehensible to his readers, and
as true as the original feeling itself, flashing vividly into being.

So Bashô began his poem by placing the cherry brumes in the first

* Indeed, as Eliot has remarked, rhythm may come as the first intimation of
a realized experience, for "a poem or a passage of a poem, may tend to realize
itself first as a particular rhythm before it reaches expression in words, and...this
rhythm may bring to birth the idea and the image...." (In "The Music of Poetry,"
Selected Prose, p. 66.)

line because he saw them first; and in the second line, the bell and Asakusa, the place toward which he first looked for it; and in the last, Ueno, to which his mind wandered. This is an outline of what Bashô has done. To translate what he experienced as the bell trailed with a rich echoing sound in a perfect circle, his haiku sings with its rhythm, as do all fully crystallized haiku.

For it is not only in haiku whose appeal is to the ear, as is this one, that rhythm is important. The unwary reader might suppose that when the subject matter of the verse deals with sound, the rhythm of the words in it becomes especially important. But whether, as in the crow haiku, the appeal is to the vision, or as in the camellia haiku, lies in action, every haiku, in becoming actual, produces its own rhythm as it creates its own form, true to the poetic experience. Since rhythm of course arises from the relationship of the words to each other, it seems appropriate to consider haiku rhythm in terms of word order, which has been previously considered in terms of turning and spatial relationships. Let us take the camellia haiku as our example:

> Brushing the leaves, fell
> A white camellia blossom
> Into the dark well.

In this haiku it will be noted how harmoniously the feeling in rhythm is expressed through the dual nature of language, its union of *sound* elements and *thought* elements, in a combination, moving as the poet's feeling for the motion of the object—the camellia in this case. I shall call the former vertical rhythm, which is the rhythm of aesthetic feeling become the pulsation of the experience in temporal order; it is expressed through the tone quality of the sound of words and through patterns of stressed and unstressed syllables. Horizontal rhythm signifies the rhythm of thought as the meaning of experience externalized in temporal order through words. It is measured or counted by the number of syllables in accordance with the flow of thought in each line, or from one line to another. Its characteristics of rhythm in each line I will call, for the sake of convenience, haiku measure.

Perhaps the reader whose experiences in poetry have been confined mainly to English will object that what I have termed horizontal rhythm is applicable only to a language like Japanese, which, lacking stressed and unstressed syllables, must depend on some other means of rhythm formation, such as syllable count. He may feel that in English, with its pattern of stressed and unstressed syllables, such a concept of rhythm divorced from meter will either be so tenuous as to be negligible or even completely inapplicable. Up to the time of the Imagist movement there would be little questioning his stand. For, until then, for the majority of readers, rhythm was felt to reside only in regularity of meter, and rare was the poet whose numbers did not sweetly flow in metric measures. So firmly indeed did meter grasp all other possible rhythmic elements in poetry, that an *Evangeline* was perhaps inevitable with its insistent dactyls gallopping over every line like a mad rider beating his horse to death.* It was from just such tyranny that the Imagists revolted, for the "idea that cadence should be substituted for meter...was at the very heart of the Imagist credo," according to Hughes.[20] Ezra Pound trumpeted: "As regarding rhythm: [we wish] to compose in the sequence of the musical phrase, not in sequence of a metronome."[21] For they felt that the high price of conformation to a regular meter resulted in the mechanical deadening of poetry, and that other rhythms were possible, which would "correspond exactly to the emotion or shade of emotion to be expressed," as Pound went on to say.[22] Such correspondence can be independent of meter, as John Hubert Scott has said: "Rhythm in general and in all its finest manifestations is independent of meter."[23] For rhythm depends upon "the feeling arising from the content," in Otsuji's words.[24] My stand is that the rhythm of the thought-flow should be the primary consideration and that vertical rhythm (i.e., stressed and unstressed syllables) should vivify and make alive the experience in the poem. Vertical rhythm or meter is not the primary rhythmic factor in poetry. The relationship between the two rhythms is not like that of a Christmas bauble on a holiday tree, but much more organic, like the flush of a beautiful face. What the Imagists did with their concept is dealt with later on in this section.

---

* It is interesting to note that as early as 1842, Edgar Allen Poe, who enjoyed the admiration of Baudelaire, pointed out that "the hexameter can never be introduced into our language, from the nature of that language itself. This rhythm demands, *for English ears,* a preponderance of natural spondees. Our tongue has few." He goes on to point out that while the Greek hexameter is impossible in English, Longfellow's lines can "well be read as mere English dactylic verses" which are "continued for two feet." (Edgar Allen Poe, "Longfellow's Ballads," in *The Shock of Recognition.* Ed. by Edmund Wilson. Garden City: Doubleday, 1947, pp. 101–2.)

It may be interesting at this point to consider how the Japanese met the problem of gaining interesting texture in rhythm only from the horizontal elements in their language. According to Otsuji, Japanese poets have depended upon two methods: repetition of line patterns in the longer tanka or waka form and groupings of syllabic combinations in the shorter haiku form.

> In Japanese, words of one, two, three, and four syllables predominate.... Possible word combinations of two and three syllables or vice versa, or three and four syllables or vice versa are the most common.... The lack of variety possible from stress must be compensated for in Japanese by various syllabic combinations. In waka the first two lines of five and seven syllables were repeated, with an additional line of seven syllables to gain variety. In a shorter form, such a repetition is ineffective. If a repetition of two and three syllables or three and two syllables is used, still this method is like child's play. Variety arising from syllabic combinations rather than from repetition as in waka is the necessary element. Therefore if one wishes to select common yet rich syllabic combinations, the combination of a seven-syllable line with two five-syllable lines, or of two five-syllable lines with a seven-syllable line comes to mind. When either of these combinations is rearranged to gain the greatest variety, the result is a 5–7–5 combination.[25]

While it is true that the haiku derives from longer poetic forms, Otsuji maintains that the 5-7-5 pattern as it appears in the longer waka, and as it appears in haiku can be differentiated: "What has been called the 5-7-5 pattern is merely a historical step showing how it branched out from waka, and even in the period of Bashô the haiku had already developed a pattern of *niku isshô* (two parts make one whole). The intervals between the three lines of 5-7-5 do not occur with the same time stress or length."[26] I have already dealt with the question of the necessity for the haiku to be the length it is—seventeen syllables—arranged in the combination of three lines of 5-7-5 syllables each. What Otsuji has to say of attaining variety in the Japanese haiku through the "beauty of syllabic rhythm" and "a more delicate variety of rhythmic waves"[27] as compared to simple line repetition in the longer forms can apply equally well I feel to haiku in English as far as horizontal rhythm is concerned, since both languages are polysyllabic. An analysis of horizontal rhythm in English would proceed somewhat as follows.

The flow of thought in the camellia haiku may be divided thus:

> Brushing the leaves
> fell

A white camellia blossom
Into the dark well.

The participial phrase *brushing the leaves* may be subdivided as we count the number of syllables in the thought flow into two parts: *brushing* and *the leaves*. So the haiku measure in the first line may be shown thus by counting the syllables as they fall within words and groups of words according to the thought pattern:

$$\underset{2}{\text{Brushing}} \quad \underset{2}{\text{the leaves,}} \quad \underset{1}{\text{fell}}$$

Accordingly, the second and third lines may be divided in the following manner:

$$\underset{2}{\text{A white}} \quad \underset{3}{\text{camellia}} \quad \underset{2}{\text{blossom}}$$

$$\underset{2}{\text{Into}} \quad \underset{1}{\text{the}} \quad \underset{2}{\text{dark well.}}$$

The above illustrates the principle of measuring rhythm in thought elements through syllable count. It should be noted that in this system words belong wholly within one group and are not divided. As is seen, the unit of horizontal rhythm is one syllable, since the unit of our thought-flow is the one-syllable word. However, a flow of only one-syllable units in continuous succession, without differences of pitch, stress, or speed (all elements of vertical rhythm) is incapable of giving rise to rhythm. Rhythm arises as the one-syllable unit moves in combinations with groups of two, three, or four syllables. However, the three- and four-syllable groups can be broken down into combinations of the simpler unit of one and two groups as follows: $3 = 1 + 2$ or $2 + 1$; $4 = 1 + 3$ or $3 + 1$ or $2 + 2$.

That is to say, any three- or four-syllable group can be broken down into the above combinations, while any of the combinations can be considered as larger groups of three or four syllables, as the flow of the thought forms and is realized. The above formulas enable us to arrive at the following basic general possibilities of thought rhythm in the first and last lines of haiku in their simplest forms:

(a) 1:2:2   Shows the road to me
(b) 2:1:2   Into the dark well
(c) 2:2:1   Brushing the leaves, fell

And in the second line, the following syllabic combinations in general are possible:

(a) 1:2:2:2   To the one who breaks the branch
(b) 2:1:2:2   Weary from travel I find
(c) 2:2:1:2   Sea-waves whirl up to my gate
(d) 2:2:2:1   In the curfew's trailing gong

These haiku measures have their own characteristics, as varied and subtle as each feeling itself. The following chart shows the general characteristics of each measure:

FIVE SYLLABLES

(a) 1:2:2:2   rising rhythm—aspiring, smooth, light, etc.
(b) 2:1:2   balanced rhythm—conclusive, calm, self-possessed, etc.
(c) 2:2:1   falling rhythm—continuous, suggestive, pregnant, etc.

SEVEN SYLLABLES

(a) 1:2:2:2   rising rhythm—aspiring, smooth, light, etc.
(b) 2:1:2:2   conclusive, light, quiet, etc.
(c) 2:2:1:2   successive, strong, suggestive, etc.
(d) 2:2:2:1   falling rhythm—forceful, fast, elastic, etc.

These are the basic characteristics of haiku measures; each will of course vary in accordance with the mood or meaning of the haiku, giving a peculiar effect to the haiku rhythm.

Now let us return to the camellia haiku:

> Brushing the leaves, fell
> A white camellia blossom
> Into the dark well.

Let us examine the effect of the haiku measure upon the harmony existing between the horizontal and vertical rhythms. The first line is characterized by the horizontal rhythm in a haiku measure of 2:2:1, as we have already seen:

$$\underset{2}{\underline{\text{Brushing}}} \quad \underset{2}{\underline{\text{the leaves,}}} \quad \underset{1}{\underline{\text{fell}}}$$

This haiku measure progresses evenly in 2:2 and at the very end changes in 1, instead of continuing as 2, which gives an irregular effect to the flow of the rhythm; and, by the meaning of the word *fell*, this irregular movement of feeling gains in meaning as a sudden drop, true to the motion of the falling of the camellia flower itself. Viewing the haiku measure in contrast with as well as in combination with the vertical rhythm, one soon sees how intricate is the design of haiku. For this haiku measure of 2:2:1 is vivified or intensified by the accenting of the words in perfect harmony with the movement of the object, the falling of the camellia flower, which, as I pointed out previously,[28] is the principal substance of the rhythm in this haiku:

Brushing the leaves, fell

Here the trochaic opening of this line is followed by an iambic movement, creating a rich and smooth trough-like action, similar to the action of *brushing* itself, with the two unaccented syllables between those two crests of the ictus, in the forward progression of thought as the haiku measure of 2:2. It is followed in succession by the accented, single syllable *fell*, making the abrupt and sudden ending that gives the true effect of the camellia flower dropping. Moreover, from the meaning of the word *fell* the rhythmic flow of the first line is made to ebb into the second line, as though one asked unconsciously: "What fell?"

A white   camellia   blossom
2   3   2

The first syllable *A* harmonizes with the one syllable of *fell* which lacked one syllable at the end of the first line, and thus satisfies the rhythmic succession of the basic measure in the first line of two. From the meaning as thought-flow, it also creates a basic measure of two when added to the single syllable *white* for the rhythmic flow of the second line. The three syllables in the word *camellia* itself give body and weight to the subject as the center of interest, and distinctly stamp on our mind a positive impression of the large, white (therefore *white* is an accented syllable) blossom as significant as possible in contrast to the background of the dark well into which it falls.

The accented forceful ending of the first line is softened by the iambic beginning of the second line and by the following feminine ending of *blossom* at the end of the second line; the whole line would be marked in the following vertical rhythm.

A white camellia blossom

The third line, with its haiku measure of 2:1:2, with the long trough created by the two unaccented and one half-accented syllables between the two crests at the beginning and the end, suggests the deep passage of the well, filled with soft darkness into which the camellia fell.

Into the dark well.

The forward movement of the thought-flow, with its conclusive character in the haiku measure, makes us feel that the falling camellia blossom
comes to rest. Finally, the last word *well*, which rhymes with the word
fell at the end of the first line, recalls the whole movement by its echo,
giving a vivid impression of finality and completeness to the haiku
cadence in a harmonious cycle.

Considering the vertical rhythm alone in this haiku, it is most
apparent that this is not metrical verse:

Brushing / the leaves, / fell /

A white / camellia / blossom /

Into / the dark well. /

Here there are three trochees, two iambs, one amphibrach, a single
accented syllable, and one three-syllable foot unnamed in classic
prosody. Since there is no dominant foot-pattern, the criticism may
arise that this is not poetry but prose, no more regular in rhythm than
is prose. But as has been shown, the poem has cadence and its rhythm
moves true to the movement of the experience. Returning to the first
line, for example, we do not need here a syncopation by which it may
be scanned in a regular iambic. Indeed we should not have it, for
there is no substitute for the natural rhythm of felt action. To attempt
to twist the natural and exact rhythm by syncopation into a formal
predetermined pattern of traditional versification is a monstrous error.
No matter how unrhythmical the single accented syllable at the end of
the first line may sound, this abrupt and sudden ending is the only one
fit rhythm to bring out exactly the effect of the blossom that drops. No
other rhythm can be substituted, it would seem, without twisting the
natural organic rhythm of the idea to be expressed.

Let us take one more example to analyze haiku rhythm. I shall use
Bashô's poem, quoted in the beginning of this chapter. The first line
follows, with appropriate markings:

Beyond cherry brumes,
2   2   1

The haiku measure of 2:2:1 gives the continuous effect appropriate as
an introduction. The iambic beginning leads our attention onward, up,
over, and through the cherry flowers, much as the poet listened for the

sound of the bell; yet, because he cannot see through the thick mist and his eye is stopped by them, we have the accented *brumes*.

The second line flows in a haiku measure of 1:2:1:4:

$$\text{Is} \quad \text{the bell} \quad \text{at} \quad \text{Asakusa}$$
$$1 \qquad 2 \qquad\quad 1 \qquad 4$$

The slight caesura between the 1:2 flow and the 1:4 flow is itself rhythmic, since the four-syllable group is a multiple of the basic measure of two and flows liquidly without any accent.* In all five unaccented syllables of the second half of the line, trailing long and smoothly, is brought out the long echoing of the temple bell, as subtly as it came through the mist of cherry blossoms, after the bell itself with its full accent was tolled. And because a succession of unaccented syllables tends to have less value than the same number in a pattern of accented and unaccented syllables, the extra syllable of the second line tends to be "lost."

The last line ends in the rising rhythm of the haiku measure of 1:3:2, which can be considered a 1:2:2 pattern, since the three syllable group is again a series of unaccented syllables and since the two vowels without an intervening consonant tend to elide to one. The haiku measure is appropriately a rising one, I feel, since the poem itself ends on a strongly accented syllable, suggesting that the temple bell has again been struck, and the echo, renewed rather than fading away, continues on beyond the poem:

$$\text{Or} \quad \text{Ueno} \quad \text{that booms?}$$
$$1 \qquad 3 \qquad\quad 2$$

The five unaccented syllables, repeating the same pattern as is in the second half of the second line, suggest the same continuing even flow of sound from the second line into the third, which is the echoing bell. Just as the echo is dying out, again the bell is struck, with the heavily accented final syllable *booms*. And as the bell again booms, the rhyme brings it again through the cherry brumes at the end of the first line, completing its own lyric cycle in cadences as rich as Bashô's experience.

Both of the haiku analyzed have been extremely irregular as regards vertical rhythm. However, if the rhythm of the pulsation is regular, the cadence in haiku will flow in a regular pattern as in the following:

* It should be noted that the Japanese language does not have marked accents, as does the English.

A crimson / dragonfly,

Glancing / the water, / casts rings

As / it passes / by.

The rhythm in the first line is iambic; so the line may be called an iambic trimeter if one wishes to deal with it in formal metrical terms. (When both vertical and horizontal rhythms are considered together, I feel that the scansion would more accurately be described as an amphibrach followed by an amphimacer.) The regularity of the rhythm translates the smooth, swift flight of the dragonfly over the surface of the pool.

In the second line, however, the rhythm changes according to the movement of the dragonfly. The opening rhythm is trochaic, suggesting that a shift is about to take place, followed by an amphibrach. The first two unaccented syllables in succession suggest the movement of the dragonfly as it veers toward the water, and pinpoints the moment of the action also. The unaccented second syllable of the word *water*, with the pause that follows it, brings out the impression of the wide expanse of the pool, while the combined effect of the larger rhythm of the line together with the formal dactylic character of the first foot (another possible scansion for the line in which the foot ending with *water* would then be trochaic) gives a tranquil atmosphere over the smooth surface of the water.

But the last two accented one-syllable feet—*casts rings*—change the whole movement, bringing out exactly what happened here. These two accented feet do not disturb the rhythm created by the combined effect of the speech rhythm if one listens to the inner pulsation. They produce ripples in the flow of the line as vivid as the rings cast on the smooth surface of the water. Thus the accent in this second line plays an important part in translating the movement of the dragonfly as subtly as possible. In the last line, it will be noted that there is a return to a marked regularity of rhythm, this time trochaic, as there is in the first line. This is significant, since it suggests delicately how the dragonfly resumes its normal flight over the water.

Thus in haiku it will be noted that there are two rhythms, vertical and horizontal, constituting together the haiku rhythm. The former is textural in its quality and is expressed through the sound of words.

The latter is structural, and is vivified and colored by the textural characteristics of the former, namely, accent, rhyme, dissonance, assonance, alliteration, vowel combinations, etc. Thus the horizontal rhythm seems to retire into these methods of emphasis in vertical rhythm, and the vibrating rhythm of the textural quality comes into the foreground.

It almost obliterated, as has been noted, other kinds of rhythm in English prosody, especially through an insistence on rhyme and meter. Yet, as the Imagists discovered, poets who would abandon the mechanical beat of meter for some other kind of rhythm will run the risk of producing only "pieces of disguised prose," as Louise Bogan puts it.* The Imagists themselves were aware that discarding a mechanical meter did not mean discarding discipline in verse. Miss Bogan has described the situation:

> Pound and his friends had learned from contemporary French poets and critics that vers libre demanded as much critical responsibility, on the part of the poet himself, as poetry written in form; that free verse should be kept by every possible technical means, from monotony and flaccidity. The lack of regular meter and rhyme should not result merely in pieces of disguised prose. This early insistence on the formal elements of free verse is interesting in the light of future developments.[29]

One of these developments was the separation in America between 1914 and 1917 of the whole vers-libre movement into "formal" and "popular" manifestations, with Amy Lowell the head of the "popular" school. For Pound, her brand of free verse lacked discipline: "Pound [sent Miss Lowell] a stern letter. . . . Imagism he insisted was built upon a core of form, and it was to this core that. . .poets. . .must adhere."[30]

But Pound and his whole tribe, for all their insistence on the "formal aspects" of free verse, were most vague when they came to actual grips with what these were. As previously quoted, Pound himself called for a rhythm according to the "musical phrase."[31] Miss Lowell, perhaps because she was even freer than Pound, said: "The unit of vers libre is not the foot, the number of syllables, the quality of the line. The unit is the strophe, which may be the whole poem, or may be only a part. Each strophe is a complete circle."[32] This seems to be about as free as

---

* As Eliot somewhat truculently remarked in 1917, two years after the first Imagist anthology: "The so-called *vers libre* which is good is anything but 'free.' " (*Selected Prose,* p. 87.)

it is possible to become. Small wonder that she came to call her own verse "polyphonous prose" and that Pound later described her school as "Amygism."[33]

Perhaps practicing poets can be forgiven their vaguenesses when they discuss what they are doing, for of course discussion of their methods is not their first job. It remains for the critics to tell us what the poets do, but even here, there seems to be much vagueness. Nor is this vagueness confined to the poetry of the Imagists alone, for as Miss Bogan has noted, the best of modern English verse has incorporated aspects of Imagist verse: "By the time that formal metrics were again brought into use... (1920)—the years of free verse experimentation had changed conventional English poetic procedures for good. The former insistent iambic beat was varied."[34] Although it is not within the scope of this inquiry to explore this area thoroughly, I believe that some such statement of a theory of rhythm as presented here is in actuality what the Imagists and exponents of free verse meant when they spoke of a verse free from an insistent meter, but still disciplined by a "core of form." A thorough survey of their practice in their best poetry will reveal, I feel, a scheme of rhythm following the above outline. I do not mean to suggest that non-haiku poets in English will conform to a basic unit of two in syllabic count or to a line of five syllables; where I feel the English poet can borrow from the haiku poet is in the concept of the two kinds of rhythm and their relationship which will provide a form that will be disciplined only by the insight itself and the nature of their language.

I will proceed to a closer analysis of the function of other characteristics of vertical rhythm.

3. Rhyme in Haiku

The use of rhyme in haiku has already been mentioned in the discussion of rhythm, for rhyme is the most obvious way to emphasize the pulsation of feeling as well as of meaning. The definite repetition of the accented vowel and subsequent sounds produces a synchronous vibration when two words rhyme with each other, which can create a frame, as it were, around a haiku, so that its edges are sharp and concrete. Through its use there can occur a sense of finality, of completion to an experience as it begins, unfolds, and comes to rest in meaningful sound. When such a consonance of sound occurs only for the sake of the sound, the effect is not refined, as in most popular jazz songs where the rhyme can be almost anticipated: if there is a *blue,* it will rhyme invariably with a *you; love* calls for a *dove; pine* for a *mine;* and so on. Yet even here, the two powerful functions of rhyme can be noted, although the rhymes can hardly be called meaningful sound. When they serve some other purpose also, as was noted in the preceding section, their use adds greatly to the total effect of the poem.

As was shown in the camellia haiku and the bell haiku, the rhymes in which one of the words is a verb can serve to re-echo the action of the poem and to complete the poetic cycle. In the camellia poem, the word *fell* makes us ask what fell:

> Brushing the leaves, fell
> A white camellia blossom
> Into the dark well.

The rhyming word *well* arouses echoes of *fell,* raising again its question, and thus completes the cycle. As was shown, the same is true of the word *booms* in the following:

> Beyond cherry brumes,
> Is the bell at Asakusa
> Or Ueno that booms?

Through its rhyme with *brumes* in the first line and from its accented meaning, producing again the voice of the temple bell as it comes through the brumes, the poetic cycle is completed. Another example is the following, again a haiku for the ear.

> A bleak gale that raves,
> Dies away, remaining only
> In the roar of waves.

At the height of the passing storm, the sounds, one imagines, of the waves and the wind were one huge roar. Gradually as it passes, its fury dies away and only the voice of the waves remains as its reminder. The rhyme here accurately re-echoes the action.

When the rhymed words are nouns, they seem in a good haiku to be the key words, as in the following example:

> Hurriedly runs rain
> Toward the sunlit grain field,
> Half across the plain.

In this poem the streaks of the rain that hide half of the plain, as it hurries toward the shining green waves of the grain, provide the key word, from which this lovely action is created as the center of the poem. Here the word *plain*, which rhymes with the word *rain*, presents the whole scene to us once more, and within the echo of their rhyme we seem to see the trees and farmhouses fade away behind the streaks of the rain as it runs with hurried steps toward the sunlit field. Another example where the rhyme serves to point out directly the object of interest in the haiku is the following:

> A crimson dragonfly,
> Glancing the water, casts rings
> As it passes by.

Here the word *by* points out the subject immediately and directly as it rhymes with the last word in the first line, the *dragonfly*, which is the center of interest and the source of the delicate haiku rhythm in this poem.

Another function of rhyme is to vivify or intensify the center of interest, instead of pointing it out directly to the reader. Let us consider the following poem:

> In the twilight gloom
> Of the redwood and the pine
> Some wisterias bloom.

There is a twilight touch in this beautiful scene; the lovely clusters of the wisteria hang against the semi-dark background of the redwood and the pine. Here the verb *bloom* brings out the rich purple clusters and the rhyme with *twilight gloom* places them in the proper light. Thus the visual contrast is vivified and the softness of the purple color of the wisteria comes out into the foreground most effectively.

The following haiku by Bashô also illustrates this point, though more indirectly:

> The autumn moon is bright;
> Sea-waves whirl up to my gate,
> Crested silvery white.

The flowery crests of the ocean waves that whirl up to the gate of Bashô's hut at Fukagawa are beautifully depicted here under the charm of the bright autumn moon. All the exquisite details of Bashô's experience are not explicitly enumerated; yet they are all in the haiku. As the sea-waves whirl up to the gate, they are vivified by the rhyme of the word *white* with the word *bright;* for through the rich echo a certain degree of intensity is added to the impression, a lustre of brightness as vivid as was Bashô's experience of it.

Intensification can arise also from a contrast in the meaning of the rhymed words as in the following:

> In the lonely night
> There the firefly glides one foot,
> Putting out its light.

Here the firefly's light holds our attention as the center of interest. It is intensified through the rhyme with the word *night*, which directly brings out the light of the firefly against its lonely darkness, creating a sharp impression.

The association of allied or kindred ideas is also a valid basis for rhyme, as the following will show:

> Luminous and cool
> Is the way a pebble sinks
> Into the blue pool.

The blue pool into which the pebble sinks with silver bubbles has a refreshing feeling in itself. The word *cool*, which rhymes with it, enlivens that feeling once more and intensifies the tone of the poem. Another example of what may perhaps be called the idea-rhyme is the following one between *bloom* and *perfume:*

> Flowers give but perfume
> To the one who breaks the branch
> From the plum in bloom.

Or *throat* and *note* in this haiku:

> Uguisu, your note
> Breaks the silvery silence,
> Rolling from your throat.

Not the least interesting of the idea-rhymes is found in this haiku by
Bashô:

> As I seek a bower,
> Weary from travel, I find
> A wisteria flower.

It is said that Bashô wrote this poem one late-spring evening when he
found a small inn after a day of hard, long travel. But note that he
does not say, "I find an inn!" Here, at the end of his weary day, he
is filled with joy by the wisteria flower, as if it were the bower he sought
in nature, which he loved with a childlike devotion. How appropriate
then that in the echo of this rhyme the flower is identified with the
bower that Bashô seeks. When a rhyme is inevitable, not as a mere
rhyme, but as part of the meaning, it fulfills its true function in haiku.
It then sounds most natural and its effect is a delightful surprise, as
rich as the sounds that echo in our imagination in the lyric cycle. Ezra
Pound, too, calls for some element of surprise in the rhyme used, but
warns against the over-obvious: "A rime must have in it some slight
element of surprise if it is to give pleasure; it need not be bizarre or
curious."[35]

We have been discussing the masculine rhyme, ending on a stressed
syllable. The impact of the accented rhyme gives a sense of concreteness
and is the strongest emphasis obtainable through sound elements in
poetry. So the use of masculine rhyme, whether to point out the key
words, echo the action, vivify or intensify the center of interst, or
clarify the meaning, gives the maximum effect to a haiku. Sometimes,
however, the clang of a direct masculine rhyme is disadvantageous in
bringing out the feeling-tone of a haiku. At such times, the poet may
use an extension of the masculine rhyme, or the feminine rhyme. The
following poem, which Issa wrote when he was about six years old, will
illustrate this point:

> With one another
> Let's play; so come, O sparrow
> Who has no mother.

The falling rhythm of the feminine rhyme adds an unutterable effect
to the feeling of this haiku. It helps to bring out, in a simple and natural
flow of thought, Issa's real feeling toward the orphan sparrow, while,

it is said, he sits alone in old clothes and watches from a distance the other children playing in their gay festival dresses. Thus when the feeling is such, the feminine rhyme is almost necessary to convey the experience most significantly, for the too-hard emphasis of the masculine rhymes destroys the haiku rhythm as well as the delicate atmosphere that the poet tries to express.

Here is another interesting example of the use of feminine rhymes:

> A lizard flicks over
> The undulating ripples
> Of sunlit clover.

In this haiku the light syllable following the stressed vowel at the end of the first line is so pertinent that it brings out the exact movement of the lizard, which seems to be the motif of the haiku rhythm. It shows vividly how the lizard scurries away, for the quickness of the action is made clear by the falling feminine rhyme, which, in its soft liquid sound, duplicates the smooth, flicking movement.

An equally deft use of the feminine rhyme shows in the word *passes* in the following haiku:

> A shower comes and passes,
> Leaving the bright summer moon
> Upon the grasses.

The active element in the verb *passes* is diminished by the falling rhythm of the additional light syllable, which gives the impression of the softness and quickness of the shower, leaving the moon in the refreshing, clean air upon the swaying grasses wet with silver shower-drops. If we change the haiku in the following manner, the difference in effect is apparent:

> Showers come and pass,
> Leaving the bright summer moon
> Upon the wet grass.

The positive masculine rhyme here is too strong and declarative to translate the lightness of the shower or the twinkling sparkle of the moonlight upon the grass. Consequently the haiku's movement as a whole suffers.

One more type of rhyme worthy of our attention is the hermaphrodite rhyme—a masculine rhyme matching the last syllable of a feminine rhyme. This type of rhyming is considered very poor and never accepted by the ear trained to listen for perfect rhyme. However, in haiku it sometimes finds a place as the best expression of the subtlety of thought in translating the meaning of feeling.

> I turned back to see,
> But the man I passed was veiled
> In mist already.

Hypothetically the word *already* might be pronounced as *ál-rea-dý*. This is clearly artificial, if not impossible, with the accent on the last syllable. It also destroys the wholeness of the poem as intended by the writer; for accent in haiku is not used for a metrical regularity or for a stamping clang of rhyme, but to reveal the rhythm of feeling. Consequently the last line begins in iambic, and the rising rhythm of the iambic foot appropriately leads us into the mist to see the man, as the poet wishes. The ending flows smoothly in amphibrach, repeating the iambic rhythm and finally closing the verse with an unaccented syllable, giving an impression that only the mist can give. The half-rhyme of the unaccented syllable—*dy*—with *see* at the end of the first line gives the effect of a faint overtone, as if we see the image of the man veiled in the spring mist.

A final use of rhyme which I wish to discuss briefly is the comic, ironic, or satirical effect obtainable through its use. The almost doggerel lilt of the following poem conveys a rueful complaint, and the function of the rhyme seems self-evident:

> Living in the town,
> One must have money even
> To melt the snow down!

Less obvious is the use of rhyme and accent in the following:

> Look, oh how fearsome
> Are the rouged fingers against
> The white chrysanthemum!

The first line is stressed as follows:

> Loōk, ŏh hōw fearsŏme

However, these markings are not finely differentiated enough to show what actually happens as one reads the line. The first strong accent is followed by an unaccented word, establishing a trochaic beat. Yet, because the second word is an exclamatory one and would normally be accented, it tends to drain accent from the third word *how*, which normally would be fully accented in a tendency to follow the established trochaic meter. When the tendency is frustrated, the fourth syllable *fear* is slightly softened in its normal heavy accent and transfers some of it to the last syllable *some*, which normally would be extremely light. Just how light the last syllable ordinarily is is shown in the following iambic line:

$$\breve{A} \ \bar{fear}\breve{some} \ \bar{girl} \ \breve{is} \ \bar{she}.$$

This phenomenon of accents occurring otherwise than they normally would seems to correspond to the surprised, wittily self-deprecatory state of mind of the person holding out her hands to the white flower. The device as used above, with a minor accent on the normally unaccented syllable, is very effective, making the haiku rhythm startling and giving a freshness that no accurate rhyming could ever give.

Before going on to a discussion of alliteration in haiku, I want to mention in passing that the use of the assonance-rhyme in haiku is very promising, since it can give rise to effects more subtle and muted than can the types of rhyming discussed above. I believe that some haiku poets will be able to use it as effectively as modern singers do in their poems, when the form becomes known to the public and to poets. I feel of course that English haiku are valid and possible without rhyme. The effect of such poems would perhaps approximate the effect of the best free verse in English; there would have to be the same strongly inevitable turning in the verse, with perhaps a greater use of assonance and alliteration than in the examples quoted above. I have preferred to use rhyme in some of both the translated and the original haiku for the effects above noted that give to my mind strength to the whole poetic structure. As to the propriety of using rhyme in translation when in the original Japanese, without exception, rhyme, as understood in English, does not exist, it would seem to me that the translated haiku must stand or fall on their merits as poems in English. As poems in English, they utilize all the poetic resources of the language, of which rhyme is one of the greatest. I have felt on the basis of some such reasoning justified in the use of it in my translations.

4. ALLITERATION IN HAIKU

Alliteration, a close kin to rhyme and older than it, occupies in haiku a special position, emphasizing its structure in a way peculiar to itself. For alliteration speaks gently where rhyme commands. The term, here used broadly, means the repetition of the same consonant sounds in words near each other. Its functions are as numerous and as important as those of rhyme in haiku and can be discussed under the following six classifications: initial, stressed, syllable, oblique, buried, and crossed alliteration.

INITIAL ALLITERATION

Initial alliteration, the simplest type, is easily recognizable. As the terms signifies, it has to deal with the same first consonants in words in close conjunction, whether they are accented or unaccented. Generally speaking, only the accented alliteration is considered as the true type; the following haiku contains two examples of it.

> A *f*alling *f*lower, thought I,
> *F*luttering *b*ack to the *b*ranch—
> Was a *b*utterfly.

The two *f*'s in the first line, together with the initial *f* of the second, constitute an accented alliteration which binds the first line together with the repetition of the sound, sharpening the impression and bringing the object out into the foreground. The initial accented *f* of the second line, in its repetitive sound as well as in its meaning and rhythm, helps the first line to flow into the rest of the verse, making a connection with the new rhythm of the *b* alliteration that follows. For the dactylic rhythm of *fluttering* not only suggests the action of the butterfly, but through its two unaccented beats carries the flow of the *f* rhythm into the second and third lines. The *b*'s in the second and third lines bind the ideas together with their same accented initial consonant sounds, marking the haiku measure, which cannot be shown in the mere regularity and repetition of rhyme.

The off-accent alliteration can also be used to couple the consonants of an accented and unaccented syllable in words near each other. For example:

*B*eyond cherry *b*rumes,
Is the *b*ell at Asakusa
Or Ueno that *b*ooms?

The *b* in *beyond* is not on an accented syllable; yet this usage is as effective and pleasing to the ear as the accented one. It may be considered, from the usage and the effect that alliteration of this kind produces, that the off-accent alliteration is comparable to the off-accent rhyme in haiku. Here the unaccented *b* in *beyond* is followed by the accented *b* in *bell* in the second line and *booms* in the third line, which helps to connect the rhythmic flow of the *b* alliteration to the end, where the accented *b* of *booms* brings the sound of the bell out as much as does the rhyme.

Another effective example follows:

*S*oothed by the *s*erene
Balminess of *s*pring, I fell
Asleep on the green.

The *s* of *serene* coupled with those of *soothed* and *spring* seems to suggest the spring mood and its balmy weather.

An example of off-accented alliteration of vowels follows:

Warm the weather grows
Gradually as one plum flower
*A*fter *a*nother blows.

Here the *a* coupling gives enough emphasis to show how mildly the warmth of the early spring is increasing as the plum blossoms are budding one by one. The accented *a* seems to suggest the fully-opened flower, and the unaccented *a* the half-opened one.

Let us note what alliteration does for the following poem:

In the lonely night
There the *f*ire*f*ly glides one *f*oot,
Putting out its light.

The accented and unaccented *f*'s in *firefly* bring out the image of the object clearly and distinctly against the background of the night. The other *f* in *foot,* at the end of the second line, repeating the same initial consonant sound after the two words of one syllable of different beginning sounds, seems to suggest the dark space between the light emitted by the firefly as it flies. Let us change the *glides* to *floats* and notice the changed effect caused by the succession of three *f*'s:

> In the lonely night
> There the *f*irefly *f*loats a *f*oot,
> Putting out its light.

The change shows that the additional *f* of *floats* seems to shorten the dark space and so destroys the intent of the poet. The characteristic effect of the flying firefly is lost.

At times, the simple initial alliteration can be used to unify the whole poem, as the following will show:

> With a *b*uzzing cry
> A *b*ee shifts on the *b*loom sought
> *B*y a *b*utterfly.

STRESSED ALLITERATION

Stressed alliteration refers to the alliteration of stressed syllables of two or more beginning consonants in words near each other, whether these stresses are at the beginning or within the words. The device is usually applied to the beginning consonants of the stressed words. When thus used, it is like the accented initial alliteration, although the impression is much sharper since two or more beginning consonants are involved. The following poem contains an illustration:

> Flowers give but perfume
> To the one who *br*eaks the *br*anch
> From the plum in bloom.

Here the *br*'s in the second line emphasize strongly the haiku measure of 1:2:2:2 and bring out the horizontal rhythm by marking it with alliteration. The *b* in the last line, coupled with them, seems to suggest once more the action of *breaking the branch,* as well as to present to the reader once more the *branch* of the blooming plum by its repetitive sound.

The haiku below illustrates several types of alliteration: stressed alliteration in *shines* and *shadows,* and initial alliteration in the second and third lines.

> Brightly *sh*ines the moon,
> And where *s*ilver *sh*adows are
> Insects *s*tring their tune.

It seems to me that this combination of alliteration gives an intricate effect to the haiku atmosphere, rendering it as immediate as the songs of the insects, singing in the silver shadows of the dew-wet blades of grass under the bright moon.

The next poem also contains two types of alliteration:

> *St*ones and trees that meet
> My eyes *gl*are *st*raight at me
> In this *gl*azing heat.

The words *stones* and *straight* are an example of stressed alliteration. The type created by *glare* and *glazing* will next be discussed.

SYLLABLE ALLITERATION

Syllable alliteration deals with the close repetition of the same syllables, whether accented or unaccented. For example, in the following poem, the *pa*'s in the second line and the *in*'s in the third give a strongly concise pattern of alliteration to the syllables, which helps to add intensity to the haiku and brings out the effect of the summer heat:

> Oh, how small, my sweet,
> Is your *pa*inted *pa*rasol
> *In* this *in*tense heat!

A similar effect is apparent in the following:

> Stones and trees that meet
> My eyes *gla*re straight at me
> In this *gla*zing heat.

The *gla* in *glare,* coupled with the *glazing* in the last line, intensifies the effect of the heat both through the alliteration and the meaning of the words; this is also helped by the stressed alliteration of the *st*'s in the first and second lines.

This type of alliteration may be considered as a "head rhyme," since the beginning consonant and the vowel immediately following it are the same sound. Hence, among the various types of alliteration, syllable alliteration gives the strongest effect to haiku rhythm.

OBLIQUE ALLITERATION

Oblique alliteration deals with the repetition of the same initial consonantal sound followed by a different consonantal sound, which shades the total effect from exactness into a similarity. For example, in the following haiku, in *small* and *sweet,* the beginning *sm* sound shades off into *sw:*

> Oh, how *sm*all, my *sw*eet,
> Is your painted parasol
> In this intense heat!

In the following poem, again, the first two consonant in *shadow* blend into the first two of *swaying* by their tonal gradation:

> The hills cast *sha*dows,
> And pampas grass is *swa*ying
> In sunlit meadows.

This close shading of the sound adds a new quality to the haiku tone, if it is used skillfully and naturally; and to the psychological effect it gives a delicate imagery of music which cannot possibly be expressed by simple initial alliteration. To illustrate this point, I shall use the following example:

> A little village here
> Is *sl*eeping, lulled by *cr*ickets
> Chirping *sw*eet and *cl*ear.

As the initial *sl* sound of *sleeping* shades off into the new *sw* one in *sweet,* and the *cr* sound into the *cl,* the effect becomes as varied and interesting as the music of the cricket itself. Here *little* and *lulled,* with their initial accented alliteration, also add further variation to the melody. The same is true in the following:

> A *sp*ring *br*eeze is *sw*eet,
> *Bl*owing over the *s*unlit *br*ook
> *S*oughing through the wheat.

Here the *sp* sound in *spring* shades off into the *sw* sound in *sweet.* In addition to this, the initial alliteration of the *s* sound in *sunlit* and *soughing,* coupled with the first two words, brings out further reverberations of the feeling, true to the tonal atmosphere of this poem. Moreover, these four words beginning with *s* alternate with the three words in oblique alliteration—*breeze, blowing,* and *brook*—so that through the interlocking pattern a unity and harmony result. In addition to the sound words, the word *sunlit* infuses the haiku with a bright light and clean air, bringing out the greenness of the wheat and making the breeze visible. The alternating repetition of sounds seems to suggest the green waves of the wheat, over which the spring breeze blows sweetly, with the murmuring sounds of the stream, so that for the moment of reading we are one with the spirit of nature captured in this haiku.

BURIED ALLITERATION

Buried alliteration, as the term signifies, deals with the same consonant or consonants, one or more of which are buried within words in close conjunction, whether they are stressed or unstressed. For example:

> Flowere*d* is her hem,
> Ankle-*d*eep in *d*affodils
> As she ga*th*ers *th*em.

The *d* forms part of a buried alliteration in *flowered, deep,* and *daffodils;* and the *th* in *gather* and *them.* Let us consider another example:

> Warm *the* wea*ther* grows
> Gradually as one plum *f*lower
> A*f*ter another blows.

Here the *th* is buried in *weather* and *the;* and the *f* in *after* and *plum flower.* This buried alliteration helps to bind the words or phrases together through its repetitive sounds in its own subtle way. This type of alliteration is fit to translate complexity in thought and delicacy in feeling.

Two more examples will be given:

> Hu*rr*iedly *r*uns *r*ain
> Towar*d* the sunlit g*r*ain fiel*d*,
> Half across the plain.

In this haiku, the *r* and *d* are buried; they are also crossed, as can be noted.

> Luminous and cool
> Is the way a pe*bb*le sinks
> Into the *bl*ue pool.

Here the *bl* is buried; this alliteration, as well as the initial alliteration of the *p* in *pebble* and *pool,* serves to focus attention on the stone as it sinks through the water.

CROSSED ALLITERATION

Crossed alliteration is the most complex type of all; in it sets of letters, whether initial or buried, are linked or crossed with each other in words close together. The pattern is easily seen in the following example:

> *St*ones and trees that meet
> My eyes *gla*re *st*raight at me
> In this *gla*zing heat.

It will be noted that the sets of letters *st* and *gla* are crossed. *W* and *th* are crossed in the following haiku:

> *W*arm *the* *w*eather grows
> Gradually as one plum flower
> After another blows.

A complex example of this type is shown in the following poem:

> A *sp*ring *br*eeze is *sw*eet,
> *Bl*owing over the *s*unlit *br*ook
> *S*oughing through the wheat.

Here the consonantal sounds are placed in this order: *sp, br, sw, bl, s, br, s.* Interlocking and alternating with each other as they do, they act more subtly upon the haiku rhythm than any other device could possibly do to translate the feeling. The next haiku is a similar type, with the alliteration in the pattern *l, sl, l, cr, sw, cl:*

> A *l*ittle village here
> Is *sl*eeping, *l*ulled by *cr*ickets
> Chirping *sw*eet and *cl*ear.

Of these six important types of alliteration which have been discussed at length, initial, stressed, and syllable alliteration are usually used to intensify or vivify the vertical rhythm, or to place emphasis upon words important to the meaning. The chief function of buried and crossed alliteration, besides emphasizing the haiku rhythm, is to add color to the rhythm and to bind or link phrases and ideas together to gain unity. Through oblique alliteration, delicate nuances in haiku tone, adding to the singing quality and variety of the verse, are possible.

5. ASSONANCE IN HAIKU

Assonance is the repetition of the same vowel sounds, whether initial or buried, in words in close conjunction, with a difference in the consonantal sounds after them. In haiku it is used chiefly to enrich a line.

The way in which assonance is used for harmonic effect is almost the same as that in which alliteration is used, the chief difference being that in the first the sounds dealt with are vowel sounds, while in the second they are consonantal sounds. Minute analysis would therefore be redundant here, since the various usages of alliteration have been discussed. A few examples will be given with some observations.

The first poem follows:

> How silent and still!
> Into the heart of rocks sinks
> The cicada's shrill.

The alliteration of the *s* sound is obvious. The assonance is significant in the way it is interwoven with the *s* sounds for harmonic effect. A similar example is next:

> Brightly shines the moon,
> And where silver shadows are
> Insects string their tune.

Here the vowel sound *i* is skillfully chained with the *s* sound; the combination thus achieved seems to suggest a kind of onomatopoetic effect, true to the singing voice of the insect under the moon.

An intricate example of the harmony of sounds, in which assonance plays a part, is the following:

> From the peony's
> Petals overbrims the hum
> Of the honey bees.

The harshness of the *s* sounds, suggesting the buzzing of the bees, is strikingly softened by the predominating vowels *o* and *e,* and further by the *m* and *n* sounds. Further interest is added to the texture by the *p, b, h* alliteration as they blend with the other sounds in the haiku.

As in crossed alliteration sets of letters are linked or crossed with each other in words close together, so assonance can be similarly treated:

> A spring breeze is sweet,
> Blowing over the sunlit brook
> Soughing through the wheat.

Here the linking of the *i* and *ee* sounds in combination with the crossed alliteration of the *s* and *b* sounds in the first line makes the music of this poem as subtle and delicate as the atmosphere it attempts to convey. An even more effective example follows:

> The nightingales sing
> In the echo of the bell
> Tolled at evening.

This haiku will reveal a delicate play of assonance. The vowel *i,* appearing at regular intervals, seems to suggest the voice of the nightingales. The rhythmic repetition of the inner vibrations of the three *i*'s in the first line seems to produce emotional values not included in the meaning of the words that contain them. In the harmony of the *o* and *e* sounds the rich sonorous booming of the temple bell seems to echo, with the clear sound of the *e* harmonizing with the slow, stately sound of the *o.* The expanding *o* of *tolled* in the last line continues the reverberating echoes, in which the *i* of the last word, rhyming with the *i* in *sing,* brings out the voice of the nightingales in the soft twilight air. Thus the *i, e, o* vowels, with their emotional values and the inner meanings of the sounds, permit us to go into the delicate, colorful vibratory realms of lyric perception and help us to grasp a much more accurate impression of the aesthetic experience.

Of course the emotional values of these vowels is not constant. But by both poet and reader, it is recognized that letters, whether consonants or vowels, produce singly and in combination a psychological effect, just as colors do. Certain values of emotional perception can be felt, and they can be used either to translate the feeling into haiku or to appreciate the haiku in which such feeling is externalized, by means of the sounds of words as well as their meaning.

CHAPTER FIVE

HISTORICAL VIEW

IN THE FOREGOING CHAPTERS I have dealt with haiku theory as it relates to the possibilities of the haiku in English. In doing so, of necessity random references to the history of the haiku in Japan have been made to clarify the questions under discussion. As has been noted, there have been some principal preoccupations which have dominated the Japanese haiku theorists: for example, the seasonal theme, haiku length, etc. It will be illuminating, I feel, to deal more systematically than has been done with the history of haiku in Japan, especially in those areas which are pertinent to an English haiku, for such an examination should reveal that what I have maintained about the inner necessity of its elements was gradually evolved and clarified throughout its history. The historical background will function in part as a sounding board for my position and, I trust, make it more meaningful.

As stated in the introduction, I have chosen to deal with my concept of haiku theory directly, rather than by tracing its development historically, since the latter method seems to me to leave many questions unanswered, as will be seen in what follows. Furthermore, it appeared to be a better method to deal with the concepts first, exploring their meanings and ramifications, in order that any historical treatment could be fully understood; that is to say, what the seasonal theme is and how it functions in a haiku must be grasped before any treatment of its gradual evolution can be easily recounted. Without some such point of departure, a historical survey would be extremely cumbersome, especially when the background of ideas is not familiar to the English-speaking reader.

1. Poetic Forms

What is haiku? What does haiku consist of? When we reflect on these questions again, keeping in mind what we have covered in the foregoing discussion, it may be answered that haiku is a poetic form of expression which employs primarily substantives and centers around groups of words usually totalling seventeen syllables in length, in and through which the poet realizes his poetic experience. We have seen that the haiku form has not developed fortuitously but rather has arisen from what is deeply rooted both in the poetic instinct of man and in the inner necessity of realizing it aesthetically. Consequently, if we give to haiku only a conceptual definition by saying that it is a poem of seventeen syllables containing among other things a sense of season or seasonal theme, there is the danger on the one hand of entertaining the idea that its form was attained only accidentally or by poetic fiat and, on the other hand, of limiting our consideration of the historical facts and the vast areas of Japanese poetry through which flow the countless streams of haiku-like expressions, giving clarity to the finally attained haiku form and making possible a realization of its meaning. The salient facts of the history of Japanese poetry and of the development of the haiku are well known and have been clearly recounted by many competent Japanese authorities. But it seems to me that a fresh account of these facts will show that the elements that make haiku what it now is are to be found in the whole stream and original impulses of Japanese poetry. Poetic experience seems to have sought this form of expression from the earliest period, and an examination of the history of Japanese poetry will show that the haiku-like expression which gradually developed into a crystallized form is noticeable to an astonishing degree in all periods.

What is this haiku-like quality which flows throughout Japanese poetry until it crystallizes in the haiku form? How did Japanese poets consciously or unconsciously develop it into the haiku as we know it now? Questions such as these relating to what may be called the haiku-like tendencies in all of Japanese poetry are extremely valuable in understanding the aesthetic principles which govern it. Tracing these characteristics will, I hope, clarify my contention that haiku developed as it did through its own inner necessity rather than through the mere chance of being the hokku or first verse of either chained verse or of haikai, which later became independent. Let us begin with the pre-haiku period.

PRE-HAIKU PERIOD

How happy am I! I have met a handsome man.
How happy am I! I have met a lovely maid.¹

These two lines recorded in the *Nihonshoki* (A.D. 720) as the greetings exchanged by the deities Izanagi and Izanami at their first meeting are very interesting. While they are not regarded as poems by the Japanese, they are classified as utterances—a terminology that is particularly revealing. For utterance connotes the short, the spontaneous, the immediate formation of words. Igarashi has termed them "sudden, emotive words": "What may be termed sudden, emotive words are for example the intimate phrases exchanged by Izanagi and Izanami, appearing in the first part of the *Nihongi*."² As the two expressions stand, one might be classified as an exclamatory question and the second as the reply or response. Such is the basis—question and answer—for the poetic form called *katauta* on which the early poems are based. As Tachibana Moribe (1781–1849), a famous poet-scholar, said of katauta: "In thinking it over [I realize that] what we call katauta are not songs to be sung, but those for conveying a question to another."³

Origuchi, in his monumental and original work, has pointed out that the katauta may well have origins deep within a primitive society and be identified with spring festivals, which I would suggest have much in common with the "vegetation rituals and fertility rites of primitive cultures," as Elisabeth Drew terms them.⁴ When we remember the broad relationships subsequently developed between such spring rites, when the resurrected god of vegetation returns to the earth, and those of puberty, the great antiquity as well as the deep-rootedness of the social setting for the katauta can be grasped. Origuchi states: "The *mondô* [question and answer] exchanged between the gods and the spirits became the *mondô* exchanged between men disguised as gods and men. The latter changed into *mondô* between men disguised as gods and the maidens of the village who welcomed them. A question or the answer to it is called a katauta. A pair of katauta making a poem is always in the form of a *mondô*."[5]

The form of a katauta consists usually of three parts arranged in the syllabic pattern, 5-7-7 or 5-7-5, varying in length from seventeen to nineteen syllables. It is extremely significant that the length of this oldest poetic form in Japanese is the length that it is. For it was used to ask a question—simply, directly, spontaneously, in one breath length. And the answer to the question is given in the same manner, in one breath. As I have shown, the maximum number of syllables that can be uttered with ease in one breath is around seventeen, while the one breath length itself arises from the nature of the material conveyed. As Igarashi has said, immediacy is one characteristic of such material: "This form of poetry [katauta] is not used when one has more time to think and to elaborate; it is used only when one has to make an immediate response, such as in answer to a question."[6] Now it seems to me that, considering the ancient utterances of Izanagi and Izanami, both seventeen syllables long, it is clear that the length of katauta arose not through mere chance but because of the type of material it dealt with: the simple question; the simple answer; or what might be called a spontaneous breath response in the utterance of words.

In the ritual setting which Origuchi describes, where katauta was used between the men-gods and the village maidens, as the game developed, a great premium was based on the questions or answers that could confound by their wit or unanswerableness. As the katauta lost its identification with such prescribed settings, nevertheless, as Igarashi points out, its characteristic wit had great influence in determining the form it took: "Katauta is used mostly in the question and answer form because, in a situation where an immediate witty response is demanded, that form that is the most extremely compressed—the briefest form a poem can possibly take—is used and becomes a unit of poetry."[7] Another example of katauta, divorced from ritual, which appears in the *Kojiki* (A.D. 712), is as follows:

> When Takeru Yamato, as recorded in the *Kiki,* crossed the Eastern country and came out to a place called Kai, [he composed the following]:
>
> > Passing across
> > The new land of Tsukuba,
> > How many nights did we sleep?

To this the old man who tended the fires replied:

> Counting my fingers,
> It has been nine times by night
> And will be ten times by day.[8]

Of course I do not mean that this ancient poetic form consisting of approximately seventeen or eighteen syllables immediately produced the haiku, but it is relevant to point out that this characteristic katauta form flows throughout the stream of Japanese poetry, undergoing many metamorphoses and crystallizations and eventuating in the haiku. Even with this simple question-answer type of poetry, it is possible to find the characteristics that are haiku: ellipsis, condensation, spontaneity, and nakedness of treatment. The pattern of seventeen syllables typical of haiku is deeply rooted. Indeed Igarashi states unequivocally that it is the unit of Japanese poetry: "Katauta is a poem of three lines in which the first two lines consist of one short and one long one; and the last line is the same length as the second line, which is added as a prop to help harmonize the rhythm. This is the unit of ancient Japanese poetry."[9]

It is in this sense that I feel haiku history should be looked upon and considered against a large background, covering a much wider area than that usually accepted as relevant by many historians and poets. For example, Shiki dismisses haiku before the Genroku period (1668–1703): "The origin of haiku can be traced as far back as the era of Genroku. Of course, I know haiku existed before then, but I do not count them for much. Collections of selected haiku started in the Genroku age also. However, those collections of selected haiku before the Genroku period do not amount to much."[10] In the light of Shiki's general position, the above view seems justified. However, without a full understanding of the deeply basic origins of haiku, its fundamental functions as a poetic form cannot be grasped. For, while it is true that in the most restricted sense of the term, haiku achieved its unique life as an independent poem after Shiki in 1891, it can hardly be assumed that it sprang suddenly into being as an identifiable entity in 1891. It will be remembered that a clear meaning of what Shiki meant by the term haiku appears in his writing from this date, when he had decided to turn his full attention to poetry. One of his friends recorded: "In the fall of 1891 Shiki called at my house in Negishi and told me that he was going to abandon his studies because of illness though he was supposed to graduate the next year...and he expressed his intention of continuing his studies on haiku after leaving the university, taking a warmer interest in it...."[11] Two years previously Shiki had written an article entitled "Haikai and Haiku," but, until the above date, he did not develop a precise meaning for the latter term. Whatever the terms used, however, the genesis of haiku lies in the very beginnings of Japanese poetry and it embodies some of its most fundamental motivations, accounting for its importance at present in the whole body of Japanese poetry. What constitutes the center of haiku, linking it with the earlier forms, is I believe the fact that it is a group of words consisting of seventeen syllables. In this sense the conversation between Izanagi and Izanami can be taken as the beginning of the poetic unit in Japanese poetry.

Of this early period, whose poetry is recorded in the *Kojiki* and the *Nihonshoki,* there remain one hundred eighty-three poems, which can be classified into four types. The first is katauta, already discussed, whose pattern tended to be 5-7-5 or 5-7-7.

Sedôka, from the point of view of its form, is a pair of katauta, i.e., 5-7-7 plus 5-7-7. Differing from katauta, however, sedôka are not necessarily in the question-and-answer pattern and were written by one person. As Origuchi states: "It became possible for one person to write a pair [of katauta]. In such a case, it is already a sedôka."[12]

The so-called chôka were built of alternating lines of five and seven syllables to an indefinite length, concluding with a seven-syllable line. It is interesting to note that, even in this longer type of poem, the lines remain fairly fixed as to length, i.e., five and seven syllables alternately. It is even more interesting to note that, within the dominant rhythm of alternating lines of five and seven syllables, there occur the katauta-like patterns of 5-7-7 or 5-7-5 within the body of the poem. An example of the first follows:

$$\underset{4(5)}{\underline{\text{At Mimuro}}} / \underset{7}{\underline{\text{where the mighty castle stands}}}$$

$$\underset{7}{\underline{\text{Lies Oiko Meadow;}}}$$

$$\underset{5}{\underline{\text{At Oiko}}} / \underset{5}{\underline{\text{with that meadow}}}\ldots{}^{13}$$

Here we see that within the chôka itself occurs the katauta pattern of

5-7-7. (The first line, although it consists of only four syllables, is taken to stand for a five-syllable line, while in the third and fourth lines, the long *O* in *Oiko* is pronounced as two syllables.) Another, even more complex example from the *Kojiki* is pointed out by Igarashi; what appears to be a chôka is shown on analysis to be a katauta and a tanka:

> O palace maiden, / the daughter of my subject,
>   5   7
> Do you bring a wine-holder? / If you hold it up,
>   7   5
> Oh, hold it in your hands; / oh, hold it firmly
>   6(7)   5
> Ever firmly in your hands, / O you wine-holding maiden!
>   7   7

If we write it this way, it may appear to be a chôka, consisting of eight lines. If we write it in the following way, however, we can clearly notice a change in the long poem:

> O palace maiden, / the daughter of my subject,
>   5   7
> Do you bring a wine-holder?
>   7
> If you hold it up, / oh, hold it in your hands,
>   5   6(7)
> Oh, hold it firmly, / ever firmly in your hands,
>   5   7
> O you wine-holding maiden!
>   7

Thus it becomes clear that this chôka is made up of a katauta and a tanka.[14]

That is to say, the first group of three lines is a katauta in the 5-7-7 pattern. The second group of five lines is a tanka, as is shown by the 5-7-5-7-7 pattern. (The fifth line, containing six syllables, is considered as a seven-syllable line.) Similar instances occur throughout the chôka found in both the *Kojiki* and the *Nihonshoki,* giving rise to the supposition that chôka, like sedôka, are based on the katauta.

The fourth form is the tanka, whose basic pattern, as above noted, is 5-7-5-7-7. The history of the mutations of the tanka itself forms such an important chapter in haiku history that it will be given at greater length in the following section.

Historically speaking, it cannot be said that there was a clearly formalized, rigid adherence to each of the above verse patterns. Although the rhythm is basically in a 5-7 pattern, it was as honored in the breach as in the observance, and poems were written by individual poets with great latitude as regards form. Consequently, it cannot be stated absolutely that katauta is a poem with a 5-7-7 pattern, or sedôka one with a 577-577 form. It may be safer to consider that a katauta tends to the norm of 5-7-7 or 5-7-5, while a sedôka tends to consist of a pair of katauta. Of them all, only tanka retained its poetic form fairly consistently.

Even with such variations from the norm as exist in the poems in the *Kojiki* and *Nihonshoki,* it is still possible to see that in these early forms the poetic unit is based on the katauta, as Igarashi insists: "At last [the Japanese] felt that the most beautiful form for Japanese poetry was to end with 5-7-7. As a result, the four great poetic forms were created —namely, katauta, sedôka, tanka, and chôka—whose essence is based on the 5-7-7 form."[15] Moreover, the katauta stands as a clearly independent entity. So well defined is it as a poetic unit that even in the sedôka, nominally one unified poem, each half of the verse pattern of 5-7-7 or 5-7-5 could stand independently in some examples of it, as Origuchi states: "Technically there is a full stop in sedôka at the end of [the first group of lines of] 5-7-7. In short, a duet-like form by two persons is written by one person."[16] An example of such a sedôka follows, taken from the *Kojiki* and attributed to the Emperor Ojin (A.D. 270–312). It is a bit irregular as regards syllabication:

> With the sweet rice-wine / brewed well by Susukori
> I have gotten drunk, most drunk.
> On this pleasing wine, / all muddled drunk,
> I have gotten drunk, most drunk.[17]

Aside from the importance of the katauta, as shown by the repetition of the whole pattern within the other three forms, another significant fact illuminates further its completely basic nature in Japanese poetry. We have seen that in this early period the 5-7 line pattern is dominant and well defined. As Chamberlain remarks of the poetry in the two earliest collections, "the normal form of the Japanese poem became fixed at 5, 7, 5, 7, 5, 7...7, the number of lines being thus always odd."[18] If this is the basic rhythm, as it well seems to be, the fact that a katauta contains just one statement of it—5-7—clearly demonstrates that the other forms are built on it. The last line, be it seven or five syllables long, fulfills the demand for an odd number of lines in all poetic forms, as Chamberlain points out above.

Thus even in the beginnings of recorded Japanese poetry and possibly before, as Origuchi suggests, the katauta-like rhythmic pattern shows distinctly the possibilities of an independent poetic form of three parts of approximately seventeen syllables. This fact seems to show that the basic element of haiku lies deep within the poetic instincts of Japan and to foretell the future poetic form we know today as haiku. Of course the seventeen-syllable pattern of haiku of the later period is not the same as that of katauta, as is self-evident. But the persistence of the total form with a norm of seventeen to nineteen syllables, divided into three lines, of which the first two have the norm of five and seven syllables respectively, for over a period of a thousand years, suggests the kind of elemental rootedness that T. S. Eliot describes in the following, where he means by "auditory imagination" that feeling for aural values in poetry without which poetry is unillumined:

> [Auditory imagination is] the feeling for syllable and rhythm, penetrating far below the conscious levels of thought and feeling, invigorating every word; sinking to the most primitive and forgotten, returning to the origin and bringing something back, seeking the beginning and the end. It works through meanings, certainly, or not without meanings in the ordinary sense, and fuses the old and obliterated and trite, the current and the new and surprising, the most ancient, and the most civilized mentality.[19]

Hence the assumption that the possibilities of the haiku lie in the katauta is not farfetched. The interesting fact is that the relationship between katauta and other poetic forms in the early period is similar to that of haiku and other poetic forms in the later period.

TANKA PERIOD

As previously noted, during the *Kojiki* and *Nihonshoki* periods, tanka alone consistently retained a well-defined form, namely, five lines in the pattern of 57-57-7. Here are seen the two characteristics that Chamberlain pointed out of Japanese verse: the alternation of lines of five and seven syllables, ending with a seven syllable line, which in chôka could continue to any length, but was limited in tanka to a total of five lines. In the above type of tanka, usually one subject was treated in the first pair of lines, a second in the second pair, while the concluding seven syllable line seems to serve as a refrain or reiteration. An example follows from the *Kojiki*:

> Many clouds unfurled
>   rise at cloud-decked Izumo;
> Round your spouse to hold
>   raise many folded barriers
>   like those barriers manifold.[20]

However, even in these two earliest anthologies, there are some examples of tanka written in the 575-77 pattern. That is to say, the first three lines form what might be called the upper hemistich, while the concluding lines of seven syllables each form a second hemistich. There is of course invariably a well-defined pause after the third line. Two types of tanka may be distinguished within this pattern, as can be determined through the structuring of the thought of the poems.

In the first type, the upper hemistich is a dependent clause or phrase —or can be so construed in English—while the lower hemistich is the independent clause. An example from the *Kojiki* follows:

> Standing there alone
>   in Sagami's fair meadow
>   all ablaze with flame,
> You, my true beloved one,
>   call and ask for me by name![21]

The second type consists of an upper hemistich which is grammatically independent of the lower; the upper usually terminates with a noun or a verb. A fairly primitive version from the *Nihonshoki* follows:

> I would speak aloud
>   at the Tsutsushiro Palace
>   in Yamashiro;
> When I look at my brother
>   fain my eyes would fill with tears.[22]

The possibilities of such a tanka pattern giving rise to an independent first hemistich of 5-7-5 are of course immediately evident. It is probable that the first hemistich represents the influence of the ubiquitous kata-uta, thus demonstrating again how basic a form it was for early Japanese poetry.

During the following Manyô period (*circa* A.D. 759) tanka became the dominant poetic form, while the katauta disappeared. As Igarashi notes: "Katauta is almost extinct except for what remains in the *Kiki.*"[23] Sedôka and chôka, however, were still written and, perhaps for this reason, tanka were mainly of the 57-57-7 type. An interesting variant is the type where pauses occur as follows: 5-75-77. It is, I feel, a transitional form between the first 57-57-7 and the 575-77 type. An example follows from the *Manyôshû*:

> When spring is come here,
>   what blooms first of all at my house
>   is the plum blossom;
> Looking at it by myself
>   would I spend the days of spring![24]

A statistical study of Tachibana Moribe[25] yields the following information, showing how a transition from the 57-57-7 form to the 575-77 is apparent:

Fourth line pause	500 poems
Second line pause	195 poems
Third line pause	50 poems

The third group comprises only 1.18 percent of the total number of poems, according to this older critic. The figures obtained by Asano are different and perhaps more accurate. (It should be noted that the pause referred to in the above tabulation denotes the dominant pause; secondary pauses may and often do occur.) Asano's figures for each volume of the *Manyôshû* follows:[26]

VOLUME	NUMBER OF POEMS	VOLUME	NUMBER OF POEMS
1	1	11	17
2	1	12	16
3	5	13	4
4	13	14	1
5	2	15	5
6	4	16	2
7	8	17	4
8	4	18	1
9	3	19	4
10	11	20	6

According to the above, the 575-77 type comprises 2.68 percent of the total number of tanka, which is approximately twice that found by the older critic. However, it still reveals how few poems were written in this pattern during the Manyô period.

Apparently, however, it became more popular for in the first Imperial anthology, the *Kokinshû*, published A.D. 905, the percentage increases greatly. Moreover, it is significant that only five chôka are included, for its virtual disappearance seems to reinforce the trend away from the simple alternation of five and seven-syllable lines. Aside from the five chôka, there are four sedôka, while the rest of the anthology consists only of tanka, numbering 1,102. Of them, 154 are of the 575-77 type, comprising 13.97 percent, as against the 2.7 percent of the *Manyôshû*. Following is a tabulation by each volume of the *Kokinshû*.[27]

VOLUME	NUMBER OF POEMS	VOLUME	NUMBER OF POEMS
1	5	11	13
2	8	12	6
3	2	13	8
4	10	14	10
5	7	15	14
6	4	16	7
7	1	17	10
8	5	18	14
9	2	19	14
10	11	20	2

Following are typical examples of the 575-77 type found in the *Kokinshû:*

> Do the spring-soft showers
>   shed tears as they fall gently,
>   blooming cherry flowers?
> None can but deplore your fair
>   petals scattering in air.[28]

> Where the soft spring haze
>   trails along the hill, I'm charmed
>   by the cherry flower;
> And in you on whom I gaze
>   there's the same enchanting power.[29]

The first part of these poems seems to have an undeniable relationship with the haiku, especially with the third line terminating with a noun —a typical haiku characteristic. In the partial independence of the first hemistich of this type of tanka, then, undoubtedly lie the roots of haiku even in this early period, while it clearly points the way to *renga* or chained verse in the succeeding age.

The increasing popularity of the 575-77 type continues to increase markedly in the later anthologies. The figures, according to Tachibana Moribe, are as follows:[30]

Gosenshû (A.D. 951)	16.7 %
Shûishû (1005)	18.51%
Shin-Kokinshû (1205)	19.01%

I shall give here his tabulation for each volume of the *Shin-Kokinshû* as a matter of some interest.[31]

VOLUME	NUMBER OF POEMS	VOLUME	NUMBER OF POEMS
1	12	11	13
2	19	12	11
3	15	13	14
4	30	14	22
5	24	15	15
6	32	16	37
7	5	17	23
8	18	18	37
9	11	19	8
10	23	20	9

An extremely important observation is to be made in regard to the tanka rhythm of the 575-77 type. In the early period, with the predominance of the 57-57-7 pattern, the pauses within the tanka were limited to those following the second and fourth lines. However, even in the earliest period of the *Kojiki, Nihonshoki,* and *Manyôshû,* the two-hemistich tanka developed so flexibly that a pause could occur at the end of any line in the upper hemistich. The dominant pause is, of course, at the end of the third line, while a minor pause could occur at the end of the first line, giving rise to the pattern 5-75-77. An example follows from the *Manyôshû:*

> While so longingly,
>> O beloved one, I wait
>> all alone for thee,
> Swaying my hut's bamboo blind
>> gently blows the autumn wind.[32]

Following is an example of the 57-5-77 type of rhythm, again from the *Manyôshû:*

> On the clouds that run
>   like rich banners o'er the sea,
>   shines the setting sun;
> So I think that on this night
>   we'll see a moon wondrous bright.[33]

The last type of variation is the poem in which the dominant third-line pause is the only one of note; the following Manyô example has the pattern 575-77:

> I am he indeed
>   come to gather violets
>   from the spring's fair mead;
> And enchanted by their sight
>   I have slept there through the night.[34]

In passing it should be noted that the flexibility of the tanka rhythm was such that it was possible to have a well-defined third-line pause, followed by a slightly less emphatic fourth-line pause also, as the following illustrates:

> Ocean waves that rush
>   and hurl like pounding thunder
>   against the rock-shore,
> Break and scatter, whirl and crush
>   with their wild tumultuous roar![35]

In considering the various pauses possible in the upper hemistich, it is apparent that, from its beginnings, this type of tanka contained all the variant possibilities of the dominant inner rhythmic constructions typical of haiku. The most typical, of course, is the first-line pause, which seems to have developed of necessity as the first hemistich became more clearly differentiated from the second; the first line then becomes in a sense an addition to the main body of the complete upper hemistich. The pause, however, is not so defined as to place the tanka in the type typified by the 5-75-77 pattern (the transitional form, as noted before), for the pause at the end of the first line is not as strong.

Igarashi has pointed out that the establishment of the 575-77 pattern in tanka represents a radical departure from the basic 5-7 rhythm of Japanese poetry, since, as I have pointed out above, the first-line pause is in effect a severing of the first line of five syllables from the basic rhythmic pattern of 7-5 in the first hemistich. He conjectures that the seed for the prevalence of the 7-5 pattern in the later periods is to be found already in the "poetic phrases appearing in the classical prose

of the *Kiki* and other writings,"[36] where a 7-5 rhythm can be occasionally found, though it is rare. Again, though rare, there are some poems
in the *Kiki* with a 7-5 rhythm,[37] examples of which have been given in
the foregoing pages. The third conjecture he offers is interesting, in that
he finds one of the impulses to the 7-5 rhythm in the songs classified as
kayo to be found in both the *Kojiki* and the *Nihonshoki*, though not in
later anthologies. Such songs are usually irregular and are not classifi-
able in the four, main forms of ancient poetry. Of them Igarashi points
out the following: "Two separate lines in a poem consisting of three
and four syllables [respectively], or four and three syllables, or five and
two, or two and five, came to be read as one line, which [with a succeeding five-syllable line] helped to establish the 7-5 rhythm."[38] A
translation of the example he cites, showing how two lines of four and
three syllables respectively could easily be read as one line, follows,
the syllabic pattern of the original being retained:

> The Emishi's
> 4
> One soldier's
> 3
> Worth a hundred strong,
> 5
> All the people say of them,
> 5
> But they did not resist us.[39]
> 7

Igarashi's conjecture that the first two lines of the song came to be
read as one line, forming thus a 7-5 rhythm with the third line, seems
most plausible.

Another reason which he forwards is one that I have offered as the
rationale for the length of the present day haiku: "The fourth reason
is due to the length of one breath—that is to say, when we read two
lines of five and seven syllables, some breath is left over, which tempts
us to read the next line of five syllables. As we repeat this type of reading
and it becomes a habit, we begin to feel at the same time a new kind
of rhythmic interest, which I believe is one of the strong reasons [for
the establishment of the 7-5 rhythm.]"[40] One feature of the new
rhythmic interest, contrasting with the dominant, heavy 5-7 rhythm,
was the first line pause in the 575-77 type of tanka, making possible a
lyric note in Japanese verse.

How haiku-like this first-line pause renders the upper hemistich is evident from the following examples of tanka found in the *Shin-Kokinshû*:[41]

> By my window-sill,
>   almost overblown, are double
>   flowers of cherry trees;
> How I hope that someone will
>   visit them before the breeze.

> Perfuming the air,
>   the blossoms of the iris
>   bloom so lush and fair;
> And the *hototogisu* sing
>   in May rains at evening.

> Spring has come, thought I,
>   in faint and rosy colors
>   flushed across the sky;
> On Mt. Kagu's lovely height
>   veils of mist are trailing white.

In the *Shin-Kokinshû*, tanka with the first-line pause occur frequently, seeming to indicate that poets could now handle this subtlety with some ease. It has a most desirable poetic effect, for the 575-77 type of tanka, while the most musical, can become too rigid and formal in movement. In order to avoid this effect, the placement of a slight pause at the end of the first line produces a light variation as delightful as the original feeling in which the very rhythm of perception is seized by the poet. For example, the marked first-line pause in the following poem by Kageki Kagawa gives us time to feel the broad expansiveness of the burgeoning spring field and to savor the delicious leisure and delight of an aimless, unhurried walk through the loveliness of spring:

> Through the field I strolled;
>   in the spring there is no end
>   to my gaiety;
> And a butterfly I told
>   to alight comes to rest on me.[42]

As in haiku, expanding within the pause is the air of the poetry, and the unsaid and the silently intimated arise.

In passing, I should like to venture the observation that, as is apparent from the preceding material, it would seem that the transition from the heavy regularity of the 57-57-7 tanka to the later pattern can be correlated with a refinement in feeling and perception arising from a corresponding development within the culture of the Japanese world between the early centuries of the material of the *Kiki* and the thirteenth century of the *Shin-Kokinshû*. Even during the era when the *Tales of Genji* were written (*circa* 1000), as is apparent from that novel, Japanese society was "extremely civilized, perhaps even decadent"; of an "almost unimaginable subtlety," it was perhaps "the most elegant society ever known," as Donald Keene characterizes it.[43] The great cultural developments of the Nara and Heian periods, with the stimulating influence of contact with Chinese thought and art, had left an indelible refinement and sophistication on Japanese verse, which is I feel shown in one way by the development of the tanka form as we have traced it. For the later form has a greater flexibility and ability to capture subtleties and nuances than does the earlier.

We can thus see the first steps toward the independence of the three-line poem known now as haiku by tracing the development of tanka through the pre-Manyô, Manyô, Kokin, and Shin-Kokin periods, noting that in the last era the first or upper hemistich of the tanka developed all the possible forms that the haiku poet came to use several hundred years later. It might then appear that the haiku developed directly from the tanka, and were this so, many cumbersome critical problems and misinterpretations of its nature might not have arisen. But such was not its simple path. Before the upper hemistich of the tanka became independent, there intervened other poetic forms which in turn contributed much to the haiku as it exists today, making it a unique poetic form. These forms were the renga and haikai.

RENGA PERIOD

During the first stages of the pre-haiku period, while the 57-57-7 tanka rhythm was changing into the 575-77 rhythm and developing nuances flexible enough to render total poetic experiences, there arose a special manner of rendering them. This is the method by which two persons compose one poem, one person writing the first hemistich and another the second. A poem thus composed by two persons is called a renga or linked verse. Needless to say, the value of linked verse lies in the relationship and genuineness of the poetic attitudes of the two persons who create the one complete tanka. What gave the strongest impetus from the structural point of view to the composition of renga was the development of the 57-57-7 tanka form into the 575-77 form, which we have already traced.

The spirit from which renga arose is the innocently competitive, such as is found in the various amusements and games indulged in during the early periods. About the ninth century, the game of "matching grasses" (*kusa-awase*) developed into that of "matching roots" (*ne-awase*); as Asano points out, "the participants vied with each other in the length of the roots of the grass they plucked and [such games] further developed into chrysanthemum contests, poppy contests..."[44] Sea shells, various utensils, and fans also figured in such games. Indeed, with the great popularity of poetry among the leisured class of the times, when it was considered a necessary accomplishment for a cultured person, it was only natural that poetry contests should have evolved in which two contestants sought to out-cap each other's verse either through greater wit, appropriateness, or with further development of beauty and poetic effect. The attitude is to be found in the earliest collections— the *Kojiki* and *Nihonshoki*—as *mondô* or question and answer in the form of katauta. As has been previously noted in Igarashi's observation: "Katauta is used mostly in the question and answer form, because in a situation where *an immediate, witty* response is demanded that form that is the most extremely compressed...is used."[45] Indeed, in the earlier periods it would almost seem that any verses in the question-and-answer form were classified as renga, as is implied in the observation of Yoshimoto Nijô (1320-1388), the editor of the *Tsukuba Mondô*, for he records in that book his answer to the question "In what period did renga begin?"

> In the *kana* preface to the *Kokinshû*, the Ebisu song sung on the Floating Bridge of Heaven, mentioned by Tsurayuki, is a renga. First the hokku of great god is as follows: "How happy am I! I have met a lovely maid." To this the goddess added: "How happy am I! I have met a handsome man." A poem composed by two persons is a renga. Is this not a hokku and an answering verse composed by two gods?[46]

In the Manyô period, which followed, the matching spirit shows clearly in the witty and sometimes skillful handling of tanka verse; a first tanka is composed by one person and the second by another. The same spirit also runs through many of the Manyô poems classified as *somonka* or love poems. This type of duet-like verse flourished quite well at this time, for many examples are included in nine books out of the twenty of the Manyô collection. Following is an example of two tanka coupled together as a pair:

A POEM SENT BY PRINCE OTSU TO LADY ISHIKAWA

> Waiting for you,
>   in the dripping dew of the hill
> I stood,—weary and wet
>   with the dripping dew of the hill.

A POEM COMPOSED BY LADY ISHIKAWA IN RESPONSE

> Would I had been, beloved,
>   the dripping dew of the hill
> That wetted you
>   while for me you waited.[47]

It is quite probable that from the matching of or competition between two complete tanka rose the practice of composing one tanka by two people. This probable compression, so to speak, was of course much abetted by the development of the 575-77 tanka form, as above noted. It is difficult to ascribe an exact date to the beginning of this practice, but since one example is included in the *Manyôshû*, we can safely assume that even in this early period it was done. The example follows:

A nun composed the first part, and Yakamochi, being asked by her to help complete it, composed the second.

> Rice fields one planted
>   by damming up the waters
>   of the Saho stream. —*A Nun*

> The rice from the first reaping—
>   Do you eat it all alone? —*Yakamochi*[48]

As is noted by Asaji Nose, the above is the "oldest attempt to compose a duet-like poem" in the tanka form by two persons.[49]

It is in the following Heian period (794–1192) that renga appeared more frequently in the numerous anthologies issued, although the name renga itself does not appear until 1127. It apparently became a fashionable pastime, forming one of the diversions of the poetry tournaments or *uta-awase* which also came into vogue in this period.[50] An example from the famous diary *Kagerô Nikki,* covering the period 974-95 follows:

> In the running spring
> The steed are cooling their hoofs;
> Envious they seem
>
> For upon the crystal stream
> The fine shadows stay and cling.[51]

The above, as well as the example from the *Manyôshû,* typifies the early renga, showing how the upper and lower hemistich were not yet grammatically independent, as they were to become in the later periods. Strictly speaking, therefore, the two poems are not renga in the sense which developed later. Neither the *Kokinshû* nor the *Gosenshû,* appearing in 905 and 951 respectively, contain renga. In the *Shûi Wakashû* (1005), however, there are six examples; in four of them the second hemistich is added, while in the other two, the first hemistich is added.[52]

Judging from the fact that renga are included in this imperial anthology, the form must already have assumed some significance, since only poetry of a certain degree of importance was generally included in this type of anthology. It is interesting to note also that the upper and lower hemistichs of the renga in the *Shûi Wakashû* now stood independent of each other, since this independence of the upper hemistich will lead to the importance of the hokku of renga. How extensively this type of verse was practiced can be estimated by the fact that several works—some earlier than the *Shûi Wakashû*—also contain renga. For example, there are two in the *Yamato Monogatari* (*circa* 987), one in the *Ochikubo Monogatari* (*circa* 987–990), two in the *Izumi Shikibu Nikki* (*circa* 1003–04), three in the *Makura no Sôshi* (*circa* 1004), one in the *Tsutsumichûnagon Monogatari* (*circa* 1060), and one in the *Kanjaku Monogatari* (*circa* 1070).[53]

Thus, renga appeared in many important classics, but not until 1127 did the term renga appear. In the *Kinyô Wakashû* the classification appears for the first time. Prior to this collection, renga had been placed in the section for tanka.

As was previously noted, during the early period a ready vying of wit dominated renga-composition. Masaharu Sasa has said the short renga had no literary pretensions: "Renga in the older period was something to be spoken in amusement only, suitable for one occasion only, and was not to be written down as literature for the future. Its aim was to arouse momentary applause, to make one laugh rather than to be moving, to surprise rather than inspire."[54] Doubtless it was this gay, light-hearted element which made for its great popularity and led to its intricate development. Poetic repartee was the virtue *par excellence;* quick wittedness was valued highly.

Some renga assume the qualities of highly ingenious riddles, such as the one appearing in the *Yamato Monogatari,* a novel of the *Gosenshû* period:

> Hikaki no Go, announcing that a poem would be composed and asking that enthusiasts gather around since they would be asked to add to a very difficult hemistich, said:

> > Why is the small deer
> > standing right in the middle
> > of the open sea?

To which, the following was added:

> > I think the autumn mountains
> > are clearly reflected there.[55]

Outrageous punning, as in conundrums, was not prohibited; the answer given by Tsurayuki in the following renga must have merited a chuckle from his audience. The poem, given in the work *Toshiyori Zuinô,* is attributed to the early tenth century:

> > How is it that here
> > deep in the mountains we can
> > hear a rowing boat?   —*Mitsune*

> > The fruit upon the branches
> > of the trees are ripening.   —*Tsurayuki*[56]

Mitsune, Tsurayuki's co-editor of the *Kokinshû,* certainly must have intended to confound by his question. However, Tsurayuki capped him neatly. For the words rendered as *are ripening* in the above translation are in Japanese *umi wataru,* which can also mean *crossing the sea.* Hence Tsurayuki's answer may be explained as follows: The fruit on the trees (deep in the mountains you mention) are ripening (or crossing the sea), thus accounting for the sound of a rowing boat.

Some feeling for the atmosphere of the society in which the short renga flourished can be grasped in the incident related in the *Makura no Sôshi*, which shows also that the valued quality of quick-wittedness could have less trivial roots than riddling or punning:

> The snow had piled deep and they all gathered in a room with the latticed windows closed and talked of many things, warming themselves around a brazier. Then the prince asked me: "What is the snow like on the peak of Koro Mountain?"
>
> At his words, I raised one of the latticed windows and rolled up the bamboo blind; and the prince looked pleased with the things I did. The people there should have read poems about the things I did and should have known what I referred to, but they did not seem to have expected me to act like this.[57]

What was referred to was the famous Chinese line that even the emperor's bamboo blind, customarily kept down since so sacred a personage must be protected from the common view, should be raised to view the snows of Koro Mountain, since it is so beautiful a sight. In the above anecdote, the expected reaction to the prince's question would have been the composition of a poem on the mountain's beauties, but when the court lady replied by rolling up the blind, thus acting out the Chinese story, she added the piquant wittiness to the situation that was the virtue of the time. By thus gracefully demonstrating her learning, also, she must have scored a triumph.

In time, the most ingenious techniques of linking one verse to another, such as parallelism, association, juxtaposition of kindred ideas or words, pivot words, puns, parodies, etc., were developed. Linking of a more subtle nature is apparent in the following, where poetic wit and skill seem more to the fore than in the previous examples:

> In the peach garden
>   the blossoms of the peach tree
>   are indeed in bloom.
>
> At the plum harbor, I fear,
>   the plum flowers are scattering.[58]

In this example, however crude and simple it may appear now, the delight seems to lie in the quick contrasting of the peach garden and the blossoms in bloom in the upper hemistich with the plum harbor and the scattering plum flowers in the lower.

Generally, however, the renga of the Heian period are rich in humor and wit, expressed either for the immediate amusement of one's company or demonstrating one's superior poetic skills and outwitting one's opponent. The central attitude of the poet of this period as far as the renga is concerned can hardly be called poetic, nor indeed was it meant to be, as Sasa has pointed out in defense of the short renga: "Renga of the old time...skillfully achieved their objectives as an amusement; judged as literature, they can be said to have failed. However, to be classed as literature was not the objective, and therefore we should not criticize them as such."[59]

The renga we have been considering up to this point have been the single-link type. However, during the later Heian period long renga of several links, eventually extending to one hundred, were written. One trend in the long renga was the re-establishment of the classical, poetic atmosphere typical of the tanka spirit, while a second trend continued the emphasis upon wit and humor, as in the short form. While it is difficult to determine the exact date of the inception of the long renga, it is safe to assume that by 1200 renga of one hundred links were composed.[60] It can thus be imagined that the shorter form of ten to twenty links was created much earlier. Those of fifty links were perhaps inspired by Chinese models of the fifty-line rhymed verse popular in China during this time. As for form, the long renga consisted of alternating links of 5-7-5 and 7-7, each link being composed by a different poet. Perhaps it was as a reaction to the levity of the earlier short renga that the longer form at first was dedicated, as noted above, to the recapturing of the sober, classical beauty of the early tanka spirit.

It seems quite clear that it enjoyed great vogue even before its grandest days in the hands of Sôgi during the fifteenth century. The first example of the longer renga that has survived is to be found in the historical tale *Ima Kagami* (1170), where several occasions of renga-making are described, with the notation that "such meetings were frequent."[61] Sasa has pointed out that the competitive spirit of the short renga persisted even into the longer renga, with bets being made on the comparative excellence of the links composed by various poets:

> One outstanding feature of the playful element in long renga was to lay wagers [on the comparative excellence of the linked verses]—a feature which should not be overlooked. During the reign of Emperor Gotoba [1183–98], it is stated that various kinds of stakes were displayed [that had been wagered at a renga meeting] which had been quite prodigious. We can see in the

diary kept by Teika [1162–1241] his statement that he won forty stakes at
a hundred-chain renga meeting held at a palace.[62]

And there survives from the same diary, *Meigetsu Ki,* covering the period
1180–1235, a description of a renga party, showing that by this time
even in spite of the elaborate formalizations of the uta-awase, the
renga too enjoyed enough status to be the nucleus for such organized
meetings. Prior to this, it seems to have been composd as a secondary
diversion at formal uta-awase, as Taizô Ebara has pointed out: "The
renga that began as a side amusement in the waka meetings gradually
developed into songs of fifty or one hundred chains, and renga assumed
its own identity apart from waka."[63] In the early thirteenth century,
from the *Yakumo Mishô,* a collection of essays on poetry by Emperor
Juntoku (1210–20) we have the following statement: "In olden times
there were no renga of fifty or one hundred links.... The way we
chain verses today begins from the middle period [last quarter of the
Heian period]."[64] Also from the thirteenth century is the *Kokin
Chomonshû* (1254), in which are included descriptions of renga
parties much along the lines of those in the *Ima Kagami.*[65]

In modern times, discoveries have been made of complete renga of
one hundred chains composed during the fourteenth century, the earliest
dating from 1332. They do not appear to have been well known in
their own time, however, and it does not appear unreasonable to assume
that they had no circulation.[66] The most notable work of the century
is the *Tsukubashû* (1356), the first collection devoted solely to renga
both short and long, which was well known both in its own day and
later. There seems to be ample evidence, therefore, that the long renga
as a verse form was widely known and enjoyed popularity in the pre-
Sôgi period.

However, a curious fact emerges. The *Tsukubashû,* the only widely
known collection of renga of this time, contained only single links of
various long renga and, until very recent times, was thought to be the
only source of such poetry for the period preceding 1356. Sasa notes
that a renga poet only fifteen years older than Sôgi himself was un-
acquainted with complete renga of earlier times: "Bishop Shinkei (1406–
78) states in his *Hitorigoto*: 'People have recorded the excellent verse of
their predecessors, but in most cases the preceding chain is not recorded.
... I regret this very much.'"[67]

It may be of interest to examine in some detail three verses of a long renga of the early period. As was noted, the earliest example survives in the historical tale *Ima Kagami*. The account runs as follows:

> Echigo no Menoto, a famed poetess, was a female retainer of a noble house where other courtiers used to gather and make what they called *kusari-renga* frequently.... At a certain meeting, Sanjo no Otodo wrote:

> It makes us remember too
>
> 7
>
> Nara's ancient capital.
>
> 7

To which the master added the following:

> Double cherry flowers,
>
> 5
>
> Golden leaves at autumn-tide—
>
> 7
>
> Now how do they fare?
>
> 5

Echigo no Menoto added the following:

> Lovely colors multiply
>
> 7
>
> Every time a shower comes.
>
> 7

They were praised for a long time. Such meetings were frequent.[68]

Asaji Nose's explanation of the rationale of the linking among the three verses given above offers a clue as to the nature of the connections made between verses in the long renga.

> The verse [given first above]...is a *tô-iku* [verse to be added to] beginning with a lower hemistich, to which is added [the second verse]. [This verse] treats of the double-cherry flowers, which is the associating word to Nara. These two verses make up one short renga. When we put the two together, they mean the following: The famous cherry trees with their double blossoms at Nara may have turned to gold and crimson, and thinking of how beautiful they are, I think of the capital at Nara. To this, Echigo no Menoto, treating the verse of the double-cherry flowers as a beginning verse, added [the third verse]. [The second and third verse together] mean: How do the leaves of the double-blossomed cherry trees look in their autumnal colors? Every time a shower comes, the colors of the autumn leaves probably deepen. The reason is that it is said that the color of the maple leaves is dyed by showers.[69]

As is apparent from Nose's explanation, each verse links to the one immediately preceding it and with it evolves a meaning through various techniques; there is no connection between separated verses within the same renga, as is apparent from an examination of the first and third verses in the example given above.

What the rules for linking were prior to the fourteenth century cannot now be determined, since no complete long renga exist. Of the recently discovered complete renga of the fourteenth century, a cursory examination reveals that the technicalities of linking differ from those of Sôgi's period,* but the same general procedure as above described prevails.

It was during the Muromachi period (1324–1549) that the classical, long renga reached its height in the hands of Sôgi (1421–1502). It was also called *kusari-renga,* or chained verse. The rules that developed governing its composition became complex in the extreme and have been described in some detail by Chamberlain, who says in part:

> Thus if the *hokku*...spoke of the spring with special reference to January, the second hemistich must also refer to January and end with a full stop. The third hemistich must introduce some idea appropriate, not to January only, but to the whole season of spring, and must end with the particle *te*... but should the second hemistich have included a *te*, then one of the particles *ni* or *ran*, or the phrase *mo nashi*, must be preferred. The fourth hemistich is a "miscellaneous" one, that is, no mention must be made in it of any of the four seasons.... No. 5 is called the "Fixed Seat of the Moon," because here the moon must in any case be made mention of; and this and Nos. 6 and 7 are termed the "Three Autumn Hemistichs,"—for the moon, which introduces these three, is the special property of autumn.[70]

Such minuteness extended not only to the subject matter of each link, but to the diction, use of homonyms, anagrams, method of writing and folding the paper on which the poetry appeared, etc. When intuitively exploited, as in the famous renga *Minase Sangin Hyakuin,* the rules, in spite of their complexity or perhaps because of it, could produce poems of "surpassing grace and beauty" which are "unlike any ever written in the West," in Donald Keene's appreciative words.[71] What will particularly concern us, however, are the rules governing the composition

---

* For example, the later period ordained that the second verse was to end with a noun or a full stop; however, in two of the earlier renga, one dated 1332 and the other 1333, the second verses both end in particles. (Cf. Ebara, *op. cit.,* pp. 410–43 *passim.)*

of the hokku or beginning verse of the renga, the form in a 5-7-5 pattern.

The term hokku itself comes from Chinese prosody. With the development of the elaborations surrounding renga composition, it came to occupy a most important place as the first verse of the whole chain. For its function was to represent the whole poem, somewhat as the theme or title of a poem represents it in the Western sense. The following opinion is ascribed to an authority of the thirteenth century: "Tanka's theme is its hokku; and renga uses hokku as its theme."[72] The importance attached to the hokku probably arose from the fact that the basic poetic attitude of the long renga was markedly different from the short one. So long as, in the two-link verse, only an effect of wit, surprise, or startling amusement was sought, this effect in itself served to bind the two parts together. As the intent of the renga became more serious and ambitious, however, it was necessary to find a more complicated significance capable of sustaining a longer flight. Witticism alone no longer justified this newer, elaborate game. And as the hokku stated, as it were, the *raison d'etre* for the whole poem, its importance in the poetic scheme of renga is understandable.

Consequently, the most competent poet in the group was selected to compose the hokku, as is stated in the *Yakumo Mishô* in the early thirteenth century: "Unless a skilled versifier is found in the party, you should not begin to write hokku."[73] For the success or failure of the renga depended to an appreciable extent on the excellence of the hokku, with its function of setting the whole tone or atmosphere of the poem. Shinkei, Sôgi's great contemporary, called for loftiness of tone, apparently mindful of the serious poetic intent of the renga: "As an authority once said, honku is generally lofty in style and proceeds smoothly in one rhythmic sweep; this may be called the most important point.... Its style should be fluent and natural."[74] It should be profound, since it is the start of a one-hundred chain poem, as a book on instructions for the composition of renga written for Toyotomi Hideyoshi in 1585 admonished the great military leader: "Since the hokku is a starting verse of a hundred-chain renga, its style should be lofty and profound, not commonplace."[75] It was considered a great honor and privilege to be delegated the task of composing the hokku, and everyone seems to have practiced writing them alone. By 1356, when the *Tsukubashû* was compiled, one complete volume—the twentieth—contained only hokku, and so we may assume that before this period they were being composed independently. Of course, at an actual renga meeting all verses were supposedly composed impromptu; but as the following exchange recorded in the *Kyûshû Mondô* by Yoshimoto Nijô indicates, it seems to have been tacitly understood that prior preparation might have been made. Of all the verses in a renga, such license would apply especially to the hokku:

> Question: [In a certain renga] there are many verses that seem to have been composed beforehand, and not at the time the renga was composed. Is this practice permissible?
>
> Answer: Since it is said that Tsurayuki [editor of the *Kokinshû* (905)] composed a tanka twenty days beforehand [for an uta-awase], should there be any reason why a renga verse should not be often thought out skillfully beforehand?... But those are not superior to the ones that sincerely come from one's heart at the time of composition.... Although those composed beforehand may not be the best, if they are very interesting, we should not dislike them.[76]

Indeed, so great was the concentration on hokku composition that by 1461 a separate term was evolved to indicate those hokku which were not written as the beginning verse of renga, as the following from the *Sazame Goto* shows: "In these days people value verses called *Kanto hokku,* which are very popular. And they try to avoid copying each other, so that many ways [of writing hokku] have developed."[77] In the same work there appears a passage suggesting that hokku were composed on given themes, much as tanka were in the older poetry contests. With such a practice, the recognition and appreciation of hokku as a poetic form, completely separate from renga, is established: "When hokku are composed on the same given theme, they tend to become the same in style, which is very unfortunate."[78]

The seed for the independence of the hokku of renga is to be found even in the days of the short, two-link verse, as the following statement from the *Toshiyori Zuinô* of the late Heian period shows: "Renga is a poem, a connection between two halves. Each part, the first or second, is rendered according to the composer's feeling. But it should be complete, with its meaning fully understood. It is not good to leave the first half incomplete for the second composer to supply the meaning."[79] Thus, even in the period of the two-link renga, the independence of each link was insisted upon. With the gradual development of the form, only those renga in which each link was at least grammatically an entity were recognized as true renga. This being so for sections within the body of the poem, it would be particularly stressed for the important hokku, as is stated in the *Yakumo Mishô*: "Hokku should be written with a full stop. . . . It should end with terms like *kana* [exclamatory conclusive] or *beshi* [conclusive form] or with [a noun] like 'spring breeze' or 'autumn wind,' etc."[80] One hundred and fifty years later, Yoshimoto Nijô was still propounding the same rule in his *Renri Hishô* of 1349: "Hokku first of all must have a full stop. Those that do not do so should not be used."[81] The custom in the short renga of providing the two seven-syllable lines first, with the first three lines being added later, undoubtedly also led to the independence of hokku. For such a practice would lead to a flexible handling of the three-line group as an entity, rather than as merely the beginning of some longer poetic form. As noted before, in the first imperial anthology in which the term renga appeared, the *Shûi Wakashû*, in two of the six renga included, the upper hemistich is added to the original lower hemistich.[82] An example of such renga composition also appears in the *Kokin Chomonshû* of 1254.[83]

Igarashi has suggested that the very rhythm of the hokku changed as appreciation and acceptance of it as a separate form developed; the change itself reinforced the trend toward independence:

> To make the haiku an independent poem, the effort exerted by masters in each period, from Yoshimoto Nijô, through Sôgi, Sôkan, Moritake, Teitoku, Sôin and down to Bashô, and the enrichment of the content helped a great deal. However, it is also due to the change occurring in the manner in which the seventeen syllables are read. The seventeen syllables in renga are read in the expectation that afterwards fourteen syllables will follow; therefore the first seventeen syllables may have been read without a break. However, after they became a hokku and people appreciated them as an independent poem, during the reading of the seventeen syllables in three lines, a kind of rhythm with pauses developed in the reading. By this kind of independent reading, they must have become a separate, settled form of poem.[84]

Another indication that appreciation of hokku as a form was firmly established lies in the number of anthologies and collections of hokku made by various poets of the later era. A partial list follows: *Nijô Dono Nichi Nichi Hokku* by Yoshimoto Nijô; *Sozei Hokku Shû* by Sozei (d. 1455); *Sôgi Hokku Shû* by Sôgi; *Shummu So* by Shôhaku (1442–1527) and *Sôchô Nichi Nichi Hokku* by Sôchô (1447–1532), two followers of the master Sôgi, who with him wrote the greatest long renga known, *Minase Sangin Hyakuin; Soboku Hokku Chô* by Soboku (d. circa 1545).[85]

These characteristic features of the hokku—its importance and independence—carried over into the later haikai period also. For as the complicated rules governing renga composition brought forth the masterpieces of the Muromachi period, the younger poets, despairing of matching them and victimized by the mannerisms, turned to the humorous renga, known as *haikai no renga*—*haikai* denoting the amusing or playful. Indeed, throughout the history of Japanese poetry the succession of the serious by the witty or comic is a common phenomenon, as Asano notes:

> Against the refined tanka, there appeared humorous renga [i.e., in the early, two link-stage]; when renga became refined, there apppeared the witty haikai; when haikai attained its final form, there appeared comical *senryu*, as can be verified through history. And accordingly it is interesting to note that always [the shift from the classical to the comic attitude] is accompanied by a lowering in the class of those who wrote poetry. As renga fell into the hands of the priests, and as gradually the popularity of the haikai overtook that of renga, it is natural that haikai was the poetry of the people.[86]

The word *haikai* itself appeared as early as the *Kokinshû* (905), where are included comical verses under such a classification. The witty type of renga is undoubtedly derived from the earliest short renga, which seems during the entire long renga period to have persisted, though not as a major form. Perhaps it could have been described as an amusing poetic trifle, as Sasa implies in the following:

> Though [haikai] did not flourish and was devalued...it did not completely die out. As a side game for renga poets, as in the previous period renga was a side game for tanka poets, it continued on, in however small a way.... Moreover, a famous renga poet of the time, Priest Kensai [d. 1510], states: "In the long renga meetings, always a *haikai no renga* is held."[87]

It is interesting to note that Kensai was not only a contemporary of Sôgi's but a good friend of his also. Sôgi, however, seems to have found haikai completely unworthy of attention and in his *Shin Tsukubashû* (1495), a collection of links from various long renga, "not even half a page was given to it."[88]

Haikai no renga is generally considered to have attained considerable stature with both Sôkan (1465–1553) and Moritake (1472–1549), and since both were adept at the classical form of renga also, in their work it is possible to find much of the latter form admixed. Indeed, throughout a considerable period of haikai history—for perhaps one hundred and fifty years—the form was not as sharply defined as were tanka and the long renga in Sasa's view: "Since Moritake and Sôkan originally were masters of classical renga, in their haikai it is natural to find traces of the renga rules. To think that they maintained especially set rules [for haikai] is a false interpretation of their intent."[89] The ideas of Sôkan and Moritake themselves seem quite at variance from what can be judged from their works; the greater seriousness in Moritake's work can perhaps be ascribed to his high religious position, for he eventually became the head priest of Ise Shrine, the heart of Japanese Shintoism.

Of Sôkan's work not much remains. Consequently, his thoughts on haikai can be adduced principally from his work *Shinsen Inutsukubashû,* compiled between 1523 and 1532, a collection of links from various *haikai no renga,* divided by seasons into four categories and into others also such as love, miscellaneous, etc. Following the renga links in each seasonal group are added hokku appropriate to the season. It seems quite apparent from an examination of this poetry that we are once again back in the air of the two-link renga period, with its pervasive insistence on the amusing and witty. Two representative hokku follow, both from the spring section:[90]

> A SERVANT CALLED WAKANA IS SCOLDED
>
> Being picked and then
> Being beaten up again
> Are the young spring greens.

The pun here is of course clear; the servant's name Wakana can also be translated as young spring greens.

The following is an ironic jest on the Buddhistic concept of *sunvata,* the ultimate reality arrived at when man ceases to be deluded by appearances or gross materiality:

> It's melted away;
> This Buddha of snow is now
> Indeed a true one.

The snow Buddha, having melted away in the early spring warmth, has attained the reality beyond form and matter.

In contrast to Sôkan's work, Moritake's statement of intent, at least, seems quite different. It appears in a prose postscript to his curious creation entitled *Haikai no Renga Dokugin Senku,* composed in 1508, which contains ten humorous renga, each consisting of one hundred chains and all written by Moritake himself. He describes the circumstances surrounding its conception: "The above one thousand chain haikai is the one I once took an oath [at the Ise Shrine] to write, but I was so occupied with other things I spent my time without doing it. . . . I consulted an oracle, vowing that with an odd number, I would write a renga; with an even number I would write a haikai. I prayed for the latter and drew a fortune stick; it was an even number."[91] Having set himself the task, he quite consciously is prepared to follow whatever the rules for haikai are, but finds that there are none: "When I composed it, I asked Shûkei [a contemporary haikai poet] what the rules and regulations concerning haikai were at the capital [Kyoto], for I had not seen them as yet. He replied saying that I should make up my own."[92] In such poetic freedom, Moritake enunciates the aim of haikai as he conceives it: "In haikai is the purpose to make people laugh for no reason? Haikai should deal with both appearance and reality and be refined; furthermore, a verse should be genuine yet humorous. Thus have the lovers of haikai taught."[92] He seems to call, then, for greater refinement and less gross humor than he perhaps found in the haikai of the day. He also claims for haikai a greater seriousness of intent than it enjoyed as an exercise for poetic ingenuity, but such seriousness is not to be unmitigated by lighter attitudes.

The apparent flexibility surrounding haikai composition persisted even into the Teitoku period (1571–1653), as is evidenced by Teitoku's words in the *Haikai Gosan* written in 1651:

> Few haikai are included in anthologies [of the preceding period], for in the period of unrest it did not flourish. Now in this glorious period, in both city and country, noblemen and country people, young and old lend their ears and are delighted to hear haikai. However, when it comes to rules, they are too often at a loss. They wage wordy battles without end. Therefore I write this book for the benefit of my followers.[93]

Whatever degree of amorphousness existed, however, it is possible to make some distinctions between haikai and renga, and to list some of the characteristics of haikai. First, it allowed the use of words, both Japanese and Chinese, that were forbidden in the classical forms such as tanka or the long renga. Teitoku himself declared that differences in diction were the only distinction between renga and haiku in defensive tones typical of haikai enthusiasts: "Since Sôkan of Yamasaki edited the *Inu Tsukuba,* it has been thought that renga is noble and haikai base. The heart of Sôkan is not so.... At the beginning there was no distinction between haikai and renga. Those that were written with graceful phrases only were called renga and those that did not shun colloquial words were called haikai."[94] Secondly, at least until the Bashô period, haikai was marked by some degree of the witty or the amusing. In the *Haikai Shogakushô* by Gentoku (1641), two characteristics of haikai, among others, which make it "a better verse form" than renga were said to be the following: "To be humorous and praise oneself is not forbidden. [Haikai] arouses amusement immediately."[95] Thirdly, at least until Teitoku, the various complications of linking observed in the long renga were relaxed for the haikai. In the same *Haikai Shogakushô,* the simplicity is praised for two reasons: "Haikai is easy for a beginner to learn and soothes the heart pained by [the difficulties of] tanka. Even if they do not know the older anthologies and writings, people can link in any manner provided it is amusing."[96] Fourthly, generally speaking, haikai before Teitoku's time were shorter than the classical renga.

With Teitoku *haikai no renga* developed to the stage where in all aspects but diction it was indistinguishable from renga, as Ebara has pointed out:

> In the period of Teitoku haikai was considered a step toward renga. The rules and regulations of haikai became the same as those of renga. Teitoku distingushed between haikai and renga by the presence or absence of *haigen.* Haigen are the colloquial or Chinese words which are not permitted in waka. Thus, in the book on haikai rules by the people of the Teitoku school, the rules are the same as those for renga.[97]

However, in the school which next dominated the haikai world, the Danrin, whose leading spirit was Sôin, a marked revolt against the complexities practiced by Teitoku's followers is again noticeable. Indeed, in 1679 Suiryû, a follower of Teitoku, complains bitterly against the debased poetic aims of the Danrin: "The haikai that is popular in the world at present belongs to the Sôin style, which deals only with the amusing and likes to use only new, base, or common words. They consider their first aim to be playfulness and only wish to make people laugh.... Their verses are only puns in the worst sense and are as light and as worthless as pumice stones."[98] Considering the pedestrian poetry fostered by the Teitoku school, the Danrin was perhaps inevitable. Bashô seemed to feel that the school had made a valuable contribution: "Had it not been for Sôin before us, the people of our time would still be licking up Teitoku's slobber. Sôin was the leader of the party of improvement."[99] Its influence was short lived and soon dissipated into other schools of poetic thought, the most important of which is represented by Bashô. Bashô, in his teachings and in his poetry, set the ideals for hokku which have persisted without serious challenge to the present.

As has been previously noted, the independence and importance of hokku as established in the classical renga period was carried over into the haikai era, as is evidenced by the collections of hokku of haikai issued during this time. Some representative titles follow. The first is of course Sôkan's previously mentioned *Shinsen Inutsukubashû.* In *Takatsukuba,* edited by Seibu in 1642, appear not only haikai of the Teitoku school but also separate groups of hokku. *Gyokukaishû* (1656) edited by Teishitsu, one of the most famous followers of Teitoku, is a similar collection. A representative collection of the Danrin school is the *Haikai Imayô-otoko,* edited by Chôchôshi in 1676, in which again are included haikai and hokku in separate groups. For the Bashô school, there is among many others the *Minashiguri* (1681) edited by Kikaku with the same type of materials.

What the rapidly changing history of *haikai no renga* from the days of Sôkan and Moritake through the Danrin school contributed to the development of hokku is most important. For hokku, as Bashô wrote it, enjoyed above all a flexibility that made it truly an instrument of poetic insight. Such flexibility extended first of all to diction. Haikai freed poetry from a circumscribed poetic speech, so that Bashô was to declare that "in the poetry of haikai ordinary words are used."[100] The implications of such usage are large, as has been previously pointed out.[101] Awareness of them was undoubtedly behind Bashô's following dictum: "The value of haikai poetry is to correct ordinary words. We must never deal with things carelessly."[102] Certainly Bashô's ability to reach such insights was facilitated by the tradition of haikai in regard to a broadened diction.

Secondly, the admission of humor or levity into haikai enlarged the whole base of experiences with which the hokku could deal. There are no longer subjects which are poetic and subjects which must be excluded from poetry; as Bashô said: "There is no subject whatever that is not fit for hokku."[103] Such freedom undoubtedly came from the extremes to which haikai swung in the one hundred eighty years preceding Bashô. The refined levity which Moritake advocated is to be found in Bashô himself in such hokku as the following:

> Oh those siestas, with my feet
> Pressed fearsomely against the wall![104]

Chamberlain's explanation is as follows: "This verse [illustrates] the poverty and simplicity of Bashô's mode of life. So fragile is the mud wall of his hut that he fears to break through it when pressing against it with his feet."[105] The levity of haikai, however, would be used more signifi- cantly, as in Issa (1763–1827), where it appears as a total pervasiveness in the insight that gives him his poetic power; for his comic vision enforces rather than destroys, as in Sôkan or Sôin, the totality of the experience he is communicating. Issa's famous radish could not have appeared in Japanese poetry without the exuberant experimenting of the haikai period:

> With the radish he
> Pulls out, a radish-worker
> Shows the road to me.[106]

Thus the modern haiku, as it was created by Bashô, owes much to the literary turmoil of the haikai period.

For our purposes, with the establishment of the independent hokku, we can consider the haiku of today defined as a form. Indeed, the general supposition is that haiku history begins with the initial verse of renga, but as I have pointed out, such an assumption limits not only the historical but the poetic significance of haiku. Its history reaches back to the very beginnings of Japanese verse and shares the basic poetic impulses underlying it. Without its earliest genesis being understood, the historical development of haiku cannot be fully grasped.

Another important characteristic of the modern haiku which, together with its independence and importance, is derived from the hokku of renga is its almost inevitable inclusion of the seasonal theme. Let us turn then to a historical consideration of this aspect of haiku.

2. Seasonal Element

Of the earliest poetry recorded in the *Nihonshoki* and the *Kojiki,* it should be noted that it is only in some of the tanka that an indication of season is made. It cannot be said to be a characteristic of katauta, sedôka or chôka. Moreover, even in the tanka, it does not appear invariably, as in what might be called the occasional tanka of felicitation, farewell, mourning, etc. Indeed, even in the modern period the seasonal theme, as understood in haiku, is not *de rigueur* in tanka. Following is an example from the *Nihonshoki:*

> I would speak aloud
>> at the Tsutsushiro Palace
>> in Yamashiro;
> When I look at my brother
>> fain my eyes would fill with tears.[107]

Rather, as the mention or suggestion of a season appears in the early tanka, it seems to have been in some cases purely fortuitous; that is to say, the tanka names some strongly seasonal, natural object, such as blossoms, snow, and so on, but only in passing and without the natural object's becoming an integral part of the movement of the poem or being sung of for its own sake. An example is found in the *Kojiki:*

> Many clouds unfurled
>> rise at cloud-decked Izumo;
> Round your spouse to hold
>> raise many folded barriers
>> like those barriers manifold.[108]

Ebara feels that this characteristic is due in part to the inability of poets during the Kiki period to "sing of nature objectively"[109] or to appreciate natural objects for their own sake. Rather, as the following examples from the *Kojiki* will illustrate, some other motive such as allegory or pride of possession is the binding force:

> From the Sai stream
>> the clouds arise and hover;
> On Mt. Unebi
>> clamorous are the tree-leaves
>> and winds are about to blow.[110]

It is said that the Empress Jimmu sang the above song when she learned that a stepson, who lived on Mt. Unebi, planned to revolt. It is a song of warning to her three natural sons.

The second *Kojiki* song is attributed to Emperor Ojin, whose reign supposedly extended from 270 to 312. He composed it as he surveyed his holdings, perhaps from some eminence giving him a broad view; it is a song of joy in the wealth and extent of his lands:

> When I view
>   Chiba's Kazunu meadow,
> The gardens are seen
>   of ten thousand houses
>   and the best lands of the realm.[111]

Although neither of these two tanka is cited by Ebara in support of his contention that the writers of the Kiki period were unable to view nature objectively, I take it that he would reject them on the grounds that they are not poems written as insights and perceptions of the natural scenes they describe; such realizations are not the creative impulse behind the verses. Perhaps it is for some such reason that he states that "we cannot find at all elements of the seasonal theme" in the poetry of this period.[112]

He points out that in the following Manyô period, however, the natural objects mentioned in the poems have greatly increased in number as compared with those of the Kiki period: "When it comes to this period, the way Japanese poets look at nature is widened and deepened. Of course, there are many excellent poems describing natural scenes. That is, writers are able to appreciate fully the beauties of nature as subjects for literary expression."[113] Such an appreciation is of course the *sine qua non* for the development of the seasonal theme, and in poems like the following from the *Manyôshû,* the tone is quite modern as far as the use of natural objects is concerned, that is, the objects become the poem:

> While so longingly,
>   O beloved one, I wait
>   all alone for thee,
> Swaying my hut's bamboo-blind
>   gently blows the autumn wind.[114]

There is an equivalence here between feeling and image which is to mark all the greatest Japanese poetry.

The following is perhaps more completely a nature poem:

> As the jet-black night
>   deepens on the river-beach
>   shining clear and bright,
> And fringed with mallotus trees,
>   repeatedly the plover cries.[115]

Here the poet's complete attention is to the scene before him as it lives and is an actuality; the poem contains this experience; or rather, the poem *is* this event.

In spite of the inclusion of many excellent nature poems in the *Manyôshû*, however, and the fact that "we can recognize fully the concept of season"[116] in the use of natural objects as subjects for poetry, as Ebara notes, the concept itself has not come to maturity in this collection: "The seasons used in the classical way—i.e., with the natural phenomena of the four seasons holding a special position as an important element in literature—cannot yet be recognized in the Manyô period."[117] The point is especially supported by the method of classification in the *Manyôshû*. While seasonal categories are listed, they are combined with other more conventional ones. Hence, instead of "Spring Songs," there are listed "Miscellaneous Spring Songs"; instead of "Summer Songs," "Summer Love Songs."[118]

While the sense of season received no further development in the poetry written during the period between the *Manyôshû* and the *Kokinshû,* in the latter anthology we find for the first time categories for the four seasons. In this respect, it may be called one of the epoch-making works of Japanese literary history, in Ebara's words.[119] For such a classification seems to recognize the importance of natural objects as subjects for poetry in the same way as love, or congratulatory, or elegiac poems were recognized. Consequently, the actual number of nature poems has increased proportionately as compared to the number in the *Manyôshû*. Further, there are refinements in the use of such natural objects as Ebara has noted. First, although the number of such objects has become limited, that fact in itself is no indication of a weakening of the concept of the seasonal theme, but rather of a strengthening, for it seems to indicate recognition of certain strongly seasonal elements which would best convey the poetic intent: "We should note that the things in nature used as subjects of poems are more or less stabilized according to the four seasons. For example, as we count the number of subjects used in the poems in the spring section, there are not more than twenty."[120] Such stabilization is marked: "[Among the spring subjects] the nightingale, the plum, and cherry blossoms account for more than half of the poems. The rest of the objects are used only in one or two poems. That is, the most loved themes for spring are almost established."[121] In twenty-eight out of the thirty-four summer poems, the cuckoo is the subject.[122]

With such stabilization, the seasonal feelings surrounding the objects becomes more marked:

> We can notice a tendency for...the seasonal feelings and associations in regard to these objects to become gradually stabilized. In this way, the plum tree or the nightingale no longer comes to our minds [simply as a plum tree or a nightingale]. But the plum tree or the nightingale can be thought of in connection with the spring. Consequently, here we can recognize fully the basic nature of the seasonal theme in renga and haikai.[123]

However marked the feelings become, nevertheless, the full development of the seasonal values of nature objects was far from complete, due probably to the ratiocinative approach of these poets to natural phenomena; they tend to think about nature rather than to experience it. The result is an ingenious rhetoric, full of courtly conceits, as in the following examples:

> Lovely cherry trees
>   veiled by haze, do not reveal
>   the colors of their bloom,
> But the vernal mountain breeze
>   steals, at least, their sweet perfume.[124]

> Do the spring-soft showers
>   shed tears as they fall gently,
>   O blooming cherry flowers?
> None can but deplore your fair
>   petals scattering in air.[125]

To illustrate the point, Ebara has traced the classification of poems dealing with the moon from the *Kokinshû* through the *Senzaishû* (1188). It will be remembered that, in modern Japanese poetry, the moon has come to be one of the strongest seasonal themes for autumn. It can of course appear in poems dealing with other seasons, but then must be specifically qualified as a summer moon, or a spring moon; or the other natural objects within the poem must be so clearly non-autumnal that it becomes evident that the autumn moon is not being treated of. Where the moon appears without qualifications, it is an autumn theme. As previously pointed out,[126] while such a poetic convention has not been developed to any great degree in the West, it is noticeable in certain instances. For example, a rose connotes the spring; when we wish to associate it with some other season, such as the summer, we speak specifically of a "summer rose."

In the early period, Ebara finds that poems with only the moon as a subject are generally classed as miscellaneous. That is to say, the seasonal meaning of the moon has not developed at all. This is true of the *Kokinshû,* with the exception of five poems, and "the moon in these five are qualified by such phrases as the 'autumn moon' or are used together with such autumn subjects as geese."[127]

In the following anthologies, the *Shûishû* (1005) and the *Goshûishû* (1083), moon-poems are still placed in the miscellaneous section, with the exception of one in the *Goshûishû* where a moon-poem without any qualifying phrase or object to indicate the autumn is found in the autumn section. Ebara comments on this "exceptional case": "We may conjecture that originally it was accompanied by a prefatory note giving evidence that this poem was written about an autumn moon. Other poems on the moon included in the autumn section contain such qualifying phrases as 'in the autumn night.' "[128]

In the *Kinyôshû* (1127), he finds twenty-nine moon-poems in the autumn section, without any other qualifying phrases. He offers the following reasons: "The editor of the *Kinyôshû* was Toshiyori, who was a new rising poet of the period. Therefore, without imitating the *Sandaishû* [*Kokinshû, Gosenshû,* and *Shûishû*], he must have classified the poems according to the meaning of seasonal themes prevalent in his time."[129] However, the following anthology, the *Shikashû,* returned to the practice of the previous three, and it is only with the *Senzaishû* (1188) that the moon-poems were generally classified in the autumn section: "In the *Senzaishû* there are twenty-eight poems with only the moon as the theme, exactly half of which are without any prefatory notes or mention of autumn in the poem."[130] The gradual clarification of the seasonal meaning of the moon apparent in this brief survey would apply to other nature-objects also, so Ebara states. Hence, he concludes: "The way of feeling natural objects as seasonal themes gradually deepened by the end of the Heian period."[131] Furthermore, the area of such seasonal themes was expanded to take in human activities connected with the seasons, such as "pulling out irises...changing clothes"[132]—an influence of the novel in Ebara's thinking. The inclusion of such themes was to become quite important for the poetry of the following periods.

Finally, with the *Shin-Kokinshû* (1205) of the Kamakura period, we find that the emotional meanings of certain seasonal objects is so well understood that in successful tanka the object can stand alone, without explanatory remarks by the writer, as Ebara has pointed out:

> Until the *Kokinshû* period, if it was said only that an insect sings or an autumn wind blows, such phrases did not affect either the readers or writers strongly by their sad and lonely feelings. It was necessary to express such sadness or loneliness. However, during the period that followed, a so-called sense of seasonal theme was cultivated in one way or another. A feeling for the seasonal theme was combined with materials such as the voices of insects or a blowing autumn wind closely enough to evoke a feeling of sadness.[133]

While not all the tanka in the *Shin-Kokinshû* show the same degree of maturity in the development of the use of seasonal objects, the overall tendency is markedly higher than in the previous anthologies. For example, the meaningful, speaking image of the last two lines in the following famous poem is complete in itself; there is a fullness of content here that is representative of Japanese poetry at its very best:

> As I look across,
>   neither flowers nor crimson leaves
>   can be well compared
> With the little huts that stand
>   on the autumn-evening shore.[134]

The absolute equivalence between the image and the emotion attained at this time as compared to the incomplete realization of natural objects during the *Kokinshû* period is well illustrated in the following. The first example, from the *Kokinshû*, documents Ebara's statement that it was necessary to declare explicitly the emotion of the poem:

> When the moon I see
>   ah, in myriad ways how sad
>   things indeed appear;
> Yet it is not just for me
>   that the autumn tide is here.[135]

To illustrate how unpoetically the moon functions in the poem, I note that it could stand as follows almost as well as in the original; the second line could well read: "Ah, in myriad ways how *glad*."

Such a substitution is not possible in the second example, from the *Shin-Kokinshû*:

> Even to the heart
> that has long renounced the world
> loneliness is known,
> When the snipe from marshes dart
> in the deepening autumn eve.[136]

It is this overall characteristic of the *Shin-Kokinshû* that Ebara perhaps has in mind when he makes the following comment: "The most notable characteristic in [the *Shin-Kokinshû*] is that many of the poems on scenery are truly objective; in contrast with the *Kokinshû* we can hardly find any expression of personal feeling."[137]

It is not to be thought of course that, during the early period, the element of season had been analyzed and distinguished from other elements within the poem, as is true at present. When it is present, as in the tanka in the *Shin-Kokinshû*, its presence is a valid argument for its poetic justification, much along the lines that Otsuji discusses. Its inclusion is not to be attributed to a conscious, explicit poetic principle, nor even to an awareness that is properly forgotten at the creative moment; that is, that when an experience is well realized, a sense of season is necessarily a part of it as a quality of the event. Indeed, when such words, plainly indicating a season, as autumn, red leaves, or plum blossoms appear in an early tanka, the reason may be, as Asano suggests, that the poem was written on a prescribed theme for a poetry contest.[138] Various competitive amusements and games of the early period such as "matching grasses" or matching the length of grass-roots led inevitably to poetry matches: "When these contests became literary, they produced uta-awase. In uta-awase, composition on a theme was practiced, and grasses or trees were most often taken as themes (in the *Kokinshû* for example.)"[139]

The unusual popularity of uta-awase can be seen from the fact that during the later Heian period (794-1192) there were two or three occasions on which were organized *roppyakuban awase*—poetry contests of six hundred matches.[140] On these occasions twelve hundred poems would be composed on various themes; selection would be made of the most worthy. In the following Kamakura period such groups were enlarged so that three thousand poems were composed at one time. The themes on which the competing tanka were written were natural objects, love (requited, unrequited, unknown, etc.), well-known holidays, reflections on philosophical themes, etc. The greater part of the themes were natural objects.

Poetry contests on such a grand scale were of necessity well organized affairs, as is evidenced by the following description, which though extremely detailed is being included in its entirety since uta-awase play such important role in the history of Japanese poetry:

> As the name uta-awase implies, poems written on announced themes or themes given out at the time were divided into A and B groups, or into right and left groups, and were judged by judges.... Participants in an uta-awase were divided into poets of the right or the left. In the early period, in a formal contest it was usual that all the participants were not poets.... From the two groups of the right and the left a chairman was either selected or appointed to preside over the meeting. Then readers, reciters, markers, and judges were appointed or requested to act in such positions....
>
> The procedure governing the first round was as follows: The reciters of the left-hand group read the first poem. Then the other participants in the left-hand group would recite the poem in a loud voice. Then the reciters of the right-hand group would read the first poem from their group, which would be repeated in a loud voice in the same manner as before by the right-hand group. The reason why it was started from the left was that the left hand was considered to have precedence over the right. According to this belief, persons of high positions or famous poets occupied the left side. Generally speaking, the writers' names were not disclosed. The nobility, who were naturally placed in the first position on the left, used other names or called themselves simply "A lady retainer."... The first poem from the left group always won the first round.[141]

The second match would follow the same procedure and all subsequent matches were decided on merit. New matches would start from the side that had lost the previous one and, in case of a tie, would start from the left. After the second and subsequent matches, the poems were defended or attacked by both sides in an effort to win the contest; such discussions could become very heated, and although the judges' decision had been given, could continue on. There are instances when the judges were asked to resign on the grounds of poetic incompetence; the discussions themselves were written down and made public:[142] "There were many such discussions that appeared during the later Heian and early Kamakura period. Among them the most famous and magnificent was by Kenjo, written at a *roppyakuban awase* judged by Shunzei."[143]

Prior to such large contests, smaller ones were held; the first of which any record remains is the *Arimimbukyôke* Uta-awase (Poetry Contest Held at the Residence of Arihara no Yukihira) in 885.[144] Ten rounds were held, two of them on the cuckoo and eight on unmet love. The emperor himself attended the *Teiji-in* Uta-awase held in 913. In the preface to the records of this contest the affair is described: "The Emperor was attired in robes of a cedar-bark color and dark-blue trousers. The men and women on the left were dressed in red robes with a cherry-blossom design. Those on the right were in blue with a willow design. [Music was provided] and the musicians sang a song entitled 'The Sea of Ise'... Every participant received an Imperial robe as a gift."[145] Among the themes set for the eight contestants were the early spring, cherry blossoms, nightingale, the spring, summer, love, etc.

Considering, then, the great vogue of the uta-awase, it is to be supposed that many of the tanka in the *Kokinshû* and some later anthologies were composed on such occasions, as indeed the prefatory notes to those in the *Kokinshû* establish. A random glance through the autumn section of the latter reveals the following:

Poem Composed at the uta-awase held at the house of Koresada.
Poem Composed at the uta-awase held at the residence of Kisai no Miya during the Kampyo Era.[146]

In the first poem, the natural objects mentioned are autumn mist and crimson leaves; in the second, crimson maple leaves. In the spring section the following are found:

Composed at the uta-awase at the residence of Kisai no Miya during the Kampyo Era.[147]
Composed at the uta-awase held at the Teiji-in.[148]

The first spring poem mentions the plum and spring; another composed at the same poetry contest includes the spring mist and flowers. The second above listed contains the cherry blossoms.

To my mind, therefore, there is little doubt that composition on a theme as practiced in the uta-awase influenced greatly the development of the concept of the seasonal theme. First, it established natural objects as fitting and varied subjects for poetry. Secondly, it helped to stabilize the seasonal meanings of these objects.

There can be no question but that many of the poems composed on such occasions must have been trivial in the extreme, with no attempt at a poetic realization of a natural object but with the mere naming of it to conform to the rules of the contest. The poetic climate of the time is

filled with conventionality and frivolity; as Chamberlain has said: "Poets
...were no longer to draw their inspiration from their own hearts, and
from the incidents of their lives:—they were encouraged to write to
order."[149] Hence we can understand the injunction of the poet Kamo no
Chômei (*circa* 1152–1216) in his *Mumyô Shô,* a book of observations on
poetry: "A theme poem should be profound. . . . You should devote yourself wholly to looking for the profound inner spirit of the thing you are
facing; but we do not find that quality in the poems in the old anthologies. . . . In an uta-awase, among poems of about the same [stylistic] merit,
those that have the deeper insight should be judged the more excellent."[150] But with the realization of the "profound inner spirit" of the
contemplated object, there must have adhered to the poem a deep sense
of a seasonal air much as Otsuji, whom I have cited so frequently in the
foregoing pages, conceived it. Thus we can see that even in this period of
Japanese poetry, the seed for the fundamental function of the concept of
the seasonal theme is present. The practice of theme composition in an
uta-awase can be supposed to have helped to establish and clarify the
concept of the seasonal word, as the term came to be understood.

As for the development of the seasonal concept in the short renga
form, as can be imagined from the intent of such verse, not much of
significance evolved. Seasonal objects such as deer, autumn mountains,
the plum and cherry blossom appear in them, but almost no use is made
of the seasonal meanings of such material. And where some glimmering
of seasonal air is seen, its presence is almost always inadvertent. This is
hardly surprising, for the comic or witty attitude expressed in the two-
link renga is basically intellectual, while a realization of seasonal meanings
is basically intuitive. It can be safely maintained, I feel, that in this area
the short renga contributed nothing of significance.

It is in the period of the long renga that a mention of season became *de
rigueur* in the hokku or beginning verse. Why it was felt necessary to
include a seasonal element in the hokku, except as the latter here mim-
icked the tanka tradition, has not been explicitly stated by early commen-
tators. As Asano remarks, "there is no special discussion of [the seasonal
idea]" recorded in the *Tsukuba Mondô,* a collection of essays on renga
compiled around 1369, or in other writings of the time: "Judging from
the ideas concerning the season in the Abutsu period, we can suppose that
poets around the time renga became recognized in the era of Yoshimoto
Nijô must have discussed the subject quite extensively. [But] in the

Tsukuba Mondô...there is no special discussion of [the seasonal idea], nor are there any other writings giving information about it."[151] However, the conjecture that the practice of theme composition in uta-awase, in the instances where natural objects were used as themes, may have had some influence on the need for inclusion of a seasonal element in the hokku of renga does not seem impossible, for as Igarashi has pointed out, uta-awase play a great role in literary history: "Judging from the history of the development of literature, uta-awase have exerted great influence. A change in this method [of holding poetry contests] produced renga."[152] The problem that seems to have most concerned the early renga theorists was not the reasons why the seasonal element was included in the hokku, but rather the need for a correspondence between the time of composition of the poem and the season treated of in the hokku. The following well-known anecdote of Abutsu shows this preoccupation:

> When the mother of Tamesuke, called Abutsu, went down to the East, a certain person asked her for a hokku, for he wanted to compose a renga on the last day of September.
>
> > Today already
> > Has become the very end
> > Of autumnal days.
>
> Thus she composed a hokku and gave it to him; and people made a hundred-chained verse. On the next day they gathered once more and asked her for another verse; she wrote a hokku and showed it to them.
>
> > Today is also
> > The first, and the beginning
> > Of the wintertime.
>
> And she said: Tanka's theme is its hokku; and renga uses hokku as its theme. Consequently the time when the renga is composed should not differ from the seasonal tide [expressed in the poem].[153]

As we have seen, the use of seasonal objects as themes in tanka composed in poetry contests was extremely popular and widespread. Abutsu, then, seems to feel that as the hokku provides the theme for the long renga, it must include one of the functions of the theme for uta-awase—namely the season. So we note that she specifically denotes the day of one renga party as the last day of autumn; the next day is the first day of winter, as she sings in her second hokku, which will then set the motif for the entire renga.

We can see how the practice of uta-awase might easily be carried over into renga composition by visualizing the actual scene of a group come together to compose a long linked verse. Following is a description of the early thirteenth century:

> Fellows of the "Mushin Shu" gathered to the East side and fellows of the "Ushin Shu" gathered to the West side. . . . A screen was placed to keep them separated and each party made renga until the folded paper was used up. After removing the screen, they gathered together.[154]

Since the purpose is cooperative rather than competitive as in the uta-awase, and since the hokku must provide a sufficiently grand and profound background to justify the lengthy work that is to follow, it was apparently felt that the seasonal tide which they actually and immediately experienced as a group fulfilled their needs.

During the early period of the long renga, which would include the time covered in Abutsu's anecdote given above,[155] it is probable that the seasonal concept in the fuller meaning developed in the tanka of the *Shin-Kokinshû* (1205) was not yet operative in the renga, as Ebara implies: "According to the anecdote of Abutsu, it is clear that hokku was considered good when the season in it was not different from that of the time in which the hokku is composed. This means merely that the seasonal element should not differ from the time of composition."[156] However, in the *Renri Hishô* of Yoshimoto Nijô, dated 1349, we have what is perhaps the earliest full discussion of the seasonal element in renga; and it is significant that his position is not different from that of the master Sôgi almost one hundred fifty years later, making possible the conjecture that there was an accepted poetic tradition in regard to this area of the renga.

Nijô first states the need for a correspondence between the time of composition and the time indicated in the hokku of renga much as Abutsu maintained: "We regret very much that the object named in the hokku does not agree with the seasonal tide."[157] He then cites examples of the objects most appropriate to given seasons, listing them by month. However, he points out that the list by no means exhausts the possibilities and that there is only one criterion for the use of seasonal elements: "We should not feel constrained if we [go beyond this list], so long as we are in harmony with the seasonal tide."[157] The criterion is apparently so important that he has posited it before: "It is good to be in harmony with the objects of nature."[158] His next statements are interesting, and I feel that while Yoshimoto Nijô does not develop his reasoning completely, it is along the same lines as Sôgi's: "When in cities, we should not name fields or mountains. Generally we should refrain from using what is not there. Scenes like the following should be avoided in the city: a deer crying in the garden."[158]

Why then must there be a correspondence between the time of composition and the season mentioned in the hokku of renga, according to this poet? Because such correspondence will help the poet to "be in harmony with the objects of nature," or in the terms I have used in earlier portions of this book, will enable him to realize fully the quality of the scene before him and—simply—enable him to create poetry.

A second function of the mention of season in the hokku of renga has been noted by Asano: "Aside from the question of rendering season in the hokku of renga, the requirement to state a particular time came from the need to show clearly the date that the renga was composed. That is to say, what was announced by the theme of or introduction to a waka was to be done by the hokku."[159] Let us examine some typical tanka titles taken from the *Kokinshû:*[160]

1. Composed at the uta-awase held at the residence of Kisai no Miya during the Kampyô Era.
2. Composed at an uta-awase held in autumn.
3. Composed at the uta-awase held at the house of Koresada.
4. On the beginning of the New Year.
5. Looking at the falling snow.
6. Composed on the sixtieth birthday of Sanzen Fujiwara.
7. On the seventieth anniversary of Bishop Henjô.
8. Composed on my return. (A love poem)
9. In reply. (A love poem)
10. Composed and sent to an acquaintance who went to Sumiyoshi.
11. Composed at the base of the waterfall on my visit to Ryumon.

The last two titles are taken from the so-called "Miscellaneous Section," which contains what in English might be called occasional poetry.

From this cursory view of tanka titles, it seems clear that while not all of them indicate the time or season of composition, a large number of them do. They tend to be quite long and explanatory, describing either the subject or the occasion for which the poem is composed.

In contrast the titles of renga often simply give the number of links in it and the place where it was composed. For example, the great masterpiece of the classical renga, *Minase Sangin Hyakuin,* whose title can be translated *A Poem of One Hundred Chains Composed by Three*

Poets at Minase, is typical. Another title, *Oharano Jikka Senku,* can be rendered *One Thousand Verses Composed on Ten Flowers at Oharano.*[161] Then there is the *Shômyôji Renga,* or *Renga Composed at the Shômyôji Temple.*[162] The scope and intent of the renga is of course much larger than that of the tanka and it is perhaps difficult to give a concise summary of it in a title as can be done for the tanka. Perhaps this is part of what Asano means by his statement that "what was announced by the theme of or introduction to a waka was to be done by the hokku."

Another strong case can be made I feel for the reason for the persistence of the convention in the hokku of renga, when we remember that the renga was usually a composition by a group. This in itself precludes such unshared experiences as that at the waterfall of Ryumon or of the parting of a friend for Sumiyoshi, tanka titles previously cited from the *Kokinshû.* As has been previously noted, the convention used of selecting as a theme not only the season but the day itself of composition ties together the group and provides the motive for their effort.

Ebara conjectures that the reason not only for the correspondence between the time of composition and the season mentioned in the hokku, but the inclusion of a seasonal theme itself is to be traced to the origins of renga as a "spontaneous amusement" and to the composition of hokku separately on a given theme as was recorded in the *Sazame Goto* of 1461:[163]

> Why is it that there is this relationship between the seasons and the hokku of renga? This is a problem that should be completely investigated. As for the reason, first of all I would like to point out that the origins of renga lie in their nature as spontaneous amusement. The renga that began as a side amusement in the waka meetings gradually developed into songs of fifty or one hundred chains, and renga assumed its own identity aside from waka. Even when not composed as a mere game, still the hokku itself retained vestiges of a play-nature. But since hokku composition as a game did not take place on well-defined occasions, the subject selected must be interesting enough for the participants, regardless of the time. In order to select a subject, the best method is the one described by Abutsu, i.e., to compose a verse according to the season when such composition took place.[164]

Whatever the basis for the practice, that it was followed can be clearly established by both the *Tsukubashû* (1356) and the *Shinsen Tsukubashû* (1495). The twentieth volume of the first collection contains only hokku, which all have some sort of seasonal reference, though they are not classified under seasonal headings. If they are grouped by their seasonal themes, the following tabulation can be made:[165]

Spring — 49	Autumn — 27
Summer — 22	Winter — 21

Hokku in the *Shinsen Tsukubashû* appear in the nineteenth and twentieth volumes, and can be grouped as follows:[166]

Spring — 88	Autumn — 77
Summer — 38	Winter — 46

Undoubtedly such a convention, like all poetic practices, can become dull and stereotyped. Indeed, there seems to be an air of the ironic and weary in Abutsu's two hokku, almost as if she were mocking the practice. Asked to compose verses on two consecutive days, she complies, throwing the group a bare seasonal fact, so to speak:

> Today already
> Has become the very end
> Of autumnal days.

And the next day, she notes, is the next day:

> Today is also
> The first, and the beginning
> Of the wintertime.[167]

As Ebara states, the seasonal element "has not yet been recognized as the important element of a poem" during the Abutsu period.[168] In the following two hokku of two of the earliest long renga extant, there seems to be a dependence on the intellectual content of the seasonal objects as that was established in the tanka by the period of the *Shin-Kokin-shû*.[169] Certainly the seasonal content of neither the moon nor the cuckoo is realized. The first hokku is from a renga composed on September 13, 1332:

> The moon's for autumn—
> And even in the autumn
> Famous is tonight's.[170]

The second is taken from a renga composed on April 25, 1355:

> Famous is the name;
> Surpassed by none in singing
> —Hototogisu![171]

From the *Tsukubashû* is another hokku in which the convention appears awkward:

> A hokku of renga composed at the house on the day of the setting-in of spring while the year is not yet changed.

> > Grasses come out too
> > And the tree-buds; the spring rain
> > Is falling today![172]

The technique here of piling on three typical aspects of the first day of spring in an effort to establish the time and the season as required seems as non-poetic as an announcement of the calendar date. The details are not fused; they are not immovable as they would be in a realized poem. Almost any other details can be substituted for those given. The effect is one of a mechanical carrying out of a rule for hokku making.

It is with Sôgi (1421-1502) that we get a fuller exploration of the function of the seasonal theme in hokku. Sound observations on it were not lacking in the earlier periods, and they will also be given in the following material to demonstrate how Sôgi was in the main stream of Japanese poetic thought. Sôgi's thought is, however, enhanced by the fortunate fact that during his lifetime the classical attitude came to full flower.

As early as the beginning of the thirteenth century Kamo no Chômei had given a sound definition of poetic realization: "You should devote yourself wholly to looking for the profound inner spirit of the thing you are facing."[173] As previously pointed out, such seems to be the meaning of Yoshimoto Nijô's statement: "It is good to be in harmony with the objects of nature."[174] With Sôgi, almost a hundred years later, we find much the same injunction: "In composing hokku you should make it your principle to go with the seasonal tide, whether it be spring, summer, autumn, or winter."[175] These three statements seem to emphasize the need for a profound interaction between the poet and his subject, for a one-ness between them that can result in the artistic insight much as Croce and Dewey insisted upon. Kamo no Chômei explicitly denounces the mechanical handling of a theme: "We do not find the quality [of profundity] in the poems in the old anthologies, but this lack is overlooked because of the excellence of their style. . . . But we should not follow such examples."[176] Rhetoric or verbal glitter alone is no substitute for the profound inner spirit of the contemplated object, he seems to mean. And when we recall the genteel prettiness of some of the tanka of the *Kokinshû,* his meaning seems to become clear.[177]

In Sôgi's *Azuma Mondô* (1470) he discusses his concept of the seasonal reference, for as Asano notes: "Sôgi. . . . wrote the book *Azuma Mondô* to discuss the seasonal question."[178] In his introductory remarks to the episode of the nun Abutsu previously given, Sôgi specifically states the necessity for a correspondence between the seasonal reference in the hokku and the season during which it is composed: "To the question of how hokku are composed, I would reply: the important thing to keep in mind in hokku-making is that the seasonal element used must be one that comes neither before nor after [the time in which the hokku is composed]."[179] In *Hakuhatsushû,* published sixty-one years after his death, he reiterates his position and states further that "going along with the seasonal tide" necessitates the correspondence: "In composing hokku you should make it your principle to go with the seasonal tide, whether it be spring, summer, autumn or winter. Between the seasonal element in your hokku and the season in which you composed the poem, there should be no difference at all."[180] It is interesting to note that Yoshimoto Nijô, in maintaining the same position, uses indeed the same terms in Japanese for the phrase "seasonal tide": "We regret very much the object named in the hokku does not agree with the seasonal tide. . . . It is good to be in harmony with the objects of nature."[181] It is not then as a mere recording of the date of composition that Sôgi advocates inclusion of the seasonal reference. His call is for profundity, not the calendar: "We must always attempt to attain composure and a profound air through the flowers, birds, snow, or the moon [that appear in our poems]."[182] As previously pointed out, Sôgi, one of the greatest poets of the long renga form, was not here enunciating revolutionary principles but those which had made the seasonal element so tenacious a part of the hokku to his day. For Kamo no Chômei too, in rejecting poems with only verbal expertise, calls for profundity: "In an uta-awase, among poems of about the same [stylistic] merit, those that have the deeper insight should be judged the more excellent."[183]

With all three of these men, then, the call for "profundity" or insight is linked with the necessity for going "with the seasonal tide" or devoting oneself to "looking for the profound inner spirit of the thing." It is not too farfetched to conclude that for them, then, the inclusion of the sea-sonal reference in the hokku and its correspondence with the time of composition was a means for attaining the realized vision that is a poem.

Sôgi, in striving for an exact correspondence, declares that even for a single season, such as spring, we must differentiate subtly; in the following quotation he is referring to the lunar calendar months: "Even among the things of spring in general, we can count things that belong only to January, or only to February, and also only to March."[184] Accordingly he lists by months the appropriate themes:

JANUARY:	frost, willow, nightingale, skylark
FEBRUARY:	ploughing the rice fields (for March also)
	easterly winds (until March)
MARCH:	peach (for March 3 only)
APRIL:	change of garments (for April 1 only)
MAY:	iris (for May 5 only)

The above is only a part of the list he makes and is included in the *Hakuhatsu-shû*.[185] In the same volume, he calls the meticulous noting of seasonal changes a sign of sincerity: "In composing hokku one must be careful about the seasonal element. For this reason a beginner when he composes a hokku must be truly sincere. There is no greater secret than to see things as they truly are, whether it be the scenery of a mountain, river, lake, etc."[186] Although the advice might be construed as an insistence on realism and exact copying, taken with his other observations, it seems rather to stress the need for devotion to the contemplated object, a knowing of it in all its particularity much as the occidental philosophers quoted heretofore envisioned. Thus Asano declares of Sôgi: "Sôgi is the poet who established definitely the necessity for having the seasonal element in renga. Details are clear in the quotations from *Hakuhatsu-shû*."[187]

Sôgi's list is among the first of the many lists of seasonal objects which were later compiled. Some of the representative ones were the following: *Hanabigusa* (1636) by Rippo, containing approximately six hundred and fifty items; *Yama no I* (1648) by Kigin, with approximately one thousand and fifty words; the *Haikai Saijiki* of 1803 with twenty-six hundred items; and the *Shinko Haikai Saijiki* of 1927 with approximately forty three hundred entries.[188] As can be noted, the tendency has been for such dictionaries of seasonal themes and words to grow larger and to contain ever increasingly subtle classifications. Following is an early example from Teitoku's *Haikai Gosan* (1651) on the word *wakaba* or "young leaves": "There are two views on this word: one makes it a spring theme; another makes it a summer theme. If flowers come out with the young leaves, then they may belong to the spring. Generally speaking, the term belongs to summer. According to the writings in the new rules, all verses [in which *wakaba* are mentioned] with no flowers in them are for the summer. These are tree leaves. Grass leaves should be for the spring."[189] This type of legislation continues even in the modern period and Shiki himself, the great reformer of the haiku during the nineteenth century, discussed seasonal terms in much the same manner: "The longest day is around the summer solstice, but in haiku *hinaga* [a long day] is a spring theme. The longest night is around the winter solstice, but in haiku *yonaga* [a long night] is an autumnal theme. . . . They should be used for spring and for autumn respectively, not for other seasons."[190]

As much abused as such compilations are by the amateur or non-poetical writer, who of course selects a theme from a dictionary much as a definition might be looked up in Webster's, they may be regarded as originating from the kind of observation of nature which Sôgi and Kamo no Chômei advocated. Furthermore, it must be kept in mind that poets in Japan are not only writers but teachers as well, with their schools and followers; the educational use of the seasonal dictionaries is of course plain, though perhaps their absolute poetic value is questionable. It is noteworthy that Bashô, with his single-minded insistence that the poet's character and purity only could produce good haiku, did not compile a dictionary of seasonal items. Although his followers compiled his oral instructions to them in such books as *Nijûgokajô* (1694), which contain certain classifications of seasonal themes, Bashô's final word is for reasonableness in the matter: "If it is clearly winter or summer from the meaning of the verse, there is no need for discussion. Too much consideration of the words used is not desirable; consider them from a reasonable point of view."[191] The master poet seems to be more interested in the insight itself and not in the hairsplitting wrangling over words as such.

With Sôgi, then, it may be considered that the groundwork for a fruitful and meaningful utilization of the seasonal element in hokku had been laid; he insisted on a correspondence between the time when the hokku was written and the seasonal element in the hokku as a means for experiencing a true insight which could result in profound poetry.

In the period following Sôgi, profundity and depth of insight in the renga was discussed in another enlightening manner. The concept of *hon-i*—"the heart of things"—was advanced to justify the need for an increasing minuteness in the observations on the seasons. An especially full discussion is recorded in the *Renga Shihô Shô* of 1585 by Shôha Nomura. Yoshio Yamada, the greatest living authority on the renga, has commented on the concept as follows:

> Then what is *hon-i?* *Hon-i* exists in the phrases and the whole air of the poem.... [As is stated in the *Shihô-Shô*], "There is an element of so-called *hon-i* in renga. Even though there are heavy rains and storms in spring, we should see in such rains and winds something quiet and tranquil. Even if we feel that a spring day is short, still the *hon-i* of spring includes length and balminess." This means that the *hon-i* of spring is something peaceful, tranquil, and balmy. Consequently when the spring appears in a link in renga, a spring-like feeling based on the *hon-i* of spring should be expressed in the phrases and atmosphere of the poem.[192]

The concept of *hon-i* serves to point out the difference between tanka and renga, which illuminates the essential nature of both forms and serves to clarify the meaning of *hon-i* itself:

> The tanka attitude toward nature is different from that of renga in its import. In renga, the poet is to write not only about the season or seasonal objects as they are or to grasp them as they are and to stop there, but also to go much deeper into the heart of the essence [of these objects]. In regard to the seasons, and the objects in the seasons as well as to human activities, there is a teaching concerning the *hon-i* of them.... For example, if we say spring, its *hon-i* lies in the point of its peacefulness and balminess.... If we speak of the summer night, shortness is its *hon-i*. Thus, to ascertain the exact nature of the seasons and the things of the seasons, and using it to compose a link is the aim [of renga]. In addition, it is taught that with this understanding, we should appreciate the verses.... In renga and among those who were interested in renga art, it was considered the most important element.[193]

Of course a sense of *hon-i* does occur in tanka, but there is no consciousness of its all-important necessity: "To go into the heart of things and to grasp the essence of the seasons, seasonal objects, and human activities is not wholly absent in tanka. But even when such aims were present, they were realized only so far as the skill and character of the poet concerned [would reach]. Generally speaking, the teaching [of *hon-i*] was not upheld as part of tanka art."[194] Why such a deeper insight into nature was demanded for renga in contrast to the tanka can be found, I feel, in the whole intent of renga as a poetic form. That intent can well be compared to the effect of a well unified picture scroll or to a piece of music, as Yamada says: "A whole renga from the visual point of view can be compared to a picture scroll; from the auditory, it can be likened to a piece of music. . . . Its beauty is based on the harmony and changes between the links, and lies in the entire accord arising from the dramatic contrasts and resolutions, the largo and allegro of the whole poem."[195]

Just as music is commonly felt to be the most intuitive of the arts— being divorced from actual reality as it is usually known and experienced —so we can consider that renga is the most intuitive of the poetic forms that the Japanese evolved. As previously noted, there is no attempt to deal consecutively or at great length with any single given subject.[196] Each verse is linked to the immediately preceding one and may be completely unconnected with any other in a precise way, but is in a successful renga immovably connected within the whole poem. Where the unity of the poem then does not arise from any rational "thought" within it, but depends wholly on deeper, intuitive connections such as in music, the absolute insistence on the quality of *hon-i* is, I feel, understandable. The concept of *hon-i* is, then, the basis for all the linking within a renga.

Perhaps because renga is an art form that uses words and because we normally expect words to be used in part at least to explain or delineate relationships, it is difficult to accomodate ourselves to a world where words name objects but do not deal explicitly with the relationships between them. The relationships are there, for each link is related to the preceding one and in another sense to all of the others, but words are not used to express them. They are indicated in another fashion. They are indicated intuitively as the *hon-i* of the object named in one verse is linked to the *hon-i* of the object named in another.

I would venture to conjecture also that it is again precisely because in one sense renga is such an amorphous form that so formidable a hedge of rules was built about it. At any rate, it is possible to realize, I think, why certain verses were made to contain certain natural objects. Can we imagine a long picture scroll in which the moon or mountains are depicted in every other section? The effect would be as unrewarding in painting as in the renga. The intent of renga is satisfyingly illuminated, I feel, by the concept of *hon-i*.

Sôgi's pregnant suggestions however were ignored by the succeeding age, when toward the end of the Muromachi era the long renga was superseded by the humorous renga or *haikai no renga,* with Sôkan and

Moritake as its foremost exponents. As has been previously noted, the latter form was characterized by its amusing and witty conceits and by a use of colloquial language and freedom in subject matter.[197] The independence of and special importance attached to the beginning verse carried over from the previous period and the practice of writing hokku apart from the rest of the verses of renga became even stronger than before. The hokku and more particularly, the seasonal element in it also shared the characteristics of the whole poem. The seasonal element in particular lost the direction toward seriousness pointed out by Sôgi and became a peg for the ingenious conceit. The following well-known hokku of Sôkan's will illustrate the point:

> If only we could
> Add a handle to the moon
> It would make a good fan![198]

Of the poem Henderson observes that it is "hardly real haiku—or real poetry even though it does suggest the perfect fullness of the moon and the cool of a summer night after a hot day. The reason that it is not haiku is that it is not even meant to express or to evoke any real emotion."[199] The seasonal word in this hokku is of course the moon, but any attempt to utilize its seasonal content is lacking. How far this attitude strays from Sôgi's injunction toward profundity or sincerity in observing the scene before one! The intent of the poet is of course quite different from Sôgi's, for, as Chamberlain has remarked, "almost all of his [Sôkan's] compositions verge on the comic."[200] The comic of course is an intellectual attitude rather than an intuitive one, and even in his more serious work, Sôkan betrays his bent:

> If it had no call,
> The heron and the snow
> Would indeed be one.[201]

Those of Sôgi's thought might find the first line antipoetical, for it is hardly a part of the poet's realization of the scene before him; it is rather the poet's thought about the scene, not the scene. Consequently the poem as a single whole is not consecrated to a realization of a winter scene, and the seasonal elements of heron and snow are once more merely "used" by the poet.

A final example from Sôkan's work as commented on and translated by Chamberlain will perhaps be sufficient. Again, if it is remembered how evocatively poetic the call of the frog has been in Japanese classical poetry, the distance Sôkan travelled from it can be measured more accurately. As Chamberlain says, the following poem compares "not inaptly the posture of the frog to that which a Japanese assumes when squatting respectfully, with his hands stretched out on the mats to address a superior:–'Oh! the frog, with its hands on the floor, lifting up (its voice in) song!' "[202] Within classical Japanese poetry, the singing of frogs is associated with a feeling of sweet quietude; and in the windless, hazy, moonlit night, its cry is associated with the happiness of country life, especially when the cry is heard in the distance. These characteristic feelings associated with the frog in spring do not arise from the above hokku. There is no sense of season in it, for the poet merely employed the frog to conform to the rule of including a seasonal element in his hokku. When the usage of seasonal words comes to a level like this, there is no poetic justification for their place in hokku.

This trend, bad as it was, continued for the next hundred years or so, as observed by Henderson:

> Haiku went from bad to worse, the making of seventeen syllable verses finally becoming little more than a parlor game in which the authors spent their time on tortured ingenuities. For instance, the foremost poet of the early Tokugawa days, Teitoku (d. 1653), wishing to celebrate a New Year's Day which happened to be the beginning of the "cow" year, wrote as follows:
>
>
>
> This morning, how
> Icicles drip!—Slobbering
> Year of the Cow!
>
>
>
> This is cleverer than it sounds in translation, for "taruru tsurara" is onomato-poetic, and "taruru" also has the meaning of "hang down." But it is trick work, emphatically "not haiku," and one can understand why even the gentle Bashô referred to verses of this sort as "Teitoku's slobber."[203]

Icicles is of course the seasonal word, and in itself has poetic values, keenly suggesting a sense of winter—none of which is utilized in the poem.

Henderson's suggestion that such poetry is "trick work" brings to mind a characteristic of Japanese poetry that seems to have persisted as a leitmotif even during the periods presently remembered as classical and that during such periods as above described emerged as the dominant tone. Such an alternation of the serious and frivolous has characterized Japanese poetry throughout its history as Asano has noted.[204] The similarity in tone between Teitoku's poem and the poems included in the tenth volume of the *Kokinshû* seems to me unmistakable. In that volume, in the section entitled "Names of Objects" can be found examples of what are emphatically "trick work," in which seasonal objects figure with no use made of their seasonal meanings. For example, in a tanka by Tsurayuki entitled *Ominaeshi,* the name of a flower, the first syllable in each line of the tanka "spells out" *ominaeshi (patrinia scabiosaefolia).*[205] Another example is to be found in the tanka captioned *Sumomonohana,* the damson plum, by the same poet, where the title is hidden, so to speak, within the poem—"...ugui*su mo mono wa* naga-mete...."[206] As can be seen, the italicized syllables contain the title. (There is a phonetic change in the reading of the syllable *ha* to *wa* within the poem.) The play element within Japanese poetry has a long tradition and at times has vitiated its more serious aspects as during the period under discussion to an alarming degree.

After the period of Sôkan and Moritake, there were no poets of note until Teitoku (1571–1653), who exercised considerable influence in his day, as can be seen in the partial list of his school which follows: "Year after year haikai in a definite form prevailed not only in the capital and its suburbs but also in various provinces. Among the many students [of Teitoku] were the Seven Wise Men—Chikashige Nonoguchi (Rippo), Shigeyori Matsunaga (Ishû), Seibu Yamamoto, Seishô Yasuhara (Tei-shitsu), Kigin Kitamura, Baisei Takase, Seiyû Miyagawa (Shôken)."[207] (Names indicated in parentheses are pen-names.) As previously pointed out, with Teitoku haikai itself became as complex as renga had ever been, a characteristic that applied to the seasonal element also, as Ebara has pointed out: "In the book on haikai rules by the people of the Teitoku school the rules are the same as those on renga.... The rules and studies in regard to the seasonal element...became even more minute and numerous than in the case of renga."[208] The school was not without its merits, in spite of its slobbering cows. Indeed, one of Teitoku's follow-ers, Teishitsu, composed a hokku much admired by Bashô, which is given in Henderson's translation:

> "Oh......!"
> That's all—upon the blossom-covered
> Hills of Yoshino![209]

The modern age, having undoubtedly benefited through the experience of Bashô's poetry, finds fault with the hokku in an interesting way, as Chamberlain reports: "Aeba Kôson, an ingenious modern critic, has pointed out a flaw in the verse:—it is not characteristic enough. *Mutatis*

mutandis, the same words might be applied to other unique scenes. . . .
[For example, we can substitute] Fuji with its snows for Yoshino with its
flowers."[210] The modern critic's view that the verse "is not characteristic
enough" is a position certainly akin to my contention that in realized
poetry, all elements in it are immovable. No substitutions can be made.
Such a quality belongs only to the deeply and genuinely realized insight.

As previously pointed out,[211] in revolt against the static conventions of
the Teitoku school and in search for some newer source of poetic inspiration, the succeeding group, the Danrin, was formed at Edo under the
leadership of Sôin. The most famous member was probably Saikaku, the
novelist. Their chief aim was to bring a new spirit into their work to free
themselves from the mannerisms long upheld by the Teitoku group as
the standard for haikai. The non-traditional, irregular form evolved by
the freedom-loving spirit of the Danrin poets must have been revolutionary and inspiring to younger poets. To the eyes of the poets and
critics of the older school[212] it must have appeared shocking, unlearnt,
and unpoetic, much as did the free-verse created under similar circumstances some thirty years ago in America and England. The poetry of the
Danrin school, judging from the entire history of haikai, is probably
something that could not be avoided. It was a part of the growth of
haikai—a product of the growing pains felt and experienced by the
Danrin poets without which the Bashô school itself could not have
developed as it did. It was a debt explicitly acknowledged by Bashô, as
previously indicated.[213]

Up to this period, the form used for hokku tended to be quite regular,
being generally the usual 5–7–5 pattern. However, with the experimental
spirit of the Danrin school, their new manner of expression and their
new attitude brought a change in the rhythmic patterns of all three
lines, as Asano concludes from a survey of their hokku: "Various haiku
forms that we have not seen much up to this period begin to appear at
this time. . . . The irregular rhythms appearing in the first line are comparatively numerous. Next are those poems in which all three lines are
irregular. Irregularities appearing in the last line may seem to be less, but
I find them comparatively great. Irregularities in the second line are
few. Poems with second line irregularities tend to have irregular rhythms
in the last line also."[214] However, the verses of Sôin, the leader of the
school, tend to conform to the older, established pattern: "Since Sôin is
the leader who initiated the haiku of irregular rhythms, in his poetry

verses with irregular lines are not lacking. However, when we see the general trend, the irregularities tend to occur for the most part in the first and second lines, and the verse as a whole appears to retain the older 5–7–5 rhythm. Furthermore, in regard to this point, Sôin may have had a certain degree of classicism and judgment."[215]

Not only in the freedom of their form, but in their other techniques also, the Danrin school sought new poetic ground. Their aim was above all to be shocking, as Chamberlain puts it: "The only question was as to who should express the most farfetched ideas in the most unexpected words. Sometimes it was a clever literary allusion,—a Confucian maxim, perhaps, masquerading in modern Japanese guise;—sometimes an astounding exaggeration; at others something new in the mere phrasing,—a horribly vulgar word, or else a solemnly classical one,—anything in short, provided that the effect was warranted to startle."[216] As is to be expected, when novelty was thus the end-all of poetic endeavor, the seasonal element in hokku became all too often merely an instrument toward this end. Some of the more tiresome examples are given by Chamberlain:

> Did it but sing, the butterfly
> Might have to suffer in a case.[217]

> The wild geese in the firmament,—
> These are Dutch letters sideways stretching.[218]

As Chamberlain points out concerning the last, the mention of the exotically foreign way of writing across the page rather than vertically, as in Japanese, would be a daring novelty as a subject for a hokku.

It is needless to point out that, in each of the examples given above, there is an attempt at cleverness that results only in triviality. Such seasonal elements as the butterfly or wild geese are used only to make an ingenious point. Even in one of Sôin's most admired haiku, the element of one-ness with the scene he contemplates seems to me lacking; in the following verse, after all, it is not the dew drops that hold his attention, but rather his thoughts on them. The translation is Chamberlain's:

> Lacking in all discernment as
> To where they light are the white dews.[219]

The verse can be interpreted as illustrating Sôin's observation on the grand dispassionateness of nature: however beautiful the dew may be, it falls everywhere—not only to enhance the loveliness of flowers or blossoms. The intent of the verse is great, but the phrase "Lacking in all discernment" is too explicit to be poetic. When the reader can so clearly separate the poet's "thought" from the objects mentioned in the poem is that not always fatal to the poetic illusion? It is much as if we were to have explained to us the trickery behind the magician's astounding deeds. The magic departs.

It should be pointed out that Sôin in his later years, apparently appalled by the excesses of his followers, gave up haikai and returned to the writing of renga.[220] Such a return was of course foreshadowed in his handling of the problems of the new rhythms of the Danrin school, as that is described by Asano.[221] At his best, he reaches that still point in haiku where the image alone speaks:

> In my scooping hands
> The leaves of the oak tree move
> In the crystal spring.[222]

It is interesting to speculate as to the reasons why the beginning verse of haikai retained the seasonal element, especially when it is remembered that haikai itself was a revolt against the classical renga which had established the seasonal convention. Curiously enough, however, the use of the seasonal element continued in the hokku of comic renga in general throughout its history. Perhaps the reason for its retention can be found in the fact that through it, a light satirical effect can be produced through mocking the classical connotations of such themes as the moon or the frog. For example, the moon suggested in the classical renga the harvest moon—sere, serious, and sometimes provoking a pleasing melancholy, but in the hands of Sôkan, it becomes the nexus for light, refined humor:

> If only we could
> Add a handle to the moon
> It would make a good fan![223]

The humor of course is deepened through the remembered classical connotations for the word "moon."

It is only with Bashô (1644–94) that Japanese poetry returns to the seriousness and grandeur of intent of the earlier period. And it is again with Bashô that the seasonal element returns to the conception that

Sôgi established, realizing its deepest meanings.* We need only to consider the first poem he is said to have written in the true style:

> On a withered bough
> A crow alone is perching;
> Autumn evening now.

This poem has been dealt with at length in the preceding pages.[224] Here in it we have all the profundity that Sôgi called for, the insight of Kamo no Chômei and the "profound inner spirit" he named as essential to the making of poetry. That Bashô himself recognized in Sôgi an expression of artistic intent he could make his own is born out in the following quotation: "Saigyô in waka, Sôgi in renga, Sesshû in painting, Rikyû in the tea ceremony—what runs through them is one."[225] Ebara's comment clarifies Bashô's meaning: "The spirit that underlies the basis of all art must be one."[226] Nor was it only Sôgi's classicism that Bashô found meaningful, as Ebara further points out: "The relationship between Bashô and Saigyô, and between Bashô and Sôgi is more congenial than the classical spirit [which it is] commonly recognized [that they share]."[227] What they did share, it seems to me, is a concept of the fundamental basis of the artistic process. For example, Sôgi's instruction to "go along with the seasonal tide"[228] is comparable I feel to Bashô's injunction on the role that nature can play for the poet: "Follow nature and return to nature."[229] Sôgi's instruction not to strive for an effect, but to let it arise naturally from the perception is explicit in the following: "When a beginner composes a hokku he should not try to use an outstanding theme, whether it is of spring, summer, autumn, or winter. The reason is that such things as flowers in the spring and the moon in autumn [i.e., the conventional seasonal themes] will come out naturally in the scenery you create in the hokku."[230] That is to say, Sôgi advises that grandiosity or unusualness of subject matter or seasonal theme will not create great or unusual poetry; rather, the theme alone is not to be the initiating force of the poem nor its objective. The above advice would have struck an answering chord in Bashô, for he says: "The style which is graceful and has one center of interest is refined. That which has

---

* The life and works of Bashô are too well known to need recounting here. The English reader is referred to both Chamberlain (*op. cit.,* pp. 176–93) and Henderson (*op. cit.,* pp. 18–36) for appreciative accounts of his poetry and life.

artistic twists and deals with strange things comes next."[231] The idea both men seem to have shared about that aspect of haiku we are analyzing here is that in the seasonal theme a valid and essential aesthetic principle is found: aesthetic realization of nature is impossible without cognizance of the season.

With Bashô, we go even further than this into that area John Gould Fletcher perhaps had in mind when he remarked that the haiku, "if understood in connection with the Zen doctrine they illuminate, make of poetry an act of life."[232] For with Bashô, communion with nature was motivated by a life-long search for what Chamberlain has termed "enlightenment" as that was understood in Zen.[233] Unless his position is understood against the deeply contemplative, religious background that was his, advice such as the following cannot fully be understood: "Let your verse resemble a willow branch struck by a light shower, and sometimes waving in the breeze."[234] For Bashô, nature was a living master, whose breath was the sense of season, and through which he discovered the "unchanging truth in fleeting form."[235]

That truth, to attain which was the quest of Zen, might be found anywhere, as Daisetz Suzuki has explained: "It can be anything from an insignificant blade of grass growing on the roadside to the golden-colored Buddha body ten feet six in height."[236] It could be found in a dragonfly, as Bashô tried to teach Kikaku, one of his followers:

One autumn day when Bashô and one of his ten disciples, Kikaku, were going through a rice field, Kikaku composed a haiku on a red dragonfly that caught his fancy. And he showed the following haiku to Bashô:

> Take a pair of wings
> From a dragonfly, you would
> Make a pepper pod.

"No," said Bashô, "that is not a haiku. You kill the dragonfly. If you want to compose a haiku and give life to it, you must say:

> "Add a pair of wings
> To a pepper pod, you would
> Make a dragonfly."[237]

It is perhaps unnecessary to point out that the truth which Bashô sought in haiku was not quite the simple moralistic teachings which later ages have sometimes ascribed to him; it may have contained those teachings, but was not limited to them. For example, Chamberlain's commentary on the following poem by Bashô is representative:

> The mallow-flower by the road
> Was eaten by a [passing] horse.

...the moral lesson conveyed in those few words was too obvious:—"Had not the mallow pressed forward into public view, the horse would never have devoured it. Learn, then, ambitious man, to be humble and retiring. The vulgar yearning for fame and distinction can lead nowhither but to misery, for it contradicts the essential principle of ethics."[238]

Truth, which could include such "moral lessons," was for Bashô the need to cultivate a soul that could add wings to a pepper pod, or in his grandest poetry, could make an autumnal crow contain the universe, or equate the sound of a frog jumping into an old pond with the quietude of an enlightened soul. For this, Bashô insisted upon the need for the heart in poetry, as he understood the term in Zen: "Verses composed by some are over-composed and lose the naturalness that comes from the heart. What comes from the heart is good. We should not prefer those that depend on rhetoric."[239] And in a letter to Banzan, a friend, he wrote: "I hear of your enthusiasm for haikai which pleases me. It is more important to write haikai from one's heart than to be a facile expert. There are many who write verses, but few who keep to the heart's rules."[240] Bashô's great contemporary, Onitsura, too expressed similar thoughts: "When I think occasionally about an excellent verse, I find no artistic touch in its phrasing, or display of colorfulness in its air; only the verse flows out effortlessly; yet profound is the heart that expressed it."[241] That insistence upon the heart—which is also an insistence upon aesthetic sincerity—is undoubtedly influenced in Bashô by his absorption in Zen, with its concept of intuition which probably goes beyond any role postulated for it in Western philosophy. Through intuition, however, it is possible to know ultimate reality, ultimate unity, and ultimate knowledge. There is no other path except through intuition. As Suzuki says: *"Prajna* [intuition] is ever seeking unity on the grandest possible scale, so that there could be no further unity in any sense. *Prajna* is pure act, pure experience."[242] Within the depths and farthest reaches of Zen, it is declared to be "beyond human understanding,"[243] but not beyond human experience. Between the intellect and intuition is an absolute difference: "There is a gap between the two; no transition is possible; hence there is a leap."[244] Steeped in such beliefs, it is not to be wondered at that Bashô would insist on what was experienced rather than what was thought. If his thought is considered against some such background, especially his thoughts on nature, it will gain considerably in depth and clarity.

Generally speaking, the Japanese concept of man's relationship with nature, which finds in Bashô's poetry a perfected expression and is to be found in other Japanese arts also—landscape gardening, certain schools of painting, flower arrangement, etc.—is not one shared by the West. For the West tends to see nature as an element apart from man and tries to fight it; because of the fear with which storms, earthquakes, and other natural disasters are confronted, nature has come to be pictured as an enemy to be subdued or mastered. On a more modern level, what with the *weltanschauung* science had fostered on the poet, the Western writer indeed found himself in an "inhuman and alien world," as Waggoner has put it.[245] As previously pointed out, the nature of the artist's relationship with the world about him has been one of the dominant problems throughout modern poetry[246] and has yet to be resolved to the satisfaction of either the poets or scientists. As early as 1903, Bertrand Russell had stated the problem in overwhelming terms:

> That man is the product of causes that had no prevision of the end they were achieving; that his origins, his growth, his hopes and fears, his loves and beliefs are but the outcome of accidental collocations of atoms; that no fire, no heroism, no intensity of thought and feeling, can preserve an individual life beyond the grave; that all the labors of the ages, all the devotion . . . all the noonday brightness of human genius are destined to extinction. . . all these things, if not quite beyond dispute, are yet so nearly certain, that no philosophy which rejects them can hope to stand. Only within the scaffolding of these truths, only on the firm foundation of unyielding despair, can the soul's habitation henceforth be safely built.[247]

Happily for the Japanese haiku writer, so pervasive is an acceptance of man's place in the scheme of the world, which yet leaves to him his dignity and aspirations, that he has not had to wage this battle. As Chisaburo Yamada has said: "Japanese art of the past was based on the typical Japanese attitude of perceiving the outer world not in opposition to the self, but regarding the self as part of the universe. The world was apprehended intuitively. This attitude did not foster empirical science in our history but created art of unique beauty—an art with no conflict between image and perception, an art of complete empathy and at the same time of abstraction."[248]

With Bashô, inclusion of the seasonal theme as a necessary element of intuitive apprehension was firmly established in the hokku. Hereafter, it will not be possible for the haiku to ignore this aspect of its history with impunity. With his work and teaching, the fundamental outlines of the history of the seasonal theme in haiku from an aesthetic point of view have been presented, and modern practice bears out this assertion, as witness the following definition of a haiku given in 1936 by a modern critic: "Haiku is a seventeen syllable poem in which a seasonal feeling is rendered."[249]

Three major refinements have been made in this area since the Meiji period which should be noted in passing. Until the time of Shiki (1866–1902), the concept of the seasonal element in haiku remained much as Sôgi had defined it; that is, the seasonal element in the poem corresponded to the time in which it was composed, as Asano points out: "From the time of renga to the days before Shiki, *toki* (the time of composition) was habitually rendered in the hokku."[250] However, with Shiki, the formal step of recognizing the independence of the seventeen syllable initial verse of renga was completed, and haiku ceased to be regarded as a part of a longer form. Consequently, the classical formalism of indicating the date of composition of a renga no longer was needed and the seasonal element of the new haiku no longer was made to correspond with the date of composition; a newer concept was evolved, as Asano points out: "The seasonal element as conceived by modern poets, who have almost disregarded the meaning that the older writers had, has a new meaning. (In other words, the seasonal element of the present has been invented by the moderns.)"[251] Shiki states the change in the modern attitude in his book *Haikai Taiyô*: "If a feature of a particular season is rendered as much as possible, quick association and deep feeling will easily arise. Of course, we should not entirely avoid thinking of the autumn during the spring, or of the winter during the summer. As your imagination wanders, let it."[252] Since the seasonal element then was no longer to be seized from actual scenes before one, Shiki postulated the concept of the seasonal theme or *kidai*. Accordingly, as he states above, it would be possible for a group of haiku writers to take a seasonal theme for winter—e.g., *samusa* or cold—and to write poems on them in the summer. Theoretically, such was not the practice before his day, although actually one can easily imagine that it was done; amateur poets, anticipating some contest or poetry meeting, must have armed themselves well in advance with hokku appropriate to any season so as always to be well prepared. Indeed in 1376 Yoshimoto Nijô discussed this question in his *Kyûshû Mondô* where recognition is given to the practice, as previously noted.[253] Perhaps Shiki's concept of *kidai* can be called a clarification of what was an actual practice, as well as a greater liberalism in the rules surrounding haiku composition. Yet it is to be noted that while his position may differ from Bashô's theoretically in this respect, as it emerged in actual poetry, the effect is quite the same. We note that in the quotation above, Shiki counsels that one advantage of the seasonal element in haiku is that "quick association and deep feeling will easily arise." Is this not the result of Bashô's use of the carp of the boy's festival of May 5 in the following:

> Altar of Benkei!
> Yoshitsune's sword!...Oh fly
> The carp in May![254]

The gallant qualities of derring-do and fealty are made to rise from the sword of "Japan's favorite hero" in Henderson's words,[255] and from the altar of his resourceful retainer by the mention of the carp; and Bashô's gay delight in the manliness of little boys whose festival it is sings in this charming verse.

It should be noted in passing that Shiki maintained in his permissive way as he had initially done concerning the possible lengths of haiku that it was possible to have haiku without a seasonal theme. However he does not appear to have defended the position with any vigor or to have thought it important: "You can compose haiku of the miscellaneous type—that is, non-seasonal haiku—if you like. It is not prohibited in haiku composition at all. However, the reason why most haiku poets do not work on composing miscellaneous haiku is that they cannot get much satisfaction from doing so."[256] In yet another remark, he seems almost to challenge those favoring non-seasonal haiku to produce great ones of this type: "The miscellaneous haiku has no association with the four seasons, so their meanings are shallow and thin, and many are not worth reciting. But a stirring and grand haiku need not rely on the seasonal element."[257] It is apparent that Shiki felt the seasonal haiku had greater possibilities than the miscellaneous type, although he discarded some of the irrelevant formalism surrounding that element.

As is apparent, *kidai* is a conceptual word. Any seasonal theme such as the hundreds listed in a seasonal dictionary merely name in the abstract certain seasonal features: the moon, the nightingale, a long night, a short day, etc. Such features however have yet to be realized poetically in an actual poem. When they are so realized, they become *kigo* or seasonal words. Indeed such was the basis for declaring that certain seasonal features belonged more fittingly to one season than another as Shiki declared: "These [seasonal themes] are not reasoned, but are just feelings."[258] Hence Otsuji, with his steadfast insistence on the aliveness of the poetic vision, declared that a seasonal theme, being conceptual, could never exist in a haiku, while a seasonal word, being immovably fixed within the poem, could never exist outside of a haiku: "Seasonal themes have been classified according to the four seasons, for the sake of convenience in editing anthologies of haiku, but aside from that they have no meaning."[259] And again: "Apart from haiku there are no seasonal words."[260]

It should be mentioned that the probable reason for Otsuji's insistent discrimination between a conceptual seasonal theme and a realized seasonal word is to be found in the degraded state of haiku between the period of Issa (1762–1826) and Shiki (1867–1902). It is comparable, as Henderson says, to the period immediately prior to Bashô: "The greater part of the nineteenth century was a bad time for haiku. . . . [Poets] fell more and more into an artificiality comparable to that which had existed before the advent of Bashô."[261] The period lacked even the doubtful grace of wit and humor such as Sôkan had displayed. And again the seasonal element in haiku while mechanically included became a dead formality; any seventeen syllable group of words containing some seasonal element listed in a dictionary was *ipso facto* accepted as a haiku or hokku. Following are two examples which do not unfairly represent the poetry of the period. The first is by Baishitsu (1769–1852):

> When I break a spray
> Of the lespedeza flower,
> All the branches move.[262]

The second is by Sôkyû (1761–1842):

> I cut the lilies,
> And side by side I place them
> On top of the grass.[263]

One can well understand why Otsuji would protest against such trivial conventionality.

In order to clarify his distinction further between the seasonal theme and a seasonal word, he developed the critical term *kikan* or seasonal feeling. For him, the seasonal feeling is the unified one-ness in a realized haiku: "The seasonal feeling is in its strictest sense no less than the unified feeling in a haiku."[264] It results from a formed vision: "When the poet's aesthetic activity melts into a unified feeling in a haiku and when his ego has disappeared, a seasonal feeling forms."[265] Permeating the whole haiku, it arises most directly from the seasonal word in it: "The seasonal word points out the central object in such a case.... The weather conditions, or an object, or the scenery most important to the creation of a unified feeling in the haiku is the seasonal word in that haiku."[266] The word which *functions* as the seasonal word in an actual haiku is the seasonal word in it, although other more readily recognizable seasonal words may be included in the poem: "The other words, whether they are seasonal themes or what have you, are not the seasonal word in this haiku."[267] The term "seasonal feeling" is undoubtedly a most useful critical term in the study of haiku, covering as it does so many areas which have been discussed separately in the foregoing pages. It is in short, as Otsuji states, a "symbol of feeling":

> Those who consider a sense of season as a feeling arising from the seasonal theme apart from haiku undoubtedly think of the sense of seasons as a conceptual symbol. In actuality, a sense of season cannot be formed without haiku, and for us who consider that it arises from the total poetic effect of the haiku itself, it is the symbol of feeling.[268]

For only as a felt object is realized can there be a seasonal feeling in the haiku. It was one of Otsuji's greatest perceptions when he distinguished between the seasonal theme, the seasonal word, and the seasonal feeling. How meaningful his thinking has been for the modern haiku is well illustrated in the accolade of Yaichi Haga, one of the greatest authorities on Japanese literature: "Those who have left such a substantial body of haiku theory [as did Otsuji] are unprecedented in the history of haiku.... [His] achievement contributed many new ideas to the haiku world."[269]

In the preceding pages I have attempted to give a short account of the development of the seasonal theme from the earliest period of the *Kiki* through the renga and haikai. It seems to me that its developmental line indicates that throughout the history of Japanese poetry, barring those periods when the aim of the dominant poetic form itself was in a sense anti-poetic, there has been a gradual clarification of a deeply aesthetic impulse. What began as a simple naming of natural objects in the early tanka period came to yield the richness of image found in the *Shin-Kokinshû*. What began as a statement of the time a renga was composed attained with Sôgi aesthetic justification as a means of reaching a deep realization of the scene before the poet. The very nature of the renga as a verse form, where the unity of the poem arises from fluid intuitive relationships between the links, a relationship dealt with in the concept of *hon-i,* gave to the seasonal element of the hokku a depth of reference which found its ultimate expression in some of Bashô's hokku. The content of the seasonal image became more finely differentiated and with him attained a quintessential statement. With the standard he set, whatever the trivial depths to which the seasonal element in haiku could fall and has actually fallen since, it became impossible for it to disappear completely. Its persistence in Japanese poetry arises I am sure from some fundamentally basic attitude within Japanese life itself, as Bashô pointed out in many ways: "The thoughts within my heart of the beauty of the things that come with each season are like endless songs as numerous as the grains of sand on a beach. Those who express such feelings with compassion are the sages of words."[270]

Perhaps this, in the last analysis, is the justification for the seasonal theme in haiku; it expresses a love and kinship with the world of nature which come as naturally to the Japanese as the seventeen syllable poem in which they celebrate their feeling in the language of poetry, and in which they possess it, as Archibald MacLeish has said:

> World turned experience, that is to say...turned life, may, at the rare and fortunate moment, speak the language of poetry.... These moments of perception are, as Rilke truly says, rare moments, but when they come it is in poetry they find their speech for only poetry can utter what they know. Other languages available to mankind may interpret them, may generalize upon our experience and ourselves. Poetry is possession of life and of the man.[271]

Indeed these moments are no less than haiku moments in which a sense of season is a life's breath, for it is the very act of life and the rhythm of living in action.

CHAPTER SIX

THE ENGLISH HAIKU: CONCLUSIONS

GENERALLY SPEAKING, the fate of haiku in the West has been an unhappy one. I do not think it is erroneous to say that with very few exceptions, it has been a much maligned form—exciting curiosity as with the Imagists, or scorn for its brevity, or dismissal for its limited areas. Nor is it difficult to understand why judgments on it have been so adverse. First, there exist the enormous difficulties of the Japanese language itself, acting as a barrier to any foreign student of Japanese poetry. Secondly, there exist the preconceived ideas of what poetry "should be" with which haiku has been approached. Thirdly, the Western mind itself, in large part, has come to devalue poetry, and indeed to devalue its own poetry, as witness the small place it occupies in the world of art today. Such devaluation, as has been suggested, is related to the larger problem of the validity and reality of values, the solution to which has yet to be formulated in a way understood and accepted by Western culture at large. Where the role of poetry is ambiguous within one's own culture, it is difficult to see how that of a foreign one can be appreciated for its positive contributions.

Considering then the usual judgments that are made of haiku, I have tried through an exploration of its basic attributes as a verse form to link it with poetry as the West understands the term. Once the intent of haiku is understood, it need not appear radically and exotically different from Western poetry. It has been to reach such an understanding that an examination of certain similarities in thinking between Western aestheticians and Japanese poets and critics was made in the initial pages of this book. It was also hoped that an inkling of the quality and direction of Japanese literary thought might be given.

The intent of haiku is contained in the concept of the haiku moment. For the haiku presents only such moments, the "high moments," as Henderson has said: "Sir Arthur Quiller-Couch has pointed out that the capital difficulty of verse consists 'in saying ordinary unemotional things, of bridging the flat intervals between high moments.' Now by its very shortness, a haiku avoids this difficulty almost automatically. . . . All haiku worthy of the name are records of high moments—higher at least than the surrounding plain. And in the hands of a master, a haiku can be the concentrated essence of pure poetry."[1] What those "high moments" are I have tried to explore through the terms and concepts developed by such Western thinkers as Dewey, Croce, Read, Brooks, etc., and by such Japanese poets and critics as Bashô, Otsuji, Asô, etc. I have found in the similarity of thought among these men ample proof of the great common ground from which all art is derived. For them, such moments contain only that instant of insight into the quality of an experience, only the image that speaks. What that image says is expressed only through the presentation of the image. What the experience is is presented only in the moment of insight. Such economy is one of the first principles of which John Gould Fletcher spoke and through which he felt haiku could be of value to the West:

> [What we can learn from the Japanese and their poetry] is something that may help to lead poetry back to first principles, which surely should come first; and should lead some of the more intelligent moderns to cast off the burden of too-conscious intellectualism that they carry. For the merit of these *haiku* poems is not only that they suggest much by saying little; they also, if understood in connection with the *Zen* doctrine they illuminate, make of poetry an act of life.[2]

The usual difficulty with the intellectualism of the Western poet in his poetry is that it thereby ceases to be poetry, i.e., it is not experienced. But the haiku poet creates his pattern of meaning by creating the poem which is wholly image and through which he expresses the heart of his experiences. Bashô, for example, demonstrates the profundity of the doctrine of Zen through the air he creates in his crow haiku without stating explicitly what that doctrine is. Creation of such symbols is the essence of the language of poetry, for what belongs to art alone—as distinguished from other disciplines—is its power, in the words of Mac-Leish, to create *"in* experience and out of experience a momentary eternity which is more like experience than experience itself."[3] Only when such experiences become live symbols, such as all haiku strive for, can one of the first principles Fletcher meant—an exploration and living of the life of meaning and value—be attained.

If the intent of haiku is understood, then its form, at once so different from any Western one and so curious in its allusiveness, is seen to be the only one in which the haiku moment can be realized. Its length of seventeen syllables corresponds to the length of the haiku moment. Its structure of three lines, comprising five, seven, and five syllables each, contains through its balanced grace the moment of resolution, of insight, of order. Its inclusion of the three elements of time, place, and object corresponds to the skeleton of experience, for it is the "naked" statement which is the aim of haiku. The element of time has become refined to the concept of the seasonal feeling as Otsuji envisioned it, and was traced through the brief historical review of its development.

I have tried to show that while the haiku deals with nature, they are not "nature poems" in the usual Western sense. In Japan, "nature poems" can include all subjects; poems on religion, on love, on social satire, on philosophical reflections, on ethics—all are written *sub specie* nature poems. For nature in Japan is not only another category of subject. Nature, in the haiku at least, is *the* subject, for human activities and affairs are a part of nature, just as man is a part of nature. For the Japanese haiku poet does not live in an "inhuman and alien world," and as has been pointed out, in recent years the West has begun to realize that it need not live in such a universe either.

Perhaps then, in the new world that will emerge in the West when the bonds imposed on our conceptions by an older scientism have been loosened, the haiku can play a role, for it will deal as in Japan not with conflicts and struggle but with insights and resolutions into a world order that is found acceptable to our humanity. At least, it is probable that new forms will have to be found to handle new attitudes, for, as Allen Tate has said, "it is probable that there is an intimate relation between a generally accepted 'picture of the world' and the general acceptance of a metrical system and its differentiations into patterns."[4]

That the haiku can come to play some role in Western poetry is I think most possible. And if that occasion comes, the haiku will be, I feel, in form much as it is in Japan, for the reasons I have explored in this book. Moreover, because of the difference in the two languages, it can develop different techniques through such textural elements as rhyme, vertical and horizontal rhythms, assonance, etc., as well as incorporate the techniques which have developed in the Japanese form.

Through the historical review of the development of the Japanese form, I have hoped to show the various elements that went into the haiku and to clarify some of the concepts previously presented of its nature.

As I stated in the Introduction, I have tried here to illuminate the nature of haiku and its methods of expression, with the hope that such an attempt may serve to make haiku art accessible to the West as well as to point out one direction by which the new form can be realized in English. It is my sincere belief that true artists will be willing to accept haiku when they understand it, for as Louise Bogan affirms without such incorporation of different aesthetic views, no culture can thrive: "It is through the acceptance of a variety of aesthetic and intellectual points of view that a culture is given breadth and density. Without such acceptance, rooted in a sincere liberality and tolerance of spirit, any cultural situation is bound to become one-sided and impoverished. The American arts in general, from the end of the thirties to the present day...have steadily been enriched by their absorption of differing standards and talents, both native and foreign. This absorption is still going on."[5]

Finally I have hoped here to reveal to Western poets the insights and experiences Japanese poets have created over the centuries. For their poetry and that of Western poets, in their basic poetic principles, can be shown to be the same, thereby providing a point of new understanding which we need more than ever. Whether this study provides such an interchange of poetics and aesthetics is another matter, but that such an exchange should continually be attempted seems self-evident.

SELECTED HAIKU

A BUTTERFLY

A falling flower, thought I,
Fluttering back to the branch—
Was a butterfly.

—Moritake

HARVEST MOON

If only we could
Add a handle to the moon
It would make a good fan!

—Sôkan

RIVER MISTS

River mists that float
On the wind, look soft and light
From the loading-boat.

—Sôin

THE CRYSTAL SPRING

In my scooping hands
The leaves of the oak-tree move
In the crystal spring.

—Sôin

UNCONFESSED LOVE

"Summer thinness, dear,"
I replied to him and then
Could not check a tear.

                    —*Kigin*

A CROW ON A BARE BRANCH

On a withered bough
A crow alone is perching;
Autumn evening now.

                    —*Bashô*

WISTERIA FLOWER

As I seek a bower,
Weary from travel, I find
A wisteria flower.

                    —*Bashô*

AT MY HUT

Beyond cherry brumes,
Is the bell at Asakusa
Or Ueno that booms?

                    —*Bashô*

THE GALAXY

Wild the rolling sea!
Over which to Sado Isle
Lies the Galaxy.

                    —*Bashô*

THE FIRST SNOW

Oh, the first soft snow!
Enough to bend the leaves
Of the jonquil low.

                    —*Bashô*

CICADA'S SHRILL

How silent and still!
Into the heart of rocks sinks
The cicada's shrill.

                    —*Bashô*

ON THE MOUNTAIN TRAIL

From the plum-scented air
Suddenly the sun comes up
On the mountain road.

                    —*Bashô*

THE CICADA

In the cicada's cry
There's no sign that can foretell
How soon it must die.

                    —*Bashô*

HARVEST MOON

The autumn moon is bright;
Sea-waves whirl up to my gate,
Crested silvery white.

                    —*Bashô*

SPRING MORNING

Season of spring days!
There a nameless hill has veils
Of soft morning haze.

        —Bashô

AUTUMN EVENING

None is traveling
Here along this way but I,
This autumn evening.

        —Bashô

SNOWY HERON

In the fresh spring breeze
How snowy is the heron
Flying through pine-trees.

        —Raizan

WINTER GALE

A bleak gale that raves,
Dies away, remaining only
In the roar of waves.

        —Gonsui

AUTUMN MOON

Is there anyone
Who will not take up his brush
With this moon tonight!

        —Onitsura

THE BELL IN WINTER RAIN

"Hark!" calls the refrain
Of the bell that sounds at night
With the wintery rain.

—*Kikaku*

EARLY SPRING

Warm the weather grows
Gradually as one plum-flower
After another blows.

—*Ransetsu*

SUMMER HEAT

Stones and trees that meet
My eyes glare straight at me
In this glazing heat.

—*Kyorai*

THE SNIPE

The snipe rise in flight
From the voice that scolds the cow
In the soft twilight.

—*Shikô*

FLOWERY DALE

Narrowly a trail
Fades away into the flowers
Blooming in the dale.

—*Fukoku*

VIOLETS

Violets abound
Within the rigid fences
Of prohibited ground!

        —Yaha

THE FIREFLY

In the lonely night
There the firefly glides one foot,
Putting out its light.

        —Hokushi

POET'S FANCY

Covered with the flowers,
Instantly I'd like to die
In this dream of ours!

        —Etsujin

THE RIVER

See the river flow
In a long unbroken line
On the field of snow.

        —Bonchô

THE SCARECROW

There is a hushed sound
Of the scarecrow, fallen down
Alone to the ground.

        —Bonchô

SPRING MORNING

From the long hallways
Voices of the people rise
In the morning haze.

—*Ryôta*

WEEPING WILLOWS

In the heart of town
Willows growing at the inn
Bend their branches down.

—*Rigyu*

THE HAZE

Far above the veil
Of the haze a boat, at times,
Rises with its sail.

—*Gakoku*

WHEAT FIELD

A spring breeze is sweet,
Blowing over the sunlit brook
Soughing through the wheat.

—*Mokudô*

HARVEST MOON AND INSECTS

Brightly shines the moon,
And where silver shadows are
Insects string their tune.

—*Bunson*

WHITE CHRYSANTHEMUM

Look, oh how fearsome
Are the rouged fingers against
The white chrysanthemum.

—*Chiyo*

PLUM BLOSSOMS

Flowers give but perfume
To the one who breaks the branch
From the plum in bloom.

—*Chiyo*

LONGING FOR A DEPARTED CHILD

I wonder how far
My small dragonfly hunter
Has wandered today!

—*Chiyo*

NIGHTINGALE

The nightingales sing
In the echo of the bell
Tolled at evening.

—*Ukô*

SPRING RAIN

In the rains of spring,
An umbrella and raincoat
Pass by, conversing.

—*Buson*

CAMELLIA-FLOWER

A camellia-flower,
As it drops, spills the water
From the yester-shower.

—Buson

THE PEONY

Scattered the peony!
One beside another pile,
Petals two or three.

—Buson

AUTUMN-TWILIGHT

The hills cast shadows,
And pampas grass is swaying
In sunlit meadows.

—Buson

IN WINTER

Willow-trees are bare—
Dried the water, and the stones
Lie scattered here and there.

—Buson

THE SCARECROW

In the setting sun
The scarecrow's shadow leans out
To the road alone.

—Shôha

PEONY FLOWER

Now, how dear to me
Seems my father's rage when I
Broke the peony.

> —*Tairô*

A BEE

With a buzzing cry
A bee shifts on the bloom sought
By a butterfly.

> —*Taigi*

FIREFLIES

"Look, O look, there go
Fireflies," I would like to say—
But I am alone.

> —*Taigi*

HARVEST MOON

The harvest moon is bright,
Rising from the windy grass
Of the moor tonight!

> —*Chôra*

PLUM FLOWERS

As I put on the light,
More plum-flowers are seen behind
Branches fair and white.

> —*Gyôdai*

GENTLE WILLOW

Angry, I came home
And found within my garden
A willow-tree.

              —Ryôta

IN WINTER

Breaking off each day
Withered river-rushes go
Drifting on their way.

              —Rankô

ORPHAN SPARROW

With one another
Let's play; so come, O sparrow
Who has no mother.

              —Issa

LIVING IN THE TOWN

Living in the town
One must have money even
To melt the snow down!

              —Issa

THE CHERRY BLOSSOMS AT UENO

Under the branches
Of the cherry-trees in bloom,
None are strangers there.

              —Issa

A RADISH WORKER

With the radish he
Pulls out, a radish-worker
Shows the road to me.

                    —*Issa*

CHRYSANTHEMUMS

Ah, into one shade
Many-hued chrysanthemums
Wither, die, and fade!

                    —*Issa*

PLUM AND A MOON

On the plum in flower
By my eave, the pale moon hangs
At the dawning hour.

                    —*Tenro*

THE MIST

I turned back to see,
But the man I passed was veiled
In mist already.

                    —*Shiki*

WILD GEESE

The wild geese take flight
Low along the railroad tracks
In the moonlit night.

                    —*Shiki*

ON THE WITHERED PLAIN

The gates alone remain
Of some great Buddhist temple
On this withered plain.

—*Shiki*

THE OCEAN MOON

From the distant bound
Of the cool, the ocean moon
Rises bright and round.

—*Shiki*

GOLDEN MAPLE SPRAY

City folk are they;
In the home-bound train they hold
Golden maple sprays.

—*Meisetsu*

A BUTTERFLY

To the wreaths that lie
Sweetly on the casket-lid,
Comes a butterfly.

—*Meisetsu*

HARVEST MOON

Underneath the moon
Of autumn, my neighbor plays
A flute out of tune.

—*Kôyô*

LEAVES

O Leaves, ask the breeze
Which of you will scatter first
From the verdant trees.

—*Sôseki*

TRAIN

Following the train,
The long black smoke is crawling
O'er the withered plain.

—*Sôseki*

SPRING DAY

(On parting from Kyoshi during my stay at Matsuyama)

What a long spring day!
Catching yawns from one another
We go each our way.

—*Sôseki*

A SHOWER

A shower comes and passes
Leaving the bright summer moon
Upon the grasses.

—*Shôu*

AUTUMN WIND

When the autumn wind
Blows there is but haiku
In all things I find.

—*Kyoshi*

CHERRY FLOWERS

The cherry flowers are now
In full bloom, and no petal
Flutters from the bough.
                    —*Kyoshi*

ON THE DEATH OF SHIKI

Shiki passed away
At the budding moonlit hour
Of the seventeenth day.
                    —*Kyoshi*

MAPLE LEAVES

I pursue the light
Of the swift-footed lantern
Through the chilly night.
                    —*Kyoshi*

IN AUTUMN

This road we follow
Will lead us to Mount Fuji
Through the pampas grass.
                    —*Hekigodô*

CHILLY NIGHT

The garden is now
Left unswept, for maple leaves
Flutter from their bough.
                    —*Hekigodô*

TEA PLANTS

In the lantern light
White are the tea-plant blossoms
By the path at night.

                    —*Hekigodô*

AUTUMN INSECTS

A little village here
Is sleeping, lulled by crickets
Chirping sweet and clear.

                    —*Getto*

SUMMER HEAT

Oh, how small, my sweet,
Is your painted parasol
In this intense heat!

                    —*Seihô*

WISTERIAS

In the twilight gloom
Of the redwood and the pine
Some wisterias bloom.

                    —*Shihôta*

HEAVY SNOW

Oh, how quietly
And how still the heavy snow
Fades into the sea!

                    —*Sazanami*

THE BALMY SPRING DAY

Soothed by the serene
Balminess of spring, I fell
Asleep on the green.
              —*Tôyôjô*

SPRING HILLS

Spring hills disappear
Sinking into the pine-grove
As I wander near.
              —*Seiran*

FROM THE HILL TOP

Some one from below
Is looking at the whirling
Of the cherry snow.
              —*Hakugetsu*

PAMPAS GRASS

Through the pampas grass
That sways and dances gently
In the breeze, I pass.
              —*Seireishi*

SUNSET

Piercing crimson red
Is the autumn setting sun
On the cockscomb head!
              —*Gochu*

INQUIRY

"Chestnut gatherers?"
They inquired in return
When we asked the way.

—*Suichikukyo*

MEIJI ERA

The snows are falling;
And far into the distance
Meiji has gone.

—*Kusadao*

NIGHTINGALE

Deep within the dale
Wrapped in veils of evening mist,
Sings the nightingale.

—*Shûoshi*

SNOWY MORN

In the morn I go
Stepping over the bamboo
Broken by the snow.

—*Shasui*

IN THE GROVE OF PLUM-FLOWERS

Night begins to come,
And the darkness falls at once
In the grove of plum.

—*Sôjô*

BON DANCE

The dancing rings become
Larger and larger to the beat
Of the quickening drum.

> —*Toyoshi*

FALLEN LEAVES

With a rustling sound
Fallen leaves pursue and pass
Others on the ground.

> —*Tatsuko*

EXPERIMENTS IN ENGLISH

by Shôson (Kenneth Yasuda)

A CAMELLIA FLOWER

Brushing the leaves, fell
A white camellia blossom
Into the dark well.

THE BLUE POOL

Luminous and cool
Is the way a pebble sinks
Into the blue pool.

AT TACOMA, WASHINGTON

Shadows from the hills
Lengthen half across a field
Of gold daffodils.

THE RAIN

Tenderly again
On the peony I hear
Whispers of the rain.

CALLA LILY

Cast by morning light,
The stamen's shadow is black
On the calla white.

THE LIZARD

A lizard flicks over
The undulating ripples
Of sunlit clover.

KATYDID

In moonlight, half-hid
By the silhouettes of leaves
Twits the katydid.

CRIMSON DRAGONFLY—I

A crimson dragonfly,
As it lights, sways together
With a leaf of rye.

CRIMSON DRAGONFLY—II

A crimson dragonfly,
Glancing the water, casts rings
As it passes by.

IN THE DAFFODIL FIELD

Flowered is her hem,
Ankle-deep in daffodils
As she gathers them.

AT PARTING

Here at parting now,
Let me speak by breaking
A lilac from the bough.

SUMMER TREES

The shadow of the trees
Almost reaches to my desk
With the summer breeze.

THE SPRING WATER

I drink—listening
To the sound of the water
Rising from the spring.

THE RAIN

Hurriedly runs rain
Toward the sunlit grain field,
Half across the plain.

AT DENSON, ARKANSAS

Against the black sky
The lightning paints the great oak
As it flashes by.

THE MISSISSIPPI RIVER

Under the low grey
Winter skies water pushes
Water on its way.

HYDRANGEA

Underneath the eaves
A blooming large hydrangea
Overbrims its leaves.

HARVEST MOON

Broken, broken, yet
Perfect is the harvest moon
In the rivulet.

WHITE SWANS
White swans, one or two,
Drew near, pushing the water
For the food I threw.

IN THE GARDEN

With the mattock I
Dig the garden where the cloud's
Shadow passes by.

A DIRGE FOR A SOLDIER

Moving in one big sway
The flowering winter peony
Scatters bright and gay.

IN THE GARDEN

On the bench I wait
For the second gust to come
Through the garden gate.

NOTES

INTRODUCTION

1. Given in Donald Keene, *Japanese Literature*. London: John Murray, 1953, p. 8.
2. Ford Madox Ford, *Joseph Conrad: A Personal Remembrance*. London: Duckworth, 1924, *passim*.
3. H. O. Henderson, *The Bamboo Broom*. Boston: Houghton, Miflin, 1934, p. 124.
4. Glenn Hughes, *Imagism and the Imagists*. Palo Alto: Stanford University Press, 1931, p. 143.
5. Quoted by Huges, *ibid.*, p. 10.
6. Horace Gregory and Marya Zaturenska, *A History of American Poetry*. New York: Harcourt Brace, 1942, p. 168.
7. In *The Asian Legacy and American Life*, ed. by Arthur E. Christy. New York: John Day, 1945, pp. 145-74.
8. *Ibid.*, p. 158.
9. *Ibid.*
10. *Ibid.*
11. Cleanth Brooks, *Modern Poetry and the Tradition*. Chapel Hill: Univ. of North Carolina Press, 1939, p. 71.
12. Bashô, *Haikai Ronshû* (Collected Haikai Theory), ed. by T. Komiya and S. Yokozawa, 3rd ed. Tokyo: Iwanami, 1951, p. 91. *(Akazôshi.)* The titles of the original works of Bashô, in which the given quotations are found, will be cited in parentheses after the bibliographical data.
13. Quoted by Fletcher, *op. cit.*, p. 159.
14. Isoji Asô, *Haishumi no Hattatsu* (The Development of Haikai Taste), 2nd ed. Tokyo: Tokyodô, 1944, p. 240.
15. Archibald MacLeish, *Poems: 1920–1934*. New York: Houghton Miflin, 1934, p. 84.
16. Kenneth Yasuda, *A Pepper Pod*. New York: Knopf, 1947.
17. Henderson, *op. cit.*, p. 124.

CHAPTER ONE

1. Bashô, *op. cit.,* p. 71. *(Kyoroku ni Okuru ben.)*
2. Quoted by Hughes, *op. cit.,* p. 47.
3. Cf. pp. 35–38.
4. Allen Tate, *Reactionary Essays on Poetry and Ideas.* New York: Scribner's, 1936, p. x.
5. Brooks, *op. cit.,* p. 78.
6. *Ibid.,* p. 182.
7. Quoted by Gregory and Zaturenska, *op. cit.,* p. 207.
8. Williams, *Spring and All, I–XXVIII.* Given in Louise Bogan, *Achievement in American Poetry.* Chicago: Henry Regnery, 1951, p. 130.
9. Bashô, *op. cit.,* p. 103. *(Hai mon Haikai Goroku.)*
10. Hughes, *op. cit.,* p. 5.

CHAPTER TWO

1. Masao Kume, *Bikushô Zuihitsu* (Bitter-Sweet Essays). Tokyo: Bungei Shunju Shinsa, 1953, p. 258.
2. Tate, *op. cit.,* p. 108.
3. Otsuji (Seki Osuga), *Otsuji Hairon-shû* (Otsuji's Collected Essays on Haiku Theory), ed. by Tôyô Yoshida, 5th ed. Tokyo: Kaede Shobô, 1947, p. 18.
4. *Ibid.,* p. 262.
5. Tate, *op. cit.,* p. 17.
6. Bashô, *op. cit.,* p. 98. *(Kurozôshi.)*
7. Otsuji, *op. cit.,* p. 30.
8. Asô, *op. cit.,* p. 234.
9. Quoted by Herbert Read, *Form in Modern Poetry.* London: Vision Press, 1953, p. 79.
10. Cf. pp. 49–50.
11. Otsuji, *op. cit.,* p. 19.
12. *Ibid.,* p. 11.
13. *Ibid.,* p. 47.
14. John Dewey, *Art as Experience.* New York: Mentor Balch, 1934, p. 44.
15. Ernst Cassirer, *Substance and Function and Einstein's Theory of Relativity.* Trans. by W. C. and M. C. Swabey. Chicago-London: Open Court, 1923, p. 272.
16. Otsuji, *op. cit.,* p. 4.
17. Benedetto Croce, *Aesthetic as a Science of Expression and General Linguistic.* Trans. by Douglas Ainslie. London: Macmillan, 1922, p. 127.
18. Otsuji *op. cit.,* p. 31.
19. Dewey, *op. cit.,* p. 89.
20. H. H. Waggoner, *The Heel of Elohim.* Norman, Okla.: Univ. of Oklahoma Press, 1950, p. 13.
21. Cassirer, *op. cit.,* p. 150.
22. Dewey, *op. cit.,* p. 89.
23. Otsuji, *op. cit.,* p. 13.

24. Benedetto Croce, *Ariosto, Shakespeare, and Corneille*. Trans. by Douglas Ainslie. London: George, Allen and Unwin, 1920, pp. 153–154.
25. Waggoner, *op. cit.*, p. 73.
26. Bashô, *op. cit.*, p. 49. *(Kurozôshi.)*
27. Dewey, *op. cit.*, p. 46.
28. Otsuji, *op. cit.*, p. 262.
29. A. C. Bradley, *Oxford Lectures on Poetry*. London: Macmillan, 1909, p. 6.
30. Brooks, *op. cit.*, p. 37.
31. Asô, *op. cit.*, pp. 190 and 192.
32. Cf. pp. xix–xx.
33. Benedetto Croce, *Essence of Aesthetic*. Trans. by Douglas Ainslie. London: Heineman, 1921, p. 16.
34. Cf. p. 8.
35. Asô, *op. cit.*, pp. 273–74.
36. Otsuji, *op. cit.*, p. 262.
37. Tate, *op. cit.*, p. 56.
38. Bashô, *Bashô Haikushû* (Collected Haiku of Bashô), ed. by Taizô Ebara, 18th ed. Tokyo: Iwanami, 1953, p. 30.
39. *Ibid.*, p. 30.
40. Given in *Bashô Kôza* (Lectures on Bashô), comp. and ed. by Taizô Ebara and Shûson Katô. Tokyo: Sanshôdô, 1943, I, p. 355.
41. T. S. Eliot, *Selected Essays*. New York: Harcourt, Brace, 1932, p. 248.
42. S. K. Langer, *Philosophy in a New Key*. Cambridge, Mass.: Harvard Univ. Press, 1942, p. 261.
43. Otsuji, *op. cit.*, p. 262.
44. Bashô, *Haikai Ronshû*, p. 69. *(Ryôshinron.)*
45. Tate, *op. cit.*, p. 88.
46. Stephen Pepper, *Aesthetic Quality*. New York: Scribner's, 1938, p. 31.
47. Croce, *Aesthetic*, p. 36.
48. Alfred North Whitehead, *Science and the Modern World*. New York: Macmillan, 1925, p. 120.
49. Dewey, *op. cit.*, p. 95.
50. Waggoner, *op. cit.*, pp. 192, 203.
51. Cf. p. 4.
52. Waggoner, *op. cit.*, p. 6.
53. Brooks, *op. cit.*, p. 174.
54. Waggoner, *op. cit.*, p. 219.
55. Otsuji, *op. cit.*, p. 131.
56. Asô, *op. cit.*, pp. 191, 270.
57. Bashô, *Haikai Ronshû*, p. 49. *(Shirozôshi.)*
58. Otsuji, *op. cit.*, p. 50.
59. W. M. Urban, *Language and Reality*. London: Macmillan, 1939, p. 495.
60. Asô, *op. cit.*, p. 191.
61. Waggoner, *op. cit.*, p. 219.
62. Otsuji, *op. cit.*, p. 4.
63. *Ibid.*, p. 47.
64. Gustave Flaubert, *La Correspondance de Flaubert*. Paris: Conard, 1926–33, II, p. 294.
65. Fletcher, Introduction to *A Pepper Pod.*, p. viii.
66. Bashô, *Haikai Ronshû*, p. 95. *(Kurozôshi.)*

67. Cf. p. 23 ff.
68. Ezra Pound, "A Few Don't's by an Imagist," *Poetry: A Magazine of Verse*, Vol. I (October-March, 1912–1913), p. 200.
69. *Kokinshû*, ed. by Hachirô Onoe. 19th ed. Tokyo: Iwanami, 1951, p. 11.
70. Bashô, *Haikai Ronshû*, pp. 64, 84. *(Haikai Mondô Aone ga Mine.)*
71. Pound, *op. cit.*
72. Croce, *Aesthetic*, p. 24.

CHAPTER THREE

1. Bradley, *op. cit.*, p. 32.
2. Otsuji, *op. cit.*, p. 20.
3. Cassirer, *op. cit.*, p. 272.
4. Croce, *Essence of Aesthetic*, p. 39.
5. Bradley, *op. cit.*, p. 15.
6. Tate, *op. cit.*, p. xi.
7. Waggoner, *op. cit.*, p. 210.
8. Brooks, *op. cit.*, p. 59.
9. Otsuji, *op. cit.*, p. 20.
10. Bashô, *Haikai Ronshû*, p. 69. *(Kyoraishô, Shûgyôkyô.)*
11. Otsuji, *op. cit.*, p. 101.
12. Fletcher, Introduction to *A Pepper Pod*, p. viii.
13. Otsuji, *op. cit.*, p. 4.
14. Read, *op. cit.*, pp. 44–45.
15. Chikara Igarashi, *Kokka no Taisei oyobi Hattatsu* (The Genesis of Japanese Poetry and Its Development). Tokyo: Kaizô, 1948, p. 99.
16. Kenkichi Yamamoto, *Junsui Haiku* (Pure Haiku). Tokyo: Sôgen-sha, 1952, pp. 69–70.
17. Bashô, *Haikai Ronshû*, p. 94. *(Kyoraishô, Shûgyôkyô.)*
18. Yamamoto, *op. cit.*
19. Asô, *op. cit.*, p. 208.
20. Otsuji, *op. cit.*, p. 257.
21. *Ibid.*, p. 20.
22. George Meredith, *The Poetical Works of George Meredith*, ed. by G. M. Trevelyan. London: Constable, 1912, p. 154.
23. Carl Sandburg, *Selected Poems of Carl Sandburg*, ed. by Rebecca West. New York: Harcourt, Brace, 1926, p. 29.
24. Robert Frost, *Poems of Robert Frost*. New York: Modern Library, 1946, p. 236.
25. Edna St. Vincent Millay, *Collected Lyrics of Edna St. Vincent Millay*. 5th ed. New York: Harper, 1943, p. 240.
26. Edgar Allen Poe, *Poems of Edgar Allen Poe*. New York: Peter Pauper Press, n.d., p. 39.
27. John Masefield, *The Collected Poems of John Masefield*. London: W. Heineman, 1936, p. 52.
28. Given in Tamio Kuribayashi, *Haiku to Seikatsu* (Haiku and Living). Tokyo: Iwanami, 1952, p. 116.
29. *Ibid.*, pp. 129–30.

30. Maxime DuCamp, *Chants Modernes*. Paris: Lévy Frères, 1855, p. 21.
31. *Ibid.*, p. 5.
32. Quoted by Hughes, *op. cit.*, p. 21.
33. Given in Kuribayashi, *op. cit.*, pp. 130–31.
34. Cf. pp. 4 and 21.
35. Tate, *op. cit.*, p. 84. My italics.
36. Kuribayashi, *op. cit.*, p. 170.
37. Tate, *op. cit.*, p. xi.
38. *Ibid.*, p. 82.
39. Cf. p. 28.
40. Given in Kuribayashi, *op. cit.*, p. 116.
41. *Ibid.*, p. 117.
42. Kiyoshi Yuyama, *Nihon Shiika Inritsu Gaku* (A Study of Rhythm in Japanese Poetry). Tokyo: Furôkaku Shobô, 1935, pp. 99–100.
43. Given in Kuribayashi, *op. cit.*, p. 159.
44. Waggoner, *op. cit.*, p. 86.
45. Otsuji, *op. cit.*, p. 67.
46. Shin Asano, *Haiku Zenshi no Kenkyû* (A Study of Pre-Haiku History). Tokyo: Chûbunkan, 1939, p. 126.
47. Otsuji, *op. cit.*, p. 84.
48. Given in Kuribayashi, *op. cit.*, pp. 134–35.
49. Asano, *op. cit.*, p. 264.
50. Otsuji, *op. cit.*, p. 43.
51. *Ibid.*, p. 59.
52. *Ibid.*, p. 43.
53. *Ibid.*, pp. 11–12.
54. *Ibid.*, p. 42.
55. *Ibid.*, p. 50. My italics.
56. Quoted by Hughes, *op. cit.*, p. 15.
57. Urban, *op. cit.*, p. 495.
58. Otsuji, *op. cit.*, p. 54.
59. Cf. p. 44.
60. Otsuji, *op. cit.*, p. 11.
61. Dewey, *op. cit.*, p. 44.
62. Yamamoto, *op. cit.*, p. 78.
63. Otsuji, *op. cit.*, p. 264.
64. Asô, *op. cit.*, p. 233.
65. Otsuji, *op. cit.*, p. 45.
66. Croce, *Essence of Aesthetic*, p. 30.
67. Dewey, *op. cit.*, p. 67.
68. *Ibid.*, p. 68.
69. Bashô, *Haikai Ronshû*, p. 68. *(Akazôshi.)*
70. Babette Deutsch, *Poetry in Our Time*. New York: Henry Holt, 1952, p. 100.
71. Read, *op. cit.*, p. 74.
72. Asô, *op. cit.*, p. 271.
73. James Joyce, *Portrait of the Artist as a Young Man*. New York: W. Haebasch, 1916, p. 72.
74. Yamamoto, *op. cit.*, pp. 71–72.
75. Dewey, *op. cit.*, p. 29.

76. Cf. pp. 21–22.
77. Kyoshi Takahama, "Haiku no Tsukuri Kata" (How to Compose Haiku), in *Arusu Fujin Kôsa* (Arusu Lectures for Women), ed. by Takeo Eitahara. Tokyo: Arusu, 1927, p. 13.
78. George Barker, "William Shakespeare and the Horse with Wings," *Partisan Review*, Vol. XX, No. 4 (July-August, 1953), p. 417.
79. Gregory and Zaturenska, *op. cit.*, p. 204.
80. Bashô, *Haikai Ronshû*, p. 96. *(Kyoraishô, Shûgyôkyô.)*
81. Otsuji, *op. cit.*, p. 6.
82. Cf. p. 53.
83. Otsuji, *op. cit.*, p. 6.
84. *Ibid.*, p. 79.
85. Cf. p. 82 ff.
86. Etsurô Ide, *Meiji Taishô Haikushi* (History of Haiku of the Meiji and Taishô Eras). Tokyo: Ritsumeikan, 1932, pp. 198–99.
87. Otsuji, *op. cit.*, p. 6.
88. Cf. *ibid.*, pp. 78–79.
89. Lightner Witner, *Analytical Psychology*. Boston: Ginn & Co., 1902, p. 74.
90. Brooks, *op. cit.*, p. 33.
91. Asô, *op. cit.*, p. 245.
92. *Ibid.*, p. 239.
93. Otsuji, *op. cit.*, p. 42.
94. Tate, *op. cit.*, p. 55.
95. Otsuji, *op. cit.*, p. 101.
96. Bashô, *Haikai Ronshû*, p. 99. *(Shokanshû.)*
97. Quoted by Ide, *op. cit.*, p. 240.
98. *Ibid.*, p. 198.
99. *Ibid.*, p. 196.
100. Kuribayashi, *op. cit.*, p. 129.
101. Cf. pp. 28 and 29.
102. Kuribayashi, *op. cit.*, pp. 128–29.
103. Cf. p. 50.
104. Kuribayashi, *op. cit.*, p. 129.
105. Cf. p. 35.
106. Cf. p. 36.
107. Cf. pp. xvii–xviii for earlier discussion and sources.
108. Quoted by Hughes, *op. cit.*, p. 215.
109. Given in Otsuji, *op. cit.*, p. 330.
110. *Ibid.*
111. Given in Ide, *op. cit.*, p. 191.
112. Given in Otsuji, *op. cit.*, p. 121.
113. *Ibid.*
114. Leone Vivante, *Notes on the Originality of Thought*. Given in Read, *op. cit.*, p. 43.
115. Given in Ide, *op. cit.*, pp. 240–41.
116. Asô, *op. cit.*, p. 248.

CHAPTER FOUR

1. Cf. pp. 41 and 47.
2. Read, *op. cit.*, pp. 44–45.
3. Millay, *op. cit.*
4. Otsuji, *op. cit.*, p. 20.
5. Brooks, *op. cit.*, p. 16.
6. Otsuji, *op. cit.*, p. 20.
7. Bashô, *Haikai Ronshû*, p. 49. *(Kurozôshi.)*
8. *Ibid.*, p. 51.
9. Quoted by Hughes, *op. cit.*, p. 39.
10. *Ibid.*, p. 17.
11. Quoted by Deutsch, *op. cit.*, p. 174.
12. *Ibid.*, pp. 173–74.
13. *Ibid.*, p. 259.
14. Louis Danz, *The Psychologist Looks at Art*. London: Longmans, 1937, p. 78.
15. Bashô, *Haikai Ronshû*, p. 90. *(Kyoraishô.)*
16. Otsuji, *op. cit.*, p. 45.
17. Cf. pp. 46–52.
18. Otsuji, *op. cit.*, p. 80.
19. Brooks, *op. cit.*, p. 59.
20. Hughes, *op. cit.*, p. 78.
21. Quoted by Louise Bogan, *op. cit.*, p. 41.
22. Quoted by Jacob Isaacs, *Background of Modern Poetry*. New York: Dutton, 1952, p. 33.
23. J. H. Scott, *Rhythmic Verse*. Iowa City: University of Iowa Press, 1925, p. 39.
24. Otsuji, *op. cit.*, p. 98.
25. *Ibid.*, pp. 77–78.
26. *Ibid.*, p. 67.
27. *Ibid.*, p. 105.
28. Cf. pp. 48–49.
29. Bogan, *op. cit.*, p. 41.
30. *Ibid.*, p. 53.
31. *Ibid.*, p. 41.
32. Quoted by Hughes, *op. cit.*, p. 71.
33. Bogan, *op. cit.*, pp. 53–54.
34. *Ibid.*, p. 41.
35. Quoted by Hughes, *op. cit.*, p. 28.

CHAPTER FIVE

1. Asano, *op. cit.*, p. 119.
2. Igarashi, *op. cit.*, pp. 117–18.
3. Given in Asano, *op. cit.*, p. 117.
4. Elisabeth Drew, *T. S. Eliot: The Design of His Poetry*. New York: Scribner's, 1949, p. 61. Especially valuable for an investigation of this area is

the work of the cultural anthropologists like Malinowski, Mead, etc. It seems to me regrettable that Dr. Origuchi's work is not available in translation for the benefit of these Western scholars.

5. Shinobu Origuchi, *Origuchi Shinobu Zenshû* (Collected Works of Shinobu Origuchi), ed. by the Society for the Commemoration of Dr. Origuchi's Work. Tokyo: Chuô Kôron, 1954, I, p. 348.

6. Igarashi, *op. cit.,* p. 69.

7. *Ibid.,* p. 48.

8. Given in Origuchi, *op. cit.,* p. 348.

9. Igarashi, *op. cit.,* p. 48.

10. Given in Asano, *op. cit.,* p. 120.

11. Katsunan Mutsu, *Memoirs of Shiki.* Given in Asano, *op. cit.,* pp. 11–12.

12. Origuchi, *op. cit.,* p. 349.

13. From the *Kojiki.* Given in Igarashi, *op. cit.,* p. 354.

14. *Ibid.,* p. 167.

15. *Ibid.,* p. 156.

16. Origuchi, *op. cit.,* p. 349.

17. Given in Igarashi, *op. cit.,* pp. 157–58.

18. Chamberlain, *op. cit.,* p. 154.

19. Quoted by Deutsch, *op. cit.,* pp. 173–74.

20. Given in Asano, *op. cit.,* p. 130.

21. Taken from Kenneth Yasuda, *Lacquer Box.* Tokyo: Nippon Times, 1952, p. 4.

22. Taken from Asano, *op. cit.,* p. 139.

23. Igarashi, *op. cit.,* p. 68.

24. *Manyôshû Zenchûshaku* (The Complete Manyôshû with Notes and Commentary), ed. by Yûkichi Taketa. Tokyo: Kaizô, 1949, V, p. 94.

25. Given in Asano, *op. cit.,* p. 143.

26. *Ibid.,* p. 144.

27. *Ibid.,* pp. 150–51.

28. Yasuda, *Lacquer Box,* p. 28.

29. *Ibid.,* p. 37.

30. Given in Asano, *op. cit.,* p. 154.

31. *Ibid.,* pp. 155–56.

32. Yasuda, *Lacquer Box,* p. 14.

33. *Ibid.,* p. 17.

34. *Ibid.,* p. 6.

35. *Ibid.,* p. 59.

36. Igarashi, *op. cit.,* p. 93.

37. *Ibid.,* p. 95.

38. *Ibid.*

39. *Ibid.* Taken from the *Jimmuki* (Record of Jimmu).

40. *Ibid.,* p. 96.

41. Yasuda, *Lacquer Box,* pp. 50, 55, 61.

42. *Ibid.,* p. 69.

43. Keene, *op. cit.,* pp. 73–78 *passim.*

44. Asano, *op. cit.,* p. 74.

45. Igarashi, *op. cit.,* p. 48.

46. Given in Masakazu Sasa, *Rengashi Ron* (On Renga History). Tokyo: Tenrai Shobô, 1928, pp. 12–13.

47. *The Manyôshû: One Thousand Poems Selected and Translated from the Japanese,* ed. and trans. by N. Sasaki, Y. Yoshizawa, *et al.* 3rd ed. Tokyo: Iwanami, 1948, p. 19. The headings for the poems are not given in this work, but are taken from the original text given by Taketa, *op. cit.,* II, pp. 62–64.
48. Given in Asano, *op. cit.,* p. 170.
49. A. Nose, S. Nakamura, I. Asô, *Renga, Haikai, Haiku, Senryû.* (Vol. IV of *Nippon Bungaku Kyôyô Kôza* [Educational Lectures on Japanese Culture]). Tokyo: Shibundô, 1952, p. 2.
50. Cf. Taizô Ebara, *Haikaishi no Kenkyû* (A Study of Haikai History). 2nd ed. Tokyo: Hoshino Shoten, 1949, p. 23.
51. Given in Asano, *op. cit.,* p. 173.
52. Nose, Nakamura, Asô, *op. cit.,* p. 11.
53. Asano, *op. cit.,* pp. 174–75.
54. Sasa, *op. cit.,* p. 18.
55. Nose, Nakamura, Asô, *op. cit.,* p. 5.
56. *Ibid.,* p. 4.
57. Given in Asano, *op. cit.,* p. 177.
58. *Ibid.,* p. 178. From the *Kinyôshû* (1128).
59. Sasa, *op. cit.,* p. 20.
60. *Ibid.,* p. 51.
61. Given in Nose, Nakamura, Asô, *op. cit.,* p. 21.
62. Sasa, *op. cit.,* p. 51.
63. Ebara, *op. cit.,* p. 24.
64. Given in Nose, Nakamura, Asô, *op. cit.,* p. 25.
65. Cf. Asano, *op. cit.,* p. 182.
66. Ebara, *op. cit.,* pp. 408–9.
67. Sasa, *op. cit.,* p. 47.
68. Given in Nose, Nakamura, Asô, *op. cit.,* pp. 20-21.
69. *Ibid.,* pp. 21–22.
70. Chamberlain, *op. cit.,* p. 160.
71. Keene, *op. cit.,* p. 36.
72. Given in Asano, *op. cit.,* p. 231.
73. *Ibid.,* p. 198.
74. *Ibid.,* p. 26.
75. *Ibid.,* p. 230.
76. *Renga Ronshû* (Collected Renga Theories), ed. by Tetsuo Izichi. Tokyo: Iwanami, 1953, I, p. 84.
77. Given in Asano, *op. cit.,* p. 204.
78. *Ibid.,* p. 73.
79. *Ibid.,* p. 196.
80. *Ibid.,* p. 198.
81. Izichi, *op. cit.,* p. 37.
82. See page 117.
83. Given in Asano, *op. cit.,* p. 182.
84. Igarashi, *op. cit.,* p. 42.
85. Asano, *op. cit.,* p. 207.
86. *Ibid.,* p. 251.
87. Sasa, *op. cit.,* pp. 96–97. Dr. Ebara also points out that the witty type of renga did not disappear completely. *Op. cit.,* p. 27.

88. Sasa, *op. cit.*, p. 96.
89. *Ibid.*, p. 106.
90. *Nihon Haisho Taikei* (Selected Works on Haikai), ed. by Toyoho Kanda. Tokyo: Nihon Haisho Taikei Kankôkai, 1926, VI, p. 39.
91. *Ibid.*, p. 32.
92. *Ibid.*, p. 33.
93. *Ibid.*, supplementary vol., p. 3.
94. *Ibid.*
95. *Ibid.*, VI, p. 479.
96. *Ibid.*
97. Ebara, *op. cit.*, p. 29.
98. In *Haikai Haja Kensei.* Kanda, *op. cit.*, VI, p. 553.
99. Bashô, *Haikai Ronshû*, p. 55. *(Kyoraishô.)*
100. *Ibid.*, p. 49. *(Kurozôshi.)*
101. See page 63.
102. Bashô, *Haikai Ronshû*, p. 51. *(Kurozôshi.)*
103. *Ibid.*, p. 49.
104. Chamberlain, *op. cit.*, p. 222. His translation.
105. *Ibid.*
106. Yasuda, *A Pepper Pod*, p. 65.
107. Given in Asano, *op. cit.*, p. 139.
108. *Ibid.*, p. 130.
109. Ebara, *op. cit.*, p. 4.
110. *Kojiki*, ed. by Shigetomo Kôda. 10th ed. Tokyo: Iwanami, 1955, p. 85.
111. *Ibid.*, p. 132.
112. Ebara, *op. cit.*, p. 4.
113. *Ibid.*
114. Yasuda, *Lacquer Box*, p. 14.
115. *Ibid.*, p. 7.
116. Ebara, *op. cit.*, pp. 8–9.
117. *Ibid.*
118. *Ibid.*, p. 7.
119. *Ibid.*, p. 10.
120. *Ibid.*, p. 12.
121. *Ibid.*
122. *Ibid.*, p. 13.
123. *Ibid.*, pp. 13–14.
124. Yasuda, *Lacquer Box*, p. 25.
125. *Ibid.*, p. 28.
126. See page 62.
127. Ebara, *op. cit.*, p. 14.
128. *Ibid.*, p. 15.
129. *Ibid.*, p. 16.
130. *Ibid.*, p. 17.
131. *Ibid.*
132. *Ibid.*
133. *Ibid.*, p. 20.
134. Yasuda, *Lacquer Box*, pp. 58–59.
135. *Ibid.*, p. 30.
136. *Ibid.*, pp. 53–54.

137. Ebara, *op. cit.,* p. 19.
138. See p. 115.
139. Asano, *op. cit.,* p. 74.
140. *Nihon Bungaku Daijiten* (Dictionary of Japanese Literature), ed. by Saku Fujimura. Tokyo: Shinchôsha, 1955, p. 72.
141. Yoshiaki Minegishi, *Uta-awaseshû* (Collected Verses from Poetry Contests). Tokyo: Asahi, 1947, pp. 4–5.
142. *Ibid.,* pp. 5–7.
143. *Ibid.,* p. 7.
144. *Ibid.,* pp. 69–73 *passim.*
145. *Ibid.,* p. 74.
146. *Kokinshû,* p. 63.
147. *Ibid.,* p. 25.
148. *Ibid.,* p. 29.
149. Chamberlain, *op. cit.,* p. 158.
150. Asano, *op. cit.,* p. 75.
151. *Ibid.,* p. 63. For the Abutsu story, see p. 152.
152. Igarashi, *op. cit.,* p. 356.
153. In Sôgi's *Azuma Mondô* (1470). Given in Asano, *op. cit.,* pp. 61–62.
154. From the *Meigetsu Ki.* Given in Asano, *op. cit.,* pp. 184–85.
155. Date of birth unknown; date of death 1283.
156. Ebara, *op. cit.,* p. 23.
157. Izichi, *op. cit.,* p. 38.
158. *Ibid.*
159. Asano, *op. cit.,* p. 76.
160. *Kokinshû passim.*
161. Yoshio Yamada, *Renga Gaisetsu* (The Outline of Renga). Tokyo: Iwanami, 1937, p. 241.
162. Nose, Nakamura, Asô, *op. cit.,* p. 52.
163. See page 125.
164. Ebara, *op. cit.,* p. 23.
165. Asano, *op. cit.,* p. 232.
166. *Ibid.,* p. 222.
167. See page 145 for sources.
168. Ebara, *op. cit.,* p. 23.
169. See page 139.
170. Given in Ebara, *op. cit.,* pp. 418–19.
171. *Ibid.,* p. 437.
172. Asano, *op. cit.,* p. 240.
173. *Ibid.,* p. 75. From *Mumyôshô.*
174. Izichi, *op. cit.,* p. 38. From *Renri Hishô.*
175. Asano, *op. cit.,* p. 62. From *Hakuhatsushû.*
176. *Ibid.,* p. 75. From *Mumyôshô.*
177. For examples see p. 137.
178. Asano, *op. cit.,* p. 62.
179. *Ibid.,* p. 61.
180. *Ibid.,* p. 62.
181. Izichi, *op. cit.,* p. 38.
182. Asano, *op. cit.,* p. 61.
183. *Ibid.,* p. 75.

184. Asano, *op. cit.*, p. 62.
185. *Ibid.*, pp. 78, 94.
186. Asano, *op. cit.*, p. 236.
187. *Ibid.*, p. 76.
188. *Ibid.*, pp. 81–82.
189. Kanda, *op. cit.*, supplementary vol., p. 29.
190. Asano, *op. cit.*, pp. 107–8.
191. Kanda, *op. cit.*, IV, p. 42.
192. Yamada, *op. cit.*, pp. 130–31.
193. *Ibid.*, pp. 219–20.
194. *Ibid.*, p. 220
195. *Ibid.*, p. 223.
196. See pages 122–23.
197. See p. 129 ff.
198. Yasuda, *A Pepper Pod*, p. 4.
199. Henderson, *op. cit.*, pp. 12–13.
200. Chamberlain, *op. cit.*, p. 168.
201. *Ibid.*, p. 168. My translation.
202. *Ibid.*, pp. 168–69. His translation.
203. Henderson, *op. cit.*, pp. 13–14.
204. See page 128.
205. *Kokinshû*, p. 98.
206. *Ibid.*
207. Asano, *op. cit.*, p. 77.
208. Ebara, *op. cit.*, p. 29.
209. Henderson, *op. cit.*, p. 15.
210. Chamberlain, *op. cit.*, p. 172.
211. See p. 132.
212. See *ibid.* for comments from the Teitoku school.
213. *Ibid.*
214. Asano, *op. cit.*, pp. 354–57 *passim*.
215. *Ibid.*, p. 357.
216. Chamberlain, *op. cit.*, p. 176.
217. *Ibid.*, p. 174.
218. *Ibid.*, p. 216.
219. Chamberlain, *op. cit.*, p. 217.
220. Asano, *op. cit.*, p. 339.
221. See page 159.
222. Yasuda, *A Pepper Pod*, p. 6.
223. *Ibid.*, p. 4.
224. See pp. xvi, 38, 47, 64–65.
225. Kanda, *op. cit.*, I, p. 572. *(Oi no Kobumi.)*
226. Taizô Ebara, *Haikai Seishin no Tankyû* (Research on the Haikai Spirit). Osaka: Akitaya, 1944, p. 331.
227. *Ibid.*, p. 332.
228. See pages 150–51.
229. Kanda, *op. cit.*, I, p. 572. *(Oi no Kobumi.)*
230. Asano, *op. cit.*, p. 236. From *Hakuhatsushû.*
231. Bashô, *Haikai Ronshû*, p. 89. *(Akazôshi.)*
232. Fletcher, Introduction to *A Pepper Pod*, p. x.

233. Chamberlain, *op. cit.*, p. 184.
234. Bashô, *Haikai Ronshû*, p. 92. *(Shomon Haikai Goroku.)*
235. *Ibid.*, p. 28. *(Aone ga Mine.)*
236. Daisetz Suzuki, "Reason and Intuition in Buddhist Philosophy," in *Essays in East-West Philosophy*, ed. by Charles A. Moore. Honolulu: Univ. of Hawaii Press, 1951, p. 20.
237. Yasuda, *A Pepper Pod*, p. ii. Cf. Chamberlain, *op. cit.*, pp. 186–87.
238. Chamberlain, *op. cit.*, p. 181.
239. Bashô, *Haikai Ronshû*, p. 98. *(Kurozôshi.)*
240. *Ibid.*, p. 58. *(Shokanshû.)*
241. Asano, *op. cit.*, p. 421.
242. Suzuki, *op. cit.*, p. 18.
243. *Ibid.*, p. 21.
244. *Ibid.*, p. 43.
245. Waggoner, *op. cit.*, p. 24.
246. See pp. 13 ff.
247. Quoted in Waggoner, *op. cit.*, pp. 23–24.
248. Chisaburo Yamada and James Laughlin, "Contemporary Japanese Art," in *Perspective of Japan: An Atlantic Monthly Supplement.* New York: Intercultural Publications, n.d., p. 34.
249. Asano, *op. cit.*, p. 70.
250. *Ibid.*, p. 92.
251. *Ibid.*, p. 81.
252. Shiki, *Masaoka Shiki Shû* (Collected Works of Masaoka Shiki), ed. by Sokotsu. (Vol. XI of *Gendai Nihon Bungaku Zenshû* [Collected Works of Modern Japanese Literature]). Tokyo: Kaizô, 1928, p. 350.
253. See pages 125–26.
254. Henderson, *op. cit.*, p. 27. His translation.
255. *Ibid.*, p. 26.
256. Shiki, *op. cit.*, p. 431. In *Zuimon Zuitô.*
257. *Ibid.*, p. 349. In *Haikai Taiyô.*
258. *Ibid.*, p. 348. In *Haikai Taiyô.*
259. Otsuji, *op. cit.*, p. 43.
260. *Ibid.*, p. 58.
261. Henderson, *op. cit.*, p. 95.
262. Fujimura, *op. cit.*, p. 819.
263. *Ibid.*
264. Otsuji, *op. cit.*, p. 59.
265. *Ibid.*, p. 58.
266. *Ibid.*, p. 59.
267. *Ibid.*
268. *Ibid.*
269. *Ibid.*, pp. 1–2.
270. Bashô, *Haikai Ronshû*, p. 73. *(Sanseijin no zu.)*
271. Archibald MacLeish, "The Proper Pose of Poetry," *Saturday Review of Literature*, Vol. XXXVIII, No. 10 (March 5, 1955), p. 49.

CHAPTER SIX

1. Henderson, *op. cit.,* p. 2.
2. Fletcher, Introduction to *A Pepper Pod,* pp. ix–x.
3. MacLeish, "The Proper Pose of Poetry," p. 49.
4. Tate, *op. cit.,* p. 55.
5. Bogan, *op. cit.,* p. 94.

BIBLIOGRAPHY

Asano, Shin 淺野 信, *Haiku Zenshi no Kenkyû* 俳句前史の研究 (A Study of Pre-Haiku History.) Tokyo: Chûbunkan. 1939.

Asô, Isoji 麻生磯次, *Haishumi no Hattatsu* 俳趣味の發達 (The Development of Haikai Taste.) 2nd ed. Tokyo: Tokyodô. 1944.

Barker, George, " William Shakespeare and the Horse with Wings," *Partisan Review,* Vol. XX, No. 4 (July-August, 1953.)

Bashô Haikai Ronshû 芭蕉俳諧論集, comp. and ed. by Komiya, Toyotaka 小宮豐隆 and Yokozawa, Saburo 橫澤三郎. (Collected Haikai Theories of Bashō.) 3rd ed. Tokyo: Iwanami. 1951. (All quotations from this volume given in the foregoing text are followed by the name of the original works in which they appeared.)

Bashô Haikushu 芭蕉俳句集, comp. and ed. by Ebara, Taizô 穎原退藏. (Collected Haiku of Bashô.) 18th ed. Tokyo: Iwanami. 1953. (Cited below.)

Bashô Kôza 芭蕉講座, comp. and ed. by Ebara, Taizô 穎原退藏 and Katô, Shûson 加藤揪邨. (Lectures on Bashô.) 10 vols. Tokyo: Sanshôdô. 1943. (Cited below.)

Bogan, Louise, *Achievement in American Poetry.* Chicago: Henry Regnery Co. 1951.

Bradley, A. C., *Oxford Lectures on Poetry.* London: Macmillan. 1909.

Brooks, Cleanth, *Modern Poetry and the Tradition.* Chapel Hill: Univ. of North Carolina Press. 1939.

Cassagne, Albert, *La Theorie de l'Art pour l'Art en France.* Paris: Hachette. 1906.

Cassirer, Ernst, *Substance and Function and Einstein's Theory of Relativity.* Trans. by W. C. and M. C. Swabey. Chicago-London: Open Court. 1923.

Chamberlain, B. H., *Japanese Poetry*. London: John Murray. 1910.

Christy, Arthur E. (editor), *The Asian Legacy and American Life*. New York: John Day. 1945. (Cited below.)

Croce, Benedetto, *Aesthetic as a Science of Expression and General Linguistic*. Trans. by Douglas Ainslie. London: Macmillan. 1922.

———, *Ariosto, Shakespeare and Corneille*. Trans. by Douglas Ainslie. London: George Allen and Unwin. 1920.

———, *Essence of Aesthetic*. Trans. by Douglas Ainslie. London: Heineman. 1921.

Danz, Louis, *The Psychologist Looks at Art*. London: Longmans. 1937.

Deutsch, Babette, *Poetry in Our Time*. New York: Henry Holt. 1952; rev. ed., Columbia University Press, 1956.

Dewey, John, *Art as Experience*. New York: Mentor, Balch. 1934.

Drew, Elizabeth, *T. S. Eliot: The Design of his Poetry*. New York: Charles Scribner's Sons. 1949.

DuCamp, Maxime, *Chants Modernes*. Paris: Lévy Frères. 1855.

Ebara, Taizô 潁原退藏 (editor), *Bashô Haikushû* 芭蕉俳句集. (Collected Haiku of Bashô.) 18th ed. Tokyo: Iwanami. 1953. (Cited above.)

———, and Katô, Shûson 加藤楸邨 (editors), *Bashô Kôza* 芭蕉講座. (Lectures on Bashô.) 10 vols. Tokyo: Sanshôdô. 1943. (Cited above.)

———, *Haikai Seishin no Tankyû* 俳諧精神の探究. (Research on the Haikai Spirit.) Osaka: Akitaya. 1944.

———, *Haikaishi no Kenkyû* 俳諧史の研究. (A Study of Haikai History.) 2nd ed. Tokyo: Hoshino Shoten. 1949.

Eliot, T. S., *Selected Essays*. New York: Harcourt Brace. 1932.

———, *The Use of Poetry and the Use of Criticism*. London: Faber and Faber. 1933.

Flaubert, Gustave, *La Correspondance de Flaubert*. 12 vols. Paris: Conard. 1926-1933.

Fletcher, John Gould, "The Orient and Contemporary Poetry," in *The Asian Legacy and American Life*, ed. by Christy, Arthur E. New York: John Day. 1945. (Cited above.)

Ford, Madox Ford, *Joseph Conrad, A Personal Remembrance*. London: Duckworth. 1924.

Frost, Robert, *The Poems of Robert Frost*. New York: Modern Library. 1946.

Fujimura, Saku 藤村 作 (editor), *Nihon Bungaku Daijiten* 日本文学大辭典. (Dictionary of Japanese Literature.) Tokyo Shinchôsha. 1955.

Gregory, Horace and Zaturenska, Marya, *History of American Poetry*. New York: Harcourt Brace. 1942.

Henderson, H. G., *The Bamboo Broom*. Boston: Houghton Miflin. 1934.

Hughes, Glenn, *Imagism and the Imagists*. Palo Alto: Stanford University Press. 1931.

Ide, Etsurô 井手逸郎, *Meiji Taishô Haikushi* 明治大正俳句史. (History of Haiku of the Meiji and Taishô Eras.) Tokyo: Ritsumeikan. 1932.

Igarashi, Chikara 五十嵐力, *Kokka no Taisei Oyobi Hattatsu* 國歌の胎生及び發達. (The Genesis of Japanese Poetry and its Development.) Tokyo: Kaizô. 1948.

Isaacs, Jacob, *Background of Modern Poetry*. New York: E. P. Dutton. 1952.

Izichi, Tetsuo 伊地知鐵男 (editor), *Renga Ronshû* 連歌論集. (Collected Renga Theories.) 2 vols. Tokyo: Iwanami. 1953.

Joyce, James, *Portrait of the Artist as a Young Man*. New York: W. Haebasch. 1916.

Kanda, Toyoho 神田豊穂 (editor), *Nihon Haisho Taikei* 日本俳書大系. (Selected Works on Haikai.) 16 vols. Tokyo: Nihon Haisho Taikei Kankôkai. 1926. (Cited below.)

Keene, Donald, *Japanese Literature*. London: John Murray. 1953.

Kojiki 古事記, ed. by Kôda, Shigetomo 幸田茂友. (Record of Ancient Matters.) 10th ed. Tokyo: Iwanami. 1955.

Kokinshû 古今集, ed. by Onoe, Hachirô 尾上八郎. (Collection of Ancient and Modern Poetry.) 19th ed. Tokyo: Iwanami. 1951.

Kume, Masao 久米正雄, *Bikushô Zuihitsu* 微苦笑随筆. (Bitter-sweet Essays.) Tokyo: Bungei Shunju Shinsha. 1953.

Kuribayashi, Tamio 栗林農夫, *Haiku to Seikatsu* 俳句と生活 (Haiku and Living.) Tokyo: Iwanami. 1952.

Langer, Suzanne K., *Philosophy in a New Key*. Cambridge, Mass: Univ. of Harvard Press. 1942.

Manyô·hú–One Thousand Poems, The 萬葉集, ed. and trans. by Sasaki, Nobutsuna 佐々木信綱, *et al*. 3rd ed. Tokyo: Iwanami. 1948. (Cited below.)

Manyôshû Zenchûshaku 萬葉集全註釋, ed. by Taketa, Yûkichi 武田祐吉. (The Complete Manyôshû with Notes and Commentaries.) 16 vols. Tokyo: Kaizô. 1949. (Cited below.)

Masaoka, Shiki 正岡子規, *Masaoka Shiki Shû* 正岡子規集, ed. by Sokotsu 鼠骨. (Collected Works of Masaoka Shiki.) (Vol. XI of *Gendai Nihon Bungaku Zenshû* 現代日本文學全集 卷十一 (Collected Works of Modern Japanese Literature.) 63 vols. Tokyo: Kaizô. 1928.

Masefield, John, *The Collected Poems of John Masefield*. London: Heineman. 1936.

Meredith, George, *The Poetical Works of George Meredith*, ed. by G. M. Trevelyan. London: Constable. 1912.

Millay, Edna St. Vincent, *Collected Lyrics of Edna St. Vincent Millay*, 5th ed. New York: Harper. 1943.

Minegishi, Yoshiaki 峯岸義秋, *Uta-awase-shû* 歌合集. (Collected Verses from Poetry Contests.) Tokyo: Asahi Shimbun Press. 1947.

Moore, Charles A. (editor), *Essays in East-west Philosophy*. Honolulu: Univ. of Hawaii Press. 1951. (Cited below.)

MacLeish, Archibald, *Poems, 1920-1934*. New York: Houghton Miflin. 1934.

————, "The Proper Pose of Poetry," *Saturday Review of Literature*, Vol. XXXVIII, No. 10 (March 5, 1955.)

Nose, Asaji 能勢朝次, Nakamura, Kusadao 中村草田男, and Asô, Isoji 麻生磯次, *Renga, Haikai, Haiku, Senryû* 連歌 俳諧 俳句 川柳. (Vol. IV of *Nippon Bungaku Kyôyô Kôza* 日本文學教養講座 卷四. (Educational Lectures on Japanese Culture.) 14 vols. Tokyo: Shibundô. 1952.

Nihon Haisho Taikei 日本俳書大系, ed. by Kanda, Toyoho 神田豊穂. (Selected Works on Haikai.) 16 vols. Tokyo: Nihon Haisho Taikei Kankôkai. 1926. (Cited above.)

Origuchi, Shinobu 折口信夫, *Origuchi Shinobu Zenshû* 折口信夫全集, ed. by the Society for the Commemoration of Dr. Origuchi's Work. (Collected Works of Origuchi Shinobu.) 25 vols. Tokyo: Chuô Kôron. 1954.

Ôsuga, Seki 大須賀績, *Otsuji Hairon-shû* 乙字俳論集, ed. by Yoshida, Tôyô 吉田東洋. (Otsuji's Collected Essays on Haiku Theory.) 5th ed. Tokyo: Kaede Shobô. 1947. (Cited below.)

Pepper, Stephen, *Aesthetic Quality*. New York: Scribner's. 1938.

Planche, Gustave, *Nouveaux Portraits Litteraires*. Paris: D'Amyot. 1854.

Poe, Edgar Allen, "Longfellow's Ballads," in *The Shock of Recognition*, ed. by Wilson, Edmund. Garden City: Doubleday. 1947.

————, *Poems of Edgar Allen Poe*. New York: Peter Pauper Press. n. d.

Pound, Ezra, "A Few Don't's by an Imagist," *Poetry: A Magazine of Verse*, Vol. I, No. 1 (October-March, 1912-1913).

Proudhon, P. J., *Oeuvres Complètes*. 20 vols. Paris: Librairie Internationale. 1867-1870.

Read, Herbert, *Form in Modern Poetry*. London: Vision Press. 1953.

Sasa, Masakazu 佐々政一, *Rengashi Ron* 連歌史論. (On Renga History.) Tokyo: Tenrai Shobô. 1928.

Sasaki Nobutsuna 佐々木信綱, *et. al.* (editors and translators), *The Manyôshû—One Thousand Poems* 萬葉集. 3rd ed. Tokyo: Iwanami. 1948. (Cited above.)

Scott, J. H., *Rhythmic Verse*. Iowa City: University of Iowa Press. 1925.

Suzuki, Daisetz T. 鈴木大拙, "Reason and Intuition in Buddhist Philosophy," in *Essays in East-West Philosophy*, ed. by Moore, Charles A. Honolulu: University of Hawaii Press. 1951. (Cited above.)

Takahama, Kyoshi 高濱虛子, "Haiku no Tsukuri Kata" 俳句の作り方 (How to Compose Haiku), in *Arusu Fujin Kôza* アルス婦人講座, ed. by Kitahara, Takeo. (Arusu Lectures for Women.) Tokyo: Arusu. 1927.

Taketa, Yûkichi 武田祐吉 (editor), *Manyôshû Zenchûshaku* 萬葉集全註釋. (The Complete Manyôshû with Notes and Commentaries.) 16 vols. Tokyo: Kaizô. 1949. (Cited above.)

Tate, Allen, *Reactionary Essays on Poetry and Ideas*. New York: Charles Scribner's Sons. 1936.

Urban, W. M., *Language and Reality*. London: Macmillan. 1939.

Waggoner, H. H., *The Heel of Elohim*. Norman, Okla: University of Oklahoma Press. 1950.

Whitehead, Alfred North, *Science and the Modern World*. New York: Macmillan. 1925.

Witner, Lightner, *Analytical Psychology*. Boston: Ginn and Co. 1902.

Yamada, Chisaburo 山田智三郎, and Laughlin, James. "Contemporary Japanese Art," in *Perspective of Japan: An Atlantic Monthly Supplement*. New York: Intercultural Publications. n. d.

Yamada, Yoshio 山田孝雄, *Renga Gaisetsu* 連歌概說. (The Outline of Renga.) Tokyo: Iwanami. 1937.

Yamamoto, Kenkichi 山本健吉, *Junsui Haiku* 純粹俳句. (Pure Haiku.) Tokyo: Sôgen-sha. 1952.

Yasuda, Kenneth, *Lacquer Box*. Tokyo: Nippon Times. 1952.

———, *A Pepper Pod*. New York: Alfred A. Knopf. 1947.

———, *Minase Sangin Hakuin* 水無瀨三吟百韻. (A Poem of One Hundred Links Composed by Three Poets at Minase.) Tokyo: Kogakusha. 1956.

Yoshida, Tôyô 吉田東洋 (editor), *Otsuji Hairon-shû* 乙字俳論集. (Otsuji's Collected Essays on Haiku Theory.) 5th ed. Tokyo: Kaede Shobô. 1947. (Cited above.)

Yuyama, Kiyoshi 湯山 清, *Nihon Shiika Inritsu Gaku* 日本詩歌韻律學. (A Study of Rhythm in Japanese Poetry.) Tokyo: Furôkaku Shobô. 1935.

INDEX

Other Titles in the Tuttle Literature Library

THE RIVER WITH NO BRIDGE *by Sué Sumii, translated by Susan Wilkinson*

THE RONIN: A Novel Based on a Zen Myth *by William Dale Jennings*

THE SQUARE PERSIMMON AND OTHER STORIES *by Takashi Atoda, translated by Millicent Horton*

THE STORY OF A SINGLE WOMAN *by Uno Chiyo, translated by Rebecca Copeland*

THE TALE OF GENJI: A Reader's Guide *by William J. Puette*

THE TEN FOOT SQUARE HUT AND TALES OF THE HEIKE: Being Two Thirteenth Century Japanese Classics *translated by A. L. Sadler*

THE TOGAKUSHI LEGEND MURDERS *by Yasuo Uchida, translated by David J. Selis*

THE WILD GEESE *by Ogai Mori, translated by Sanford Goldstein and Kingo Ochiai*

THIS SCHEMING WORLD *by Saikaku Ihara, translated by Masanori Takatsuka and David C. Stubbs*

TWENTY-FOUR EYES *by Sakae Tsuboi, translated by Akira Miura*

VITA SEXUALIS *by Ogai Mori, translated by Kazuji Ninomiya and Sanford Goldstein*

WHEN I WHISTLE *by Shusaku Endo, translated by Van C. Gessel*

WONDERFUL FOOL *by Shusaku Endo, translated by Francis Mathy*

Kenneth Yasuda, an American of Japanese descent, has been emeritus professor of East Asian languages and cultures at Indiana University since 1984. A graduate of the University of Washington, he was the first American to receive a Doctor of Literature degree in Japanese literature from Tokyo University. His numerous other publications include *A Pepper Pod,* a collection of original haiku and translations in English; *A Lacquer Box,* translations of tanka; and a translation of *Minase Sangin Hyakuin,* the most famous collection of *renga* linked poetry. In 1974 Dr. Yasuda was awarded the Japanese Imperial Decoration of the Sacred Treasure, Third Order.